I0007680

LINEAR ALGEBRA & MATRIX THEORY FOR FINANCE

Hayden Van Der Post

Reactive Publishing

To my daughter, may she know anything is possible.

CONTENTS

COPYRIGHT © 2025 REACTIVE PUBLISHING. ALL RIGHTS RESERVED.

No part of this book may be reproduced, stored in a retrieval system, or transmitted in any form or by any means—electronic, mechanical, photocopying, recording, or otherwise—without prior written permission of the publisher, except for brief quotes used in reviews or articles.

Published by Reactive Publishing

The information provided in this book is for educational and informational purposes only. The author and publisher assume no responsibility for errors, omissions, or contrary interpretation of the subject matter herein.

PREFACE

I n an era where data drives decision-making, the synergy between mathematics and finance has never been more vital. This book, Linear Algebra & Matrix Theory For Finance: A Practical Guide for Quantitative Analysts and Traders, was conceived to bridge the gap between sophisticated mathematical theories and their profound applications in the financial world. Whether you're embarking on your academic journey in finance, a seasoned quantitative analyst, a pragmatic trader, or an ambitious student, this book aims to be your indispensable companion.

From the outset, my goal in writing this book was not solely to impart technical knowledge but to take you on a journey—one where the abstract beauty of linear algebra merges seamlessly with the tangible realities of finance. Imagine transforming complex equations into financial models that can predict market movements, optimize portfolios, and manage risks. This is not mere theory; this is actionable intelligence, the lifeblood of financial innovation.

A Personal Motivation

Several years ago, as a budding quantitative analyst, I found myself overwhelmed by the myriad of mathematical tools at my disposal. Despite the plethora of textbooks lining the shelves, none seemed to translate the rigor of linear algebra into the practical language of finance. I yearned for a resource that demystified complex concepts, showed their real-life applications, and equipped me with the tools to make data-driven decisions. This book is the culmination of that quest, enriched by years of experience, research, and collaboration with industry experts.

The Leading the way in Spirit

Financial markets are intricate systems, brimming with opportunities for those equipped with the right tools. Linear algebra and matrix theory hold the keys to unlocking these opportunities. From enhancing portfolio performance to developing robust risk management systems, the applications are endless. This book embodies the pioneering spirit required to navigate and conquer the financial landscape, ensuring you are well-prepared to tackle both present challenges and future uncertainties.

A Practical Approach

What sets this book apart is its pragmatic approach. Each chapter carefully intertwines theoretical concepts with practical applications in finance. We've covered everything from basic notions such as vectors and matrices to advanced topics like singular value decomposition and machine learning techniques. With step-by-step guides, real-world examples, and case studies, the material is designed to be digestible and immediately applicable.

For the Quantitative Analyst and Trader

Linear Algebra is the backbone of quantitative analysis. For the financial analyst, this book offers a comprehensive toolkit. Whether you're analyzing market models, optimizing strategies, or pricing derivatives, you'll find detailed explanations and applications aligned with industry standards and innovations. For the trader, every chapter presents opportunities to refine trading strategies, leveraging mathematical insights to improve accuracy and performance.

A Nod to Historical Context

Understanding the evolution of linear algebra in financial applications emphasizes both the depth and the breadth of its utility. This book briefly reflects on the historical context, honoring the pioneers whose contributions laid the groundwork for modern financial mathematics. By appreciating this legacy, we can better grasp the transformative power of linear algebra in today's dynamic markets.

Preparing for the Future

Finance is continuously evolving, driven by technological advancements and market complexity. This book does not merely provide a static repository of knowledge but fosters a mindset geared towards innovation and lifelong learning. Each chapter culminates in discussions on emerging trends, ensuring you remain at the forefront of financial technology.

Structure and Accessibility

The structure of the book is meticulously designed to facilitate learning and application. Beginning with foundational concepts, it progressively delves into more intricate topics, ensuring a smooth and logical learning curve. Technical jargon is explained in plain language, and complex theories are broken down with intuitive examples.

As you begin this journey, embrace the challenges and opportunities. Mathematics is a lens to interpret and influence finance. Let this book guide and inspire you as you explore new frontiers in finance.

Linear algebra and finance are an unstoppable duo, driving innovation and efficiency in an increasingly data-centric world. Linear Algebra & Matrix Theory For Finance: A Practical Guide for Quantitative Analysts and Traders is more than just a textbook; it is a doorway to a deeper understanding and a brighter future in finance. I wholeheartedly invite you to open this door, step inside, and embark on a transformative journey that will empower you for years to come.

Thank you for choosing this book. I am confident that it will equip you with the knowledge, skills, and inspiration to excel in the dynamic world of finance. Let's begin this exciting journey together.

Yours sincerely,

Hayden Van Der Post

CHAPTER 1: INTRODUCTION TO LINEAR ALGEBRA IN FINANCE

Overview of Linear Algebra

L inear algebra is a foundational pillar in mathematics, intricately linked to finance, where numbers tell the stories of markets and investments. Its core strength lies in managing multi-dimensional data structures, making it essential for quantitative analysis. Linear algebra goes beyond simple arithmetic, utilizing vectors and matrices to solve complex problems with precision.

Vectors, in their most basic form, are lists of numbers that denote points in space. In financial contexts, however, they become representations of asset portfolios or streams of cash flows over time. Matrices serve as comprehensive organizers, arranging data into rows and columns that can be manipulated to uncover patterns and insights hidden within the numbers. Picture a matrix as a vast table—a grid where every entry holds significance.

Operations like addition, multiplication, and transformation applied to these structures allow for efficient analyses that would otherwise be cumbersome. Take this example, in portfolio optimization, linear algebraic techniques such as matrix multiplication and inversion help determine optimal asset allocations that minimize risk while maximizing returns.

Linear algebra's capabilities extend further, enabling the modeling of complex systems through linear equations. These equations can express relationships between various economic variables or constraints within a financial model. Efficiently solving these systems yields critical solutions for decision-making under uncertainty—a familiar landscape for finance professionals.

The utility of linear algebra goes beyond data comprehension; it also facilitates data transformation. Concepts like eigenvalues and eigenvectors—arising from linear transformations—decompose market data into components that reveal underlying trends and volatility factors. This decomposition is crucial in risk assessment and management, where understanding market dynamics is vital.

Beyond theoretical considerations, the practical applications of these principles are extensive. In algorithmic trading, matrices assist in back-testing strategies against historical data, ensuring robustness before real-world execution. In credit risk modeling, linear algebra helps stress test scenarios to predict potential defaults and losses.

This mathematical framework also supports advances in machine learning—a field increasingly significant in finance. Algorithms trained on large datasets leverage linear algebra for tasks such as classification and regression analysis, driving innovative solutions in predictive analytics.

Exploring linear algebra is like navigating an intricate labyrinth; each turn offers an opportunity to uncover new insights or optimize existing strategies. This overview only scratches the surface—preparing you for a detailed exploration ahead where theory meets application in meaningful ways within the realm of finance.

Importance in Financial Applications

Linear algebra holds immense significance in finance, deeply influencing both theoretical constructs and practical applications. Its role is pivotal in the efficient analysis of large datasets, a critical requirement in today's data-driven financial markets. This analytical capability forms the backbone of decision-making processes that drive investment strategies and risk management frameworks.

Asset pricing models offer a clear illustration of linear algebra's value. These models frequently rely on matrix formulations to evaluate multiple factors simultaneously. Take, for instance, the Capital Asset Pricing Model (CAPM), which calculates an asset's expected return based on its market-related risk. In this context, matrices handle covariances between assets, transforming complex relationships into manageable computations.

In quantitative finance, linear algebra is instrumental in optimizing portfolios by minimizing risk for a given level of expected return. Markowitz's mean-variance optimization exemplifies this by using matrix operations such as multiplication and inversion to solve for asset allocation weights. Linear algebra not only facilitates finding solutions but also ensures efficiency—a crucial factor for time-sensitive decisions.

Credit risk modeling is another area where linear algebra proves invaluable. Techniques like stress testing allow financial institutions to assess vulnerability by applying linear transformations to matrices representing financial positions and market factors. This approach helps predict potential losses under various scenarios, enhancing proactive risk management.

Matrix theory also plays a crucial role in derivative pricing models. The renowned Black-Scholes model for option pricing, though primarily based on calculus and probability theory, incorporates linear algebra through matrices for volatility estimations and scenario analysis. This integration enables accurate pricing of derivatives by considering multiple influencing variables concurrently.

In algorithmic trading, where speed and accuracy are vital, linear algebra supports back-testing trading algorithms against historical data through matrix operations that identify patterns indicative of profitable strategies. This capability provides traders with insights that refine strategies and enhance execution precision.

More broadly in risk management, eigenvalue analysis—a core component of linear algebra—helps identify principal components within datasets, revealing market volatility drivers. Such insights empower financial professionals to construct more resilient portfolios capable of withstanding fluctuations.

The integration of machine learning techniques into finance further underscores the importance of linear algebra. Predictive modeling algorithms often rely on matrix operations for tasks like data normalization or regression analysis, uncovering actionable insights that inform strategic decision-making across various financial domains.

Linear algebra serves as a foundational element upon which modern finance is built, offering a framework that facilitates innovation while ensuring analytical rigor and strategic formulation. As you explore these concepts throughout this book, view them not just as tools for comprehension but as empowering resources that enable you to navigate complex financial landscapes with confidence and authority.

This seamless integration into financial applications

highlights not only mathematical elegance but also practical necessity—a testament to how foundational principles can significantly influence real-world outcomes when applied judiciously amidst the ever-evolving challenges and opportunities in finance.

Key Concepts and Terminology

Understanding the key concepts and terminology of linear algebra is crucial for applying it effectively in finance. This knowledge serves as the foundation for more complex analyses and practical applications.

At the heart of linear algebra are vectors, fundamental elements that represent quantities with both magnitude and direction. In finance, vectors can describe various data points, such as asset returns over time or asset weights within a portfolio. They form the basic building blocks for more complex structures like matrices.

Matrices, which are essentially arrays of numbers organized in rows and columns, succinctly represent large datasets. They enable simultaneous operations on multiple data points, which is particularly beneficial in finance where numerous variable relationships are analyzed together. Take this example, a covariance matrix can illustrate how different asset returns correlate, offering insights into diversification benefits.

Scalars, single numbers used to scale vectors or matrices, play a key role in financial contexts. They may represent a single interest rate applied uniformly across different investments. The interaction between scalars and vectors or matrices through multiplication is a common operation that adjusts financial data according to specific factors or conditions.

Matrix operations such as addition, subtraction, and multiplication are central to data manipulation techniques. Adding or subtracting matrices facilitates the comparison of different datasets, while multiplication transforms data to reveal deeper insights, like projecting future values based on historical trends.

The idea of an inverse matrix is critical in solving systems of equations—a frequent requirement in financial modeling. Inverses help efficiently untangle relationships when determining unknown variables that satisfy multiple equations simultaneously.

Determinants add another layer of understanding by offering insights into matrix properties such as invertibility. A non-zero determinant indicates that a matrix has an inverse; in financial terms, this suggests that solutions exist for specific market conditions or pricing models.

Eigenvalues and eigenvectors are essential tools for simplifying complex datasets by identifying principal components. These components capture significant features within data, aiding tasks like risk assessment or performance analysis by focusing on key drivers rather than noise.

Familiarity with these terms and their interrelations is vital because they recur throughout financial computations. The language of linear algebra—built upon these concepts—enables precise communication about mathematical models and their implications for financial strategies.

As we delve deeper into linear algebra's application within finance, these foundational concepts will repeatedly emerge, supporting more advanced topics like optimization algorithms or predictive modeling techniques. Understanding these terms ensures clarity as we progress to intricate analyses and helps ground each layer of complexity in solid understanding.

This conceptual foundation not only clarifies theoretical discussions but also empowers practical applications, allowing seamless integration of linear algebraic techniques into financial problem-solving processes. Mastery of this terminology grants the fluency needed to navigate both academic discussions and real-world financial challenges with ease and precision.

Historical Context

Understanding the historical context of linear algebra enriches our appreciation for its crucial role in today's financial systems. This mathematical discipline has evolved significantly, transitioning from abstract origins to concrete applications that underpin modern finance.

The journey of linear algebra began with ancient civilizations tackling the challenge of solving systems of linear equations. Take this example, the Babylonians developed methods to address quadratic equations, marking an early step toward grasping linear relationships. Over the centuries, these foundational ideas became more sophisticated, driven by the efforts of mathematicians like René Descartes and Carl Friedrich Gauss.

In the 19th century, linear algebra emerged as a distinct field with the introduction of matrices and determinants. Mathematicians such as Arthur Cayley and James Joseph Sylvester formalized these concepts, establishing a framework that would support future innovations. They recognized matrices not merely as computational tools but as objects of intrinsic mathematical interest, laying the groundwork for applying these structures across various scientific domains.

As the 20th century unfolded, technological advancements accelerated the development and application of linear algebra. The advent of computers transformed it into a practical tool for handling large-scale calculations with unprecedented speed and accuracy. This transformation opened new possibilities in fields such as physics, engineering, and notably, finance—where quick computation of large datasets became invaluable.

Linear algebra's role in finance began subtly but gained momentum during the rise of quantitative analysis in the late 20th century. As markets grew more complex and data-driven decision-making became crucial, financial professionals turned to mathematical techniques to gain insights and optimize strategies. Tools like covariance matrices helped analysts understand asset correlations better, while eigenvalue decomposition facilitated principal component analysis—a method for reducing dimensionality in large datasets.

The introduction of the Black-Scholes model in 1973 exemplified how linear algebra could revolutionize financial analysis. By modeling derivative prices through partial differential equations and matrix transformations, it enabled traders to assess risk and price options more accurately— a breakthrough demonstrating the power of mathematics in real-world finance.

Today, as data science and machine learning continue to advance within finance, linear algebra remains at the forefront of innovation. Its principles form the backbone of algorithms that drive automated trading systems and predictive analytics. This evolution from theoretical abstraction to practical application underscores its enduring relevance.

Reflecting on this history reveals how linear algebra has transitioned from abstract mathematics to an indispensable tool in financial strategy formulation. Its evolution showcases a narrative of adaptation and integration—where ancient techniques have been refined into cutting-edge solutions tailored for contemporary challenges.

The Role of Quantitative Analysts

Quantitative analysts, commonly known as "quants," are pivotal in the financial industry, combining mathematics, finance, and technology to develop models that guide data-driven decision-making, manage risk, and optimize returns. These professionals design intricate financial strategies grounded in linear algebra.

In the high-speed realm of finance, quants convert extensive raw data into actionable insights. Their deep understanding of linear algebra allows them to build models that detect patterns and forecast market behaviors. By employing matrix operations, quants efficiently analyze multidimensional data sets—an essential capability for navigating modern market complexities.

Matrix theory forms the backbone of quantitative analysis, enabling quants to quickly evaluate correlations between various financial instruments. Take this example, covariance matrices help measure how assets move in relation to each other, aiding in portfolio optimization and risk management. Using these techniques, quants construct diversified portfolios that aim to maximize returns while minimizing risk exposure.

Eigenvalues and eigenvectors are crucial in principal component analysis (PCA), a method quants use to reduce dimensionality in large data sets without significant information loss. PCA isolates key factors driving market changes, streamlining data analysis and emphasizing critical variables. This approach not only boosts computational efficiency but also sharpens strategic decision-making.

In derivative pricing, quantitative analysts employ linear algebra to create sophisticated models like the Black-Scholes formula. These models use matrix transformations to simulate various financial scenarios, providing traders with pricing strategies based on mathematical precision rather than speculation. Through these applications, quants ensure financial products are accurately valued and aligned with market dynamics.

Quants also leverage machine learning algorithms—deeply rooted in linear algebra—to automate trading strategies and enhance predictive analytics. Techniques like regression analysis utilize matrices to fit models to historical data and forecast future trends. By continuously refining these models through iterative learning processes, quants improve their market movement forecasts and proactively adjust trading positions.

Beyond modeling, quantitative analysts serve as interpreters between complex mathematical theories and practical financial applications. They translate abstract concepts into strategies that stakeholders can understand and implement effectively. This bridge-building is vital for aligning technical insights with business goals, ensuring firms remain competitive in a data-driven landscape.

In an environment where precision meets creativity, quants are responsible not only for deploying existing mathematical tools but also for innovating new solutions tailored to emerging challenges. Their contributions highlight the dynamic nature of finance, where success depends on continuous learning and adaptation.

Through the lens of linear algebra, quantitative analysts drive forward-thinking strategies that transform our understanding and interaction with financial markets. Their expertise underscores the indispensable role of mathematics in navigating modern finance's intricacies—demonstrating its transformative power time and again.

Practical Uses in Trading

In the dynamic world of financial trading, practicality is paramount. The integration of linear algebra with trading strategies exemplifies the direct application of mathematical principles to the art and science of making profitable trades. This intersection is not merely theoretical; it is at the core of modern trading floors where swift decision-making and accuracy are crucial.

Traders utilize linear algebra to develop models that predict market movements with precision beyond what manual analysis can achieve. Take this example, matrix theory is employed to identify price patterns across various securities.

By transforming historical price data into matrices, traders can apply algorithms to detect anomalies or recurring patterns, uncovering opportunities that might otherwise remain hidden.

Volatility modeling offers another practical application in trading environments. Quants use covariance matrices to assess how individual asset volatilities affect overall portfolio risk. This information allows traders to dynamically adjust their positions, hedging against potential downturns while capitalizing on anticipated upswings.

Algorithmic trading thrives on speed and accuracy, relying heavily on linear algebra. Algorithms designed with these principles can execute high-frequency trades in milliseconds, responding to market stimuli faster than any human could. Vectorized operations enable rapid computation of large datasets, allowing traders to efficiently identify arbitrage opportunities across markets.

Portfolio optimization also has its roots in matrix manipulation. By configuring portfolios as vectors in a multi-dimensional space, traders can apply optimization techniques like mean-variance analysis to balance risk against expected return effectively. This often involves calculating eigenvalues of covariance matrices to pinpoint the principal components driving asset correlations and movements.

Factor models are crucial for risk management and strategy formulation. They are extensively used in creating synthetic benchmarks or replicating indices, relying on decomposing asset returns into factors using linear regression techniques based on matrix operations. These models help traders determine which factors most significantly influence portfolio performance.

In derivatives trading, pricing complex instruments like options benefits from linear algebra's computational power. Traders use numerical methods to solve partial differential equations represented in matrix form, estimating option prices under varying conditions with remarkable speed and accuracy.

Stress testing, essential for ensuring financial stability, employs scenarios constructed via matrix transformations to simulate extreme market conditions and assess their impacts on portfolios or institutions' balance sheets. This proactive approach enables traders to reinforce their strategies against unforeseen market turmoil.

And, real-time data feeds, crucial for intraday trading, are best managed through efficient data structures derived from linear algebraic formulations. Traders leverage this continuous stream of information using algorithms optimized for quick recalculations and adjustments based on incoming data points.

The seamless integration of these mathematical concepts into practical trading applications underscores the indispensable role of linear algebra in achieving financial success. Through these mechanisms, traders enhance their strategic arsenal and reinforce their competitive edge in an ever-evolving marketplace where mathematics is as integral as economics itself.

Structure of the Book

The structure of this book is thoughtfully designed to guide you through the complexities of linear algebra and its significant applications in finance. As you progress, you'll deepen your understanding while gaining practical tools for immediate use. We begin with foundational concepts, ensuring you have a solid base before venturing into more advanced topics where the true potential of these mathematical tools is realized.

Our journey starts by establishing core principles of linear algebra, specifically tailored for financial applications. This groundwork is essential for appreciating how these mathematical constructs are applied in trading and risk management. From grasping the basics of scalars, vectors, and matrices to understanding their role in representing financial data, each chapter builds on the previous one.

As we delve further, you will explore chapters focused on matrix operations—integral components of algorithmic trading strategies. Here, practical examples are seamlessly woven with theory, demonstrating how these operations can streamline data analysis and improve decision-making. This integration ensures that you not only learn the concepts but also apply them effectively.

Next, we examine matrix types and their financial implications, providing the advanced understanding needed for sophisticated modeling techniques. You will learn about special matrices such as identity and diagonal matrices, along with operations like transposition and inversion—essential for building reliable financial models.

The book then introduces determinants and eigenvalues, crucial concepts for assessing risk and portfolio stability. These chapters break down the complexities of calculating determinants and using eigenvectors for market predictions, illustrated through real-world scenarios that show how these elements contribute to robust financial strategies.

To ensure thorough coverage, we delve into advanced topics like singular value decomposition (SVD) and matrix factorizations—powerful techniques foundational to many modern analytics methods in finance today. These sections aim to expand your toolkit, enabling you to confidently tackle large-scale data sets and complex financial instruments.

Throughout this journey, case studies act as anchor points —demonstrating successful applications of linear algebra in various finance sectors. By examining real-world examples where theory is effectively transformed into practice, you'll gain invaluable insights into industry best practices.

Finally, we explore cutting-edge advancements in matrix theory relevant to today's rapidly evolving financial landscape. This forward-looking perspective encourages continuous learning and adaptation—key qualities for thriving in an industry driven by innovation.

Each chapter is a stepping stone towards mastering the potential of linear algebra within finance. With every page turned, your analytical skills sharpen, equipping you with the expertise needed to excel as a quantitative analyst or trader at the forefront of modern finance.

CHAPTER 2: BASIC CONCEPTS AND NOTATION

Scalars, Vectors, and Matrices

S calars, vectors, and matrices form the backbone of linear algebra, serving as the essential language for modeling and analyzing financial systems. Grasping these elements is crucial—not just as an academic exercise, but for their practical applications in the algorithms that drive trading decisions and risk assessments.

A scalar is the simplest of these concepts—a single number representing a quantity or measurement. In finance, scalars might denote interest rates or stock prices at a specific moment. When combined into vectors and matrices, these basic units gain power and flexibility.

Vectors build upon scalars by extending them into multiple dimensions. Picture an arrow in space; this represents a vector with both direction and magnitude. In a financial context, vectors can depict a portfolio's weight distribution among various assets. For example, a portfolio consisting of stocks, bonds, and commodities can be represented as a single vector, encapsulating their proportions. This abstraction allows for operations like scaling (multiplying by a scalar) or adding vectors (summing portfolios), simplifying complex calculations.

Matrices take this concept further by organizing numbers into rows and columns, generalizing vectors to higher dimensions. They can efficiently represent entire datasets. In finance, matrices might encapsulate historical price data for multiple assets or encode correlation coefficients between them, enabling sophisticated analyses such as predicting future trends based on past behaviors.

The interaction between these elements showcases their power. Consider matrix multiplication: multiplying a matrix by a vector transforms the vector according to the matrix's specifications—similar to applying a set of financial rules to a portfolio. Take this example, if market data is organized as a matrix and applied to your portfolio vector, you simulate how market changes impact your holdings.

To see these concepts in action, consider using matrices to calculate a portfolio's expected return. Suppose each asset's expected return is stored as one vector and its allocation as another. Multiplying these vectors yields the portfolio's expected return—demonstrating linear algebra's direct application in finance.

In practice, tools like Python simplify these computations using libraries such as NumPy:

```python
import numpy as np


\#\# Define expected returns as a vector
expected_returns = np.array([0.05, 0.07, 0.04]) \# Returns for stocks A, B, C
```

\#\# Define portfolio weights

weights = np.array([0.4, 0.4, 0.2]) \# Allocation percentages for stocks A, B, C

\#\# Calculate the expected return of the portfolio

portfolio_return = np.dot(expected_returns, weights)

print("Expected Portfolio Return:", portfolio_return)
` ` `

This snippet illustrates how easily matrices and vectors facilitate intricate financial calculations—a testament to their utility.

Scalars provide simplicity; vectors introduce dimension; matrices deliver structure—together forming an indispensable framework for financial analysis. As we delve deeper into this framework throughout the book, remember that these fundamental constructs empower every advanced application in quantitative finance.

Mastering their roles will enhance your analytical skills and transform how you interpret and act upon financial data—a crucial step toward becoming an adept quantitative analyst or trader in today's dynamic markets.

The Language of Mathematics

The language of mathematics forms the backbone for articulating complex ideas with precision and clarity, particularly in the financial sector, where accuracy is crucial. In finance, mathematical language is indispensable for modeling markets, predicting trends, and making informed decisions.

Mathematical notation allows us to express ideas succinctly.

Symbols such as Σ for summation or $\prod$ for product are compact representations that efficiently convey complex operations. This efficiency is vital in finance, where professionals must navigate vast datasets and intricate models swiftly and effectively.

Equations serve as the sentences that convey relationships between variables. Consider the simple equation $E(R) = \Sigma(w\_i * r\_i)$, where $E(R)$ represents the expected return of a portfolio, w_i are the weights of individual assets, and r_i are their respective returns. This concise expression encapsulates an entire investment strategy in one line—a feat only achievable through mathematical language.

Beyond equations, graphs and charts visually represent data relationships. A plot of asset price movements over time can provide immediate insights into volatility and trends—insights that might be obscured within rows of numerical data alone.

Transitioning from spoken or written language to mathematical syntax involves adopting a mindset that prioritizes logical structure over narrative flow. This shift enables clear communication across global markets in finance, where ambiguity can lead to costly misinterpretations.

Financial analysts often operate under tight deadlines, requiring swift comprehension. Mathematical language facilitates this by offering universally understood shorthand across cultures and languages. A correlation matrix can communicate asset relationships without lengthy explanations.

For example, expressing volatility through standard deviation rather than descriptive prose conveys a precise measure easily compared across different scenarios. In Python, calculating standard deviation becomes straightforward with libraries like NumPy:

```python
```

```
import numpy as np

\#\# Sample asset returns
returns = np.array([0.05, 0.07, 0.04])

\#\# Calculate standard deviation
volatility = np.std(returns)
print("Portfolio Volatility (Standard Deviation):", volatility)
```
` ` `

This code snippet illustrates how mathematical functions simplify complex financial analyses into digestible outputs—highlighting the practical benefits of mathematical fluency in finance.

Mastering this language requires practice and discipline, but its rewards are substantial. It enables analysts to distill complexity into actionable insights efficiently, enhancing analytical rigor and empowering strategic decision-making based on empirical evidence rather than speculation.

As we explore linear algebra's role in finance further, remember that proficiency in mathematics isn't just about memorizing formulas—it's about developing an intuitive grasp of how numbers interact within financial ecosystems. Embracing this perspective transforms numerical data into a dynamic narrative—a narrative that informs strategies and drives success in competitive markets.

In the end, it's not just about speaking mathematics fluently but understanding its nuances deeply enough to leverage it effectively within the ever-evolving landscape of finance—a skillset invaluable throughout your career as a quantitative analyst or trader.

Notation and Symbols in Linear Algebra

In linear algebra, notation and symbols serve as essential components that weave together the intricate web of mathematical concepts. They provide a universal language that allows practitioners to express complex ideas concisely and precisely. This is especially relevant in finance, where linear algebra forms the backbone of models that drive decision-making.

Consider matrices, a fundamental concept in linear algebra. Typically represented by uppercase letters such as A or B, a matrix is a rectangular array of numbers or expressions organized into rows and columns. The dimensions of a matrix, denoted as m x n, indicate m rows and n columns. Understanding this notation is crucial because it sets the stage for various operations.

Vectors, often denoted by lowercase letters like v or w, are equally important. In finance, they can represent data points such as asset prices or returns over time. Take this example, a vector might capture the closing prices of a stock over several days: $v = [100, 102, 101]$. This simple representation becomes powerful when used in calculations that inform investment strategies.

The notation extends to operations on these elements. The dot product of two vectors v and w is expressed as $v \cdot w$, involving the multiplication of corresponding elements followed by summing the results—a key calculation for understanding correlations between financial variables. Similarly, matrix multiplication is shown by placing two matrices side by side (e.g., AB), though it requires careful attention to dimension compatibility—an essential detail for financial models.

Beyond these basics are more intricate symbols like lambda (λ) for eigenvalues or sigma (σ) for singular values. Eigenvalues arise from equations involving determinants—another fundamental concept—and offer insights into market stability or asset performance through their magnitudes.

Symbols also represent special matrices: I for identity matrices acting as multiplicative neutrals; 0 for zero matrices serving as additive neutrals; and D for diagonal matrices frequently used in financial optimization problems due to their computational simplicity.

This notation facilitates expressing linear transformations— an important concept when considering how asset portfolios respond to market changes. A transformation matrix T might convert an initial state vector x into a transformed state vector y = Tx, modeling shifts in portfolio values under varying conditions.

Understanding the roles of these symbols goes beyond mere recognition; it involves appreciating their functional purpose within mathematical expressions that describe real-world phenomena. This comprehension enables analysts to decode complex models swiftly and accurately—a necessity in high-stakes environments where every second counts.

For example, consider this Python illustration:

```python
import numpy as np

\#\# Define a matrix A
A = np.array([[1, 2], [3, 4]])

\#\# Define a vector v
v = np.array([5, 6])

\#\# Matrix-vector multiplication
result = np.dot(A, v)
```

```
print("Resulting Vector:", result)
` ` `
```

This example shows how symbolic representation translates into actionable computational tasks that drive financial analysis.

Mastering notation is more than an academic exercise; it equips you with tools to navigate financial landscapes efficiently and effectively. As you deepen your understanding of these symbols' roles within linear algebra's framework, you'll gain fluency in interpreting complex data structures critical to informed decision-making in finance's dynamic arena.

The clarity that comes from mastering these notations can transform seemingly impenetrable walls of numbers into narratives rich with strategic insights—a transformation at the heart of success in quantitative analysis.

Matrix Operations

Matrix operations are fundamental to linear algebra applications in finance, providing the computational power necessary for complex calculations. These operations are not just theoretical; they are practical tools essential for building financial models and strategies.

Let's begin with matrix addition, a simple yet effective operation. For two matrices of the same dimensions, A and B, their sum is calculated by adding corresponding elements. In a financial context, this could represent the combination of different datasets, such as aggregating returns from multiple portfolios. Imagine matrices A and B as 2x3 matrices representing returns over two months for three assets. Their addition results in a matrix offering a comprehensive view of total returns.

Next, consider scalar multiplication, where each matrix

element is multiplied by a constant (scalar). This operation resembles adjusting all asset values by a fixed percentage —helpful for simulating uniform market conditions or proportionally scaling risk assessments.

Matrix multiplication is perhaps the most crucial operation due to its extensive applications in financial modeling. Unlike addition or scalar multiplication, matrix multiplication requires adherence to specific dimension rules: if A is an m x n matrix and B is an n x p matrix, their product AB will be an m x p matrix. This operation facilitates the transformation of datasets across different analytical contexts, such as applying transformation matrices to asset return vectors to project potential market scenarios.

To see these concepts in action, consider this Python example:

```python
import numpy as np

\#\# Define matrices
A = np.array([[1, 3], [2, 4]])
B = np.array([[5, 6], [7, 8]])

\#\# Matrix addition
C = A + B
print("Matrix Addition Result:", C)

\#\# Scalar multiplication
D = 2 * A
print("Scalar Multiplication Result:", D)
```

\#\# Matrix multiplication

E = np.dot(A, B)

print("Matrix Multiplication Result:", E)

` ` `

This code snippet illustrates how basic operations are translated into computational tasks that yield critical insights for decision-making.

Transpose operations add another layer of utility by flipping matrices along their diagonal. This rearrangement can convert column vectors into row vectors—a particularly useful feature when aligning datasets for comparison or performing covariance calculations between different financial metrics.

The inverse of a matrix offers additional functionality. Only square matrices with non-zero determinants have inverses; these are known as non-singular or invertible matrices. The inverse is crucial for solving systems of linear equations and optimizing portfolios under constraints.

Additionally, special types like identity matrices, which act as multiplicative neutrals, and diagonal matrices, which simplify complex calculations due to their structure where all non-diagonal elements are zero, play significant roles in computations.

Each matrix operation serves more than an academic purpose; it influences real-world applications where precision and efficiency are vital. Financial models heavily rely on these operations not only for accuracy but also for optimizing performance—a crucial factor in high-frequency trading algorithms or risk management systems.

The seamless application of these operations transforms data into strategic insights within seconds—an essential capability in today's fast-paced financial markets. Mastery over these techniques empowers you to manipulate datasets efficiently and draw meaningful conclusions that drive successful investment strategies.

Each operation uniquely contributes to building robust models capable of navigating volatile markets—a testament to how fundamental understanding can lead to transformative results in quantitative finance analysis.

Vector Spaces

Vector spaces are the foundation of linear algebra, providing the framework for analyzing and interpreting data in quantitative finance. They are essential for modeling, risk management, portfolio optimization, and simulating market conditions.

At their core, vector spaces consist of vectors and the operations of addition and scalar multiplication. These operations must adhere to rules like closure, associativity, and distributivity, ensuring consistent and reliable mathematical manipulation. Far from being abstract, these properties allow for robust modeling of financial data in various scenarios.

Take this example, consider modeling returns on multiple assets. Each asset's returns can be represented as vectors within a vector space. This allows us to perform operations such as adding returns from different assets or scaling them according to market conditions or investor preferences.

A key concept in vector spaces is the basis—a set of vectors that spans the entire space. Any vector in the space can be expressed as a linear combination of these basis vectors. In finance, selecting an appropriate basis is like choosing a strategic framework for analyzing market trends or pricing derivatives. Techniques like principal component analysis (PCA) often identify a new basis that reveals significant variance directions, offering insights into underlying market drivers.

Orthogonality adds another dimension to our analytical toolkit. Orthogonal vectors are independent and carry no redundant information, a critical feature when diversifying portfolios to minimize risk without compromising potential returns.

For a practical demonstration, consider an Excel example to compute orthogonal projections:

1. Set Up Data: Enter two vectors in columns A and B.

2. Compute Dot Product: Use =SUMPRODUCT(A2:A6,B2:B6) to calculate the dot product.

3. Calculate Projection: In another column, apply =A2*(dot_product/sum(A2:A6^2)) to each element.

4. Validate Orthogonality: Sum the projection column; if it's zero (or close), the vectors are orthogonal.

This exercise shows how orthogonality can decompose complex datasets into simpler components.

Subspaces, or vector spaces within larger spaces, help isolate segments of financial data with unique behaviors or trends. In credit risk modeling, subspaces might represent distinct credit rating categories or economic sectors.

Additionally, understanding the null space and column space aids in solving equations common in finance tasks like regression analysis or optimization problems. The null space contains solutions to homogeneous equations—useful for scenarios nullifying certain financial impacts—while the column space represents feasible outcomes based on input variables.

Each interaction within vector spaces shapes how we perceive and predict market dynamics. This foundational knowledge empowers us to construct models that efficiently manage information flow and anticipate future trends with greater precision.

Mastering vector spaces impacts decision-making processes crucial for financial success. Recognizing patterns within these spaces enables analysts to deploy strategies responsive to real-time market shifts, enhancing competitive advantage in an ever-evolving landscape.

By delving into the intricacies of vector spaces, you gain the ability to transform financial data into actionable intelligence —a cornerstone skill for any quantitative analyst aiming for excellence in today's finance-driven world.

Encapsulation of Financial Data

The encapsulation of financial data through linear algebra is a powerful tool for managing complexity in modern finance. By organizing information into matrices and vectors, analysts can transform vast amounts of raw data into structured formats that facilitate analysis and decision-making. This process enhances both the accessibility and functionality of data.

Consider the multitude of data points associated with a multinational portfolio: asset prices, currency exchange rates, interest rates, and economic indicators, all of which fluctuate over time. By encapsulating this data within a matrix, analysts can streamline computations and perform comparative analyses. Take this example, each row could represent different assets while columns denote time periods. This setup enables operations like covariance analysis or scenario simulations, offering insights into the temporal relationships between financial variables.

In Excel, this encapsulation can be implemented as follows:

1. Data Input: Populate a spreadsheet with asset prices over several months.

2. Matrix Construction: Use Excel's built-in functions to arrange this data into a matrix format.

3. Statistical Analysis: Apply functions such as =COVARIANCE.P(range1, range2) to compute covariances between assets.

4. Visualization: Create charts from matrix calculations to visually interpret trends or correlations.

This approach transforms raw data into actionable insights by uncovering patterns that might not be evident through traditional methods.

Encapsulation also aids in portfolio optimization by helping evaluate risk-return trade-offs. Organizing returns and volatilities in matrices allows analysts to apply algorithms for identifying efficient frontiers—portfolios that offer the highest expected return for a given risk level or the lowest risk for a specified return target.

In coding environments like Python or R, matrices are used similarly but enable more complex computations due to advanced programming capabilities:

```python
import numpy as np


\#\# Create matrix from asset returns

returns_matrix = np.array([[0.02, 0.03], [0.01, 0.04], [0.05, -0.02]])


\#\# Calculate mean returns

mean_returns = np.mean(returns_matrix, axis=0)


\#\# Compute covariance matrix

cov_matrix = np.cov(returns_matrix.T)
```

```
print("Mean Returns:", mean_returns)

print("Covariance Matrix:", cov_matrix)
```
` ` `

This Python script illustrates how encapsulation facilitates deriving key statistical measures essential for risk assessment and portfolio construction.

The abstraction provided by encapsulation reduces cognitive load by hiding unnecessary details while presenting only relevant aspects needed for analysis—similar to focusing on a map's legend rather than its intricate features.

Also, encapsulation supports scalability; as datasets grow with additional variables or dimensions (such as geographical regions or industry sectors), matrices can expand accordingly without losing coherence or analytical power.

And, it benefits algorithmic trading where speed is vital. Algorithms operate more efficiently on pre-structured datasets, minimizing computational overhead during real-time market conditions.

Understanding how financial data is encapsulated within mathematical constructs provides clarity amid uncertainty—a critical capability when navigating volatile markets or making informed investment decisions under pressure.

By adeptly utilizing linear algebra techniques like encapsulation, finance professionals can elevate their analyses beyond surface-level evaluations into strategic foresight—paving the way toward superior performance outcomes across diverse financial domains.

Key Properties of Matrices

Matrices are fundamental tools in finance, offering essential properties for structuring, analyzing, and interpreting data.

Understanding these properties enables quantitative analysts to derive deeper insights from datasets, facilitating informed decision-making and strategic planning.

Matrix addition and scalar multiplication are basic yet powerful operations. They allow analysts to combine and scale financial data sets effectively. For example, by adding matrices that represent asset returns from different portfolios, analysts can evaluate cumulative performance or identify synergies between investment strategies. Scalar multiplication, on the other hand, helps adjust entire datasets for factors like inflation rates or currency exchange fluctuations.

Transposition is another key property. It involves flipping a matrix over its diagonal, which is useful for aligning data in comparative analyses. Take this example, transposing a return matrix—where rows represent different assets and columns represent time periods—enables the evaluation of correlations across time for individual assets. This provides insights into volatility or co-movement trends.

Symmetric matrices are particularly important in finance because they appear in covariance matrices. A symmetric matrix is one where the transpose equals the original matrix, simplifying computations in risk management practices such as variance analysis and portfolio optimization, where stable covariance estimates are crucial.

Determinants offer insight into a matrix's characteristics and implications for financial systems. The determinant provides a numerical value that indicates singularity—whether a matrix can be inverted (non-singular) or not (singular). In financial applications like asset pricing models or credit risk evaluations, understanding determinant values helps ensure robustness against computational errors when solving linear equations involving multiple variables.

Inverse matrices further extend this understanding by allowing solutions to complex systems of equations—

an essential process when assessing interdependencies among financial instruments or calculating optimal hedging strategies. An inverse exists only if the determinant is non-zero, highlighting the importance of understanding these underlying properties before proceeding with advanced calculations.

The rank of a matrix indicates its dimensionality—the number of independent rows or columns—and is critical for financial modeling accuracy. A full-rank matrix signifies maximum information content without redundancy; conversely, lower ranks suggest potential dependencies or collinearity issues among variables—a common challenge in regression analyses with multicollinearity concerns.

Eigenvalues and eigenvectors capture intrinsic attributes such as variance directions and are pivotal concepts within matrices. They are instrumental in principal component analysis (PCA), which reduces dimensionality while preserving essential patterns within high-dimensional datasets typical in finance.

Lastly, positive definiteness characterizes matrices used extensively in risk assessment frameworks like Markowitz's Modern Portfolio Theory (MPT). A positively definite covariance matrix ensures meaningful variance calculations —allowing investors to accurately gauge portfolio risks during allocation decisions amid market volatility.

These properties introduce unique facets essential to comprehensive financial analysis—from simplifying computational tasks through symmetry exploitation to guiding complex model constructions via inverse applications. Mastery of these matrix properties equips professionals with refined analytical capabilities necessary for addressing immediate challenges and anticipating evolving trends across dynamic market landscapes—a pursuit central to sustained success in competitive environments marked by rapid change and intricate interdependencies among global economic forces.

Row and Column Interpretations

Interpreting the rows and columns of matrices is crucial for understanding financial data structures. Each row and column represents unique information, and when combined, they provide a comprehensive overview. In finance, this approach is not only beneficial but essential for meaningful analysis.

Rows in a matrix typically represent individual entities, such as different financial instruments or time periods. Take this example, imagine a matrix where each row corresponds to a specific stock, while the columns denote various attributes like price, volume, and volatility. By examining these rows, analysts can easily compare attributes across different stocks, identifying patterns or anomalies that might indicate trading opportunities.

Conversely, columns are often used to depict specific attributes across multiple entities or time frames. In historical data analysis, each column might track the performance of a single attribute—such as daily closing prices—over several days. This lets you detailed trend analysis over time, aiding in forecasting and strategy development.

The dual nature of matrices—where rows represent distinct entries and columns denote specific characteristics —enables multifaceted interpretations. This versatility is vital in complex scenarios like portfolio analysis, where the performance of various assets needs simultaneous assessment. A well-constructed matrix can reveal correlations between assets, guiding investment decisions towards diversification or concentration based on market conditions.

And, understanding row-column dynamics facilitates advanced operations like matrix multiplication—a cornerstone of quantitative finance models. This operation involves pairing rows from one matrix with columns from another to produce meaningful results, such as covariance matrices used for risk assessment. Proficiency in this area allows analysts to construct and manipulate financial models accurately and efficiently.

Practical applications highlight these interpretations. Consider a covariance matrix where both rows and columns represent different assets within a portfolio. Each element then indicates how two assets move relative to one another —a critical factor in risk management strategies aimed at minimizing volatility while maximizing returns.

At its core, mastering the interpretation of rows and columns within matrices empowers financial professionals to transform abstract data into actionable insights. This foundational yet powerful skill enables the dissection of complex datasets that define modern financial markets. As you continue developing your expertise in matrix operations, remember that each row tells its own story and each column offers its perspective; together, they form a narrative essential for informed decision-making in the fast-paced environment of finance.

Practical Applications in Finance

The practical application of linear algebra in finance illustrates how abstract mathematical concepts can be transformed into actionable financial strategies. At the heart of this is the use of matrices and vectors, which enable analysts to efficiently process large datasets and convert raw numbers into strategic insights.

One key area where linear algebra is invaluable is portfolio optimization. In this context, matrices are employed to represent returns, risks, and correlations among various assets. A classic illustration is the Markowitz mean-variance optimization model, where analysts construct matrices for expected returns and covariances between asset pairs. By applying linear algebra techniques to solve these matrices, they can determine the optimal portfolio allocation that either maximizes returns for a specific risk level or minimizes risk for a set return.

Risk management also reaps significant benefits from matrix applications. Take this example, Value at Risk (VaR) calculations often rely on historical data organized in matrix form. This helps analysts to evaluate potential portfolio losses by examining past performance data, thus offering insights into worst-case scenarios and informing risk mitigation strategies.

In trading algorithms, linear algebra is crucial for developing models that predict price movements based on multiple variables. Regression analysis, a fundamental tool for traders, involves solving systems of linear equations to model relationships between market factors and asset prices. This method allows traders to forecast future price trends by leveraging historical correlations and external influences.

Additionally, linear algebra finds compelling application in option pricing models such as Black-Scholes, which involves stochastic calculus—a field deeply rooted in matrix theory. Matrices here are used to simulate various market conditions and assess option pricing under different volatility scenarios, ensuring traders can swiftly adapt to market changes.

Financial institutions also utilize linear algebra for stress testing and scenario analysis, constructing complex financial models to predict portfolio performance under adverse economic conditions. By structuring these models with matrices representing different economic indicators, analysts can simulate potential impacts across various portfolios.

Beyond strategic applications, operational efficiencies are achieved through matrix computations in automated trading systems. These systems demand real-time processing of enormous data volumes—a task ideally suited to matrix operations due to their computational efficiency and scalability.

In the end, the integration of linear algebra tools in finance highlights their essential role in converting data into strategic advantages. As you deepen your understanding of these mathematical techniques, you'll uncover more nuanced ways to apply them to specific financial challenges—whether optimizing portfolios or enhancing predictive accuracy in trading models. This seamless blend of mathematics and financial strategy not only facilitates improved decision-making but also positions professionals at the forefront of innovation in an ever-evolving industry landscape.

Challenges in Understanding Notation

Navigating the intricacies of linear algebra often begins with understanding its specialized notation, a task that can pose considerable challenges. In finance, where time is critical, quickly grasping these symbols is essential for leveraging mathematical techniques effectively. Transitioning from recognizing symbols to applying them seamlessly within financial contexts requires both familiarity and practice.

The initial hurdle is often the sheer volume of notational conventions in linear algebra. Vectors are typically denoted by bold lowercase letters like "v," while matrices are represented by uppercase bold letters such as "A." While this distinction seems straightforward, it becomes complex when handling multiple matrices and vectors simultaneously. The challenge intensifies when these symbols appear in various equations across different financial contexts.

Subscripts and superscripts add another layer of complexity. Subscripts usually indicate elements within a vector or matrix —such as "a_{ij}" representing the element in the ith row and jth column of matrix A—while superscripts might denote time periods or iterations in financial models. For newcomers, a clear understanding of these conventions is crucial to avoid misinterpretations.

Shorthand notations for matrix operations also contribute to confusion. Operations like transposition or inversion are abbreviated with symbols such as "T" for transpose or "-1" for inverse. Although standard in linear algebra, these operations require careful attention to ensure they are applied correctly in financial computations, as improper use can lead to significant errors in analysis and decision-making.

In financial applications, notation is pivotal in describing constraints and relationships between variables. Take this example, inequality constraints often appear in optimization problems, expressed using symbols like "<=" or ">=". Understanding how these constraints translate into matrix form is vital for accurately modeling financial scenarios and deriving optimal solutions.

Despite its importance, notation is not universally standardized across all financial literature or software platforms. This lack of uniformity can cause discrepancies when integrating mathematical models into different systems or collaborating with international teams. Familiarizing oneself with various notation systems and their interpretations becomes a practical necessity for finance professionals operating in diverse environments.

To effectively navigate these challenges, adopting a systematic approach to learning notation is beneficial. Engaging with examples that incorporate real-world data can deepen comprehension and retention of these abstract concepts. Utilizing software tools that visually display matrix manipulations can also bridge gaps in understanding by offering dynamic representations of mathematical operations.

In the end, while mastering notation may initially seem daunting, it serves as the foundation for all subsequent linear algebra applications. By investing time in thoroughly understanding this symbolic language, professionals position themselves to unlock the full potential of linear algebraic methods within financial analysis and beyond. This fluency in notation will enhance analytical precision and foster innovation and adaptability across complex financial landscapes.

CHAPTER 3:
SYSTEMS OF LINEAR EQUATIONS

*Representation of
Financial Systems*

I n the world of finance, mastering systems of linear
equations is essential for modeling complex scenarios.
These equations form the backbone of financial modeling,
enabling analysts to simulate and solve intricate problems
with precision. By encapsulating relationships between
multiple financial variables, linear equations provide a
structured framework for problem-solving.

Take, for instance, a portfolio consisting of three assets. Each
asset is associated with an expected return, a risk factor, and
a capital allocation. These relationships can be represented
using a system of linear equations, where each equation
corresponds to a specific financial constraint or objective. The
goal might be to maximize returns while keeping risks within
acceptable limits, all while adhering to budget constraints.

Suppose we have three assets with expected returns
represented as the vector $r = [r1, r2, r3]$, risk factors as the

vector f = [f1, f2, f3], and capital allocations denoted by the vector x = [x1, x2, x3]. The total return from the portfolio is a linear combination: Total Return = r1x1 + r2x2 + r3x3. Similarly, constraints like risk exposure are expressed with another equation: Total Risk = f1x1 + f2x2 + f3x3 ≤ Risk Limit.

To solve these equations efficiently, matrices are used. By organizing coefficients into matrix form, we convert our system into the AX = B format. Here, A is the coefficient matrix capturing relationships between variables; X is the vector representing decision variables like asset allocations; B is the result vector indicating targets such as desired returns or maximum risk thresholds.

In financial systems involving large datasets and multiple constraints—such as derivative pricing or credit scoring—these representations greatly simplify computations. Take this example, when modeling interest rate movements across different maturities in a bond portfolio or calibrating options pricing models using stochastic volatility frameworks, matrix formulations offer clarity and computational efficiency.

Beyond structuring problems, this mathematical representation provides insights into financial systems' behaviors. Consider an investment bank evaluating market conditions for strategic asset allocations across global markets; analyzing sensitivities—how small changes in one variable influence others—is crucial for informed decision-making.

The process extends beyond setting up these systems; interpreting solutions effectively is equally important. Solutions not only satisfy all conditions but also reveal optimal strategies under given circumstances. In finance contexts like arbitrage opportunities or identifying undervalued securities amidst fluctuating markets, extracting actionable intelligence from such solutions translates directly into competitive advantage.

As we explore practical applications throughout this book—whether examining intricate portfolio strategies or assessing economic models' robustness—it becomes clear that mastering these foundational techniques enhances both analytical depth and strategic acumen across diverse contexts in modern finance's dynamic landscape.

Gauss Method

The Gauss Method, also known as Gaussian elimination, is a fundamental technique for solving systems of linear equations and is particularly relevant in financial modeling. Its strength lies in its ability to systematically simplify complex matrices, making it essential for handling the large datasets typical in finance.

Imagine an investment firm analyzing multiple market factors to forecast asset prices. They use a system of equations to represent relationships between historical price data and influencing variables such as interest rates and economic indicators. By applying the Gauss Method, these equations are transformed into an equivalent but more manageable echelon form, simplifying the process of finding solutions that satisfy all constraints.

Let's examine a simple system with three variables and three equations. The initial step in Gaussian elimination involves manipulating the equations so that the matrix achieves an upper triangular form. Start with the first equation and use it to eliminate variables from subsequent rows through strategic row operations—multiplying entire rows by scalars and adding or subtracting them from other rows to maintain equivalence.

Consider a coefficient matrix A and a corresponding vector B representing desired outcomes:

[A = pmatrix 2 & 1 & -1 \ -3 & -1 & 2 \ -2 & 1 & 2 pmatrix]

[B = pmatrix 8 \ -11 \ -3 pmatrix]

The goal is to transform A into an upper triangular matrix by applying row operations to ensure that elements below the leading diagonal become zeroes. Take this example, add multiples of the first row to successive rows to clear elements beneath the first pivot (the initial leading entry). After executing these operations:

$$A' = \begin{pmatrix} 2 & 1 & -1 \\ 0 & 1/2 & 1/2 \\ 0 & -3/2 & 3/2 \end{pmatrix}$$

As the matrix approaches this form, back substitution becomes feasible. Solving from the bottom equation upwards allows for deducing values for each variable sequentially, ultimately providing a complete solution set for X—the vector embodying decision variables like asset allocations or risk metrics.

In practical finance applications such as optimizing portfolios or pricing derivatives under uncertain conditions, using the Gauss Method ensures robustness by accurately computing complex interdependencies among numerous factors simultaneously.

Beyond merely providing solutions, Gaussian elimination offers insights into system characteristics like consistency and dependency among equations—vital considerations when constructing reliable financial models or assessing systemic risks across interconnected markets.

Implementing this method not only enables analysts to solve algebraic challenges efficiently but also enhances their capacity to interpret results critically within broader strategic contexts. Whether evaluating hedging strategies against currency fluctuations or optimizing return-risk trade-offs amidst volatile markets, mastering techniques like Gaussian elimination is essential for informed decision-making at every level of financial analysis and strategy formulation.

The ongoing exploration of linear algebraic methods

promises further revelations about how these mathematical frameworks underpin sophisticated financial systems worldwide—inviting deeper dives into practical implementations that redefine possibilities in modern finance's ever-evolving landscape.

Matrices in Linear Systems

Matrices play a crucial and transformative role in linear systems, providing a structural framework that simplifies complex relationships, especially within financial data. By building on the principles of Gaussian elimination, matrices are not just computational tools; they act as lenses through which analysts can discern underlying patterns and dependencies.

Take, for example, an investment firm equipped with a matrix representation of asset price forecasts. This matrix captures various influencing factors, with each row representing an equation where variables interact to form a cohesive system. Transforming these equations into matrix form goes beyond convenience—it translates abstract relationships into tangible forms that can be precisely manipulated and analyzed.

When dealing with large-scale financial models, such as those used in risk management or credit scoring, matrices allow analysts to efficiently handle vast datasets. Take this example, evaluating the impact of interest rate changes on various asset classes can be modeled within a matrix, facilitating simultaneous evaluation and comparison across an entire portfolio.

A key feature of matrices in linear systems is their ability to reveal consistency or inconsistency within data. A consistent system indicates at least one solution that satisfies all equations simultaneously, which is essential for validating financial models before deployment. Conversely, an inconsistent system—where no single solution fits all constraints—alerts analysts to potential discrepancies or errors in assumptions or data inputs.

Matrix operations such as addition, multiplication, and inversion become instrumental when refining financial strategies. Matrix multiplication, for example, allows for the combination of different datasets or scenarios to forecast market trends under various conditions. By adjusting parameters within this matrix framework, traders can simulate outcomes and optimize decision-making processes.

The integration of technology further enhances these capabilities. Software like Python's NumPy library supports robust matrix operations, enabling rapid computations even with extensive datasets. Consider this basic example of matrix multiplication using NumPy:

```python
import numpy as np

\#\# Define two matrices
A = np.array([[2, 1], [3, 4]])
B = np.array([[1, 2], [5, 6]])

\#\# Perform matrix multiplication
C = np.dot(A, B)

print(C)
```

This script multiplies two matrices A and B to yield a new matrix C—a process analogous to evaluating combined effects of different market forces on asset prices.

Also, matrices are essential in sensitivity analysis—examining how changes in input variables affect outputs—by providing a compact representation of derivative calculations critical for managing financial risks under uncertainty.

Beyond problem-solving, matrices are integral to predictive modeling and data compression. Techniques like Singular Value Decomposition (SVD) use matrix algebra to distill high-dimensional data into core components that retain essential information while discarding noise—a significant advantage in understanding the inherent complexity of financial markets.

As we explore these applications further, the integration of linear algebraic methods into finance continues to reveal new pathways for innovation and efficiency. Matrices remain at the forefront of this evolution, bridging theoretical constructs with real-world demands and paving the way for insights that drive both academic inquiry and industry advancement alike.

Applications in Portfolio Analysis

In portfolio analysis, the abstraction of matrices intersects with the tangible world of finance, transforming mathematical structures into practical insights. By employing matrices in portfolio management, investors and analysts can systematically evaluate asset performance, optimize allocations, and manage risk—key elements for financial success.

Imagine a portfolio made up of several assets, each with its own expected return and variance. Here, matrices become essential tools for modeling the relationships between these assets. The covariance matrix, for example, captures how asset returns are interdependent, helping analysts understand the impact of one asset's movements on others. This is crucial for building portfolios that aim to maximize returns while minimizing risk.

One fundamental application of matrices in portfolio analysis is the mean-variance optimization framework introduced by

Harry Markowitz. This model focuses on identifying the optimal asset weights that minimize portfolio variance for a given expected return. In mathematical terms, this involves solving a system of linear equations represented by matrices, with the covariance matrix being central to the process.

To illustrate this concept in practice, consider the following Python example that demonstrates how matrices can facilitate such optimizations:

```python
import numpy as np

from scipy.optimize import minimize


\#\# Define expected returns and covariance matrix

expected_returns = np.array([0.12, 0.10])

cov_matrix = np.array([[0.005, -0.002], [-0.002, 0.004]])


\#\# Define objective function for minimization

def portfolio_variance(weights):

return np.dot(weights.T, np.dot(cov_matrix, weights))


\#\# Constraints: weights sum to 1

constraints = ('type': 'eq', 'fun': lambda x: np.sum(x) - 1)


\#\# Bounds: weights must be between 0 and 1

bounds = ((0, 1), (0, 1))


\#\# Initial guess: equal distribution
```

```
initial_guess = np.array([0.5, 0.5])

\#\# Minimize portfolio variance
result = minimize(portfolio_variance, initial_guess,
method='SLSQP', bounds=bounds,
constraints=constraints)

optimal_weights = result.x
print("Optimal Weights:", optimal_weights)
` ` `
```

This script determines the optimal allocation for two assets to minimize variance while adhering to certain constraints— a practical demonstration of matrix applications in real-world portfolio management.

Beyond optimization, matrices empower analysts to conduct sensitivity and robustness assessments through stress testing and scenario analysis. By adjusting matrix elements that represent market conditions or economic variables, analysts can simulate various scenarios and their potential impacts on portfolio performance—an essential tool for proactive risk management.

Also, techniques like Eigenvalue Decomposition offer deeper insights by identifying principal components within datasets, uncovering dominant patterns influencing market behavior. This information guides strategic decisions about which factors require more attention when reallocating resources or hedging positions.

Incorporating advanced matrix techniques not only enhances individual portfolio strategies but also strengthens comprehensive risk assessment frameworks used across financial institutions. As models evolve with technological advancements like machine learning—which distills large datasets into actionable intelligence—matrices remain indispensable for navigating complexity and providing clarity.

The synergy between linear algebraic methods and financial analysis creates an environment where decisions are based on quantitative rigor rather than intuition alone. This aligns with the goal of achieving sustainable growth while mitigating exposure to volatile market forces.

In this continuous interplay between theory and practice lies the potential to revolutionize traditional investment strategies—setting new standards for efficiency and effectiveness within modern finance landscapes. By maintaining a focus on foundational principles that drive innovation, we look ahead to explore further opportunities and challenges in the dynamic world of finance.

Consistent and Inconsistent Systems

Understanding financial data requires a keen grasp of the systems of equations that govern asset interactions and market dynamics. These systems of linear equations can be categorized as either consistent or inconsistent, a distinction that has significant implications for portfolio analysis and financial modeling.

A consistent system has at least one set of solutions that satisfies all the equations simultaneously. In finance, this could represent a scenario where asset allocations align perfectly with specified return objectives and risk constraints. Conversely, an inconsistent system lacks any solution set that fulfills every equation, often indicating conflicting or unrealistic financial assumptions.

To better understand these concepts, consider a practical example using Python:

```python
```

```
import numpy as np

\#\# Define a matrix A representing asset relationships
A = np.array([[2, 1], [1, -1]])

\#\# Define vectors representing desired outcomes
b_consistent = np.array([5, 1])
b_inconsistent = np.array([5, 3])

\#\# Solve for x in the consistent system Ax = b_consistent
x_consistent = np.linalg.solve(A, b_consistent)
print("Consistent Solution:", x_consistent)

\#\# Attempt to solve for x in the inconsistent system Ax = b_inconsistent
try:
x_inconsistent = np.linalg.solve(A, b_inconsistent)
except np.linalg.LinAlgError:
print("Inconsistent System: No solution exists")
` ` `
```

In this script, A captures the linear relationships between assets or variables in a portfolio. The vector b_consistent illustrates a scenario where these relationships can be satisfied by some allocation strategy, leading to a consistent system with a viable solution. On the other hand, b_inconsistent represents conflicting conditions that result in an unsolvable system, highlighting the importance of coherent assumptions in financial modeling.

Recognizing whether a system is consistent or inconsistent can guide analysts in refining their models and assumptions. Encountering an inconsistent system might prompt reevaluation of input data or exploration of alternative strategies to achieve desired outcomes.

Distinguishing between consistent and inconsistent systems is also crucial for stress testing and scenario planning. By systematically altering constraints and observing resultant system behaviors, analysts can identify robust strategies resilient to various market conditions—a cornerstone of effective risk management.

Tools like matrix rank are pivotal in diagnosing system consistency. If the rank of the coefficient matrix equals that of the augmented matrix (formed by appending the outcome vector), the system is consistent; otherwise, it is inconsistent. This method provides an analytical approach to verifying assumptions before implementation—ensuring strategic decisions rest on sound quantitative foundations.

As we delve deeper into linear algebra's applications in finance, understanding these nuances enhances modeling accuracy and fosters adaptive thinking essential for thriving amid ever-changing economic landscapes. Each step deeper into these mathematical constructs offers potential for transformative insights—empowering financial professionals to navigate complexity with precision and confidence.

Testing Solutions

In the intricate realm of financial equations, once consistent and inconsistent systems are distinguished, the next logical step is to test solutions. This stage involves verifying whether proposed solutions meet the required conditions, ensuring that financial models are both reliable and robust.

Testing solutions begins with substitution, a straightforward method where each solution is plugged back into the original equations. For example, in a consistent system derived from asset allocation models, proposed weights are substituted into constraints to validate portfolio balance and expected returns. If any equation fails to hold true, the solution is deemed invalid.

To illustrate this process, consider the following Python scenario:

```python
import numpy as np


\#\# Define matrix A and solution vector x_consistent from previous example
A = np.array([[2, 1], [1, -1]])
x_consistent = np.array([2, 1.5])


\#\# Desired outcome vector b
b = np.array([5, 1])


\#\# Verify the solution by substituting x_consistent back into the equation Ax = b
b_test = np.dot(A, x_consistent)
is_valid_solution = np.allclose(b_test, b)


print("Solution is valid:", is_valid_solution)
```

This script checks if x_consistent truly satisfies the original set of equations represented by matrix A and vector b.

The function np.dot() performs matrix multiplication to reconstruct the output vector from the solution. If b_test matches b, then the solution passes this essential validation step.

Beyond substitution, sensitivity analysis plays a crucial role in solution testing. By slightly tweaking input parameters and observing outcome variations, analysts can assess model robustness. Small changes in asset returns or risk parameters might significantly alter outcomes in some models, prompting further refinement to enhance stability under various scenarios.

Residual analysis adds another layer of assurance. It involves calculating the difference between actual outcomes and those predicted by the model. Minimal residuals suggest high model accuracy, while large discrepancies indicate potential issues needing attention.

Testing solutions not only confirms feasibility but also uncovers insights about model behavior under different market conditions. Understanding how sensitive a solution is to input variations aids in developing contingency plans for unforeseen events—an indispensable component of strategic financial planning.

Employing computational tools enriches this testing phase by enabling rapid simulations across diverse scenarios. Numerical libraries like NumPy or financial software platforms such as MATLAB or R allow analysts to perform extensive validations efficiently—transforming raw data into actionable intelligence.

In the end, testing solutions is more than mere verification; it's about enhancing confidence in financial models' ability to deliver consistent results amidst uncertainty. Each successful test reinforces assumptions made during modeling while illuminating paths toward greater precision and adaptability within dynamic market environments.

The robust ability to test and validate solutions equips financial professionals with insights necessary for making informed decisions—creating an environment where innovation meets reliability at every step of the analysis journey.

Financial Interpretation of Solutions

In finance, interpreting solutions to linear systems goes beyond simple validation; it's about extracting actionable insights that can significantly shape strategic decision-making. After confirming the validity of a solution, understanding its financial implications becomes crucial.

One effective way to interpret solutions is by examining them through portfolio optimization. When solving linear equations related to asset allocations, each element of the solution vector represents a proportion of capital assigned to different assets. These proportions aren't just numbers—they form an optimal strategy balancing risk and return according to investor preferences. For example, if a solution suggests a significant allocation toward low-risk assets, it might indicate a market sentiment that prioritizes safety over potential high returns.

To visualize this, consider using Excel for optimizing a three-asset portfolio. By leveraging Excel's Solver tool, you can see how changes in market conditions affect suggested allocations:

1. **Set Up the Model:
2. Enter historical returns for three assets in columns A through C.
3. Define expected returns and a covariance matrix on another sheet.
4. **Improve Using Solver:
5. Set the target cell (portfolio variance) to minimize.

6. Ensure the sum of asset weights equals 1.

7. Solve for asset weights that optimize the trade-off between return and risk.

This interactive setup allows each solver-derived weight to reflect a strategic position based on past performance trends and volatility expectations.

Understanding sensitivity in financial contexts further enriches interpretation. Solutions are dynamic and influenced by market variables like interest rates or geopolitical factors. Sensitivity analysis tools help quantify how these shifts impact outcomes, offering foresight into scenarios that might necessitate tactical adjustments in investment strategies.

Consider a Python-based approach using sensitivity analysis:

```python
from scipy.optimize import linprog


\#\# Coefficients for objective function (risk minimization)
c = [0.02, 0.01, 0.03]


\#\# Coefficients for constraint equations
A_eq = [[1, 1, 1]]
b_eq = [1]


\#\# Bounds on variables representing no short-selling
bounds = [(0, None), (0, None), (0, None)]


\#\# Linear programming to find optimal asset allocation
result = linprog(c, A_eq=A_eq, b_eq=b_eq, bounds=bounds)
```

```
print("Optimal Asset Allocation:", result.x)
` ` `
```

In this analytical framework, altering c reflects different risk assumptions, indicating how asset reallocation mitigates evolving risks across economic climates.

Interpreting solutions also requires a contextual understanding—recognizing patterns aligned with macroeconomic indicators or business cycles enhances strategic positioning. Take this example, solutions suggesting a shift towards more liquid assets during recessions may indicate prudent risk aversion consistent with broader economic contractions.

Lastly, decision-makers must consider ethical implications when acting on financial interpretations. Transparency and adherence to regulatory guidelines ensure decisions not only achieve profitability but also uphold integrity in competitive markets.

Thus, interpreting solutions involves a blend of quantitative rigor and qualitative foresight—empowering financial professionals to transform complex models into coherent strategies poised for success amid uncertainty. By adeptly interpreting and acting on these insights, data-driven models become impactful real-world financial decisions.

Complexity and Algorithmic Methods

Navigating the intricate world of financial modeling requires more than mathematical prowess; it demands a deep understanding of algorithmic complexity. In finance, where time is money, optimizing algorithms for speed and efficiency offers a decisive edge. A thorough grasp of computational complexity enables analysts to develop solutions that are not only accurate but also efficient enough for real-time trading environments.

Algorithmic complexity often revolves around how running time or space requirements grow with input data size. For example, when solving systems of linear equations, solutions must be both correct and swift. While Gaussian elimination is straightforward for small matrices, it becomes computationally expensive as matrix size increases. This is where Big O notation becomes essential—it serves as the universal language for discussing algorithm scalability.

Consider linear programming in portfolio optimization. The simplex algorithm, a cornerstone method, can struggle with large datasets due to its exponential worst-case complexity. Yet, it remains practically efficient for many real-world problems. In contrast, interior-point methods offer polynomial-time guarantees, advantageous for the massive datasets common in finance.

A practical demonstration using Python can illustrate these methods:

```python
from scipy.optimize import linprog

\#\# Objective function coefficients
c = [-0.10, -0.05, -0.07]

\#\# Equality constraints matrix
A = [[1, 1, 1]]
b = [1]

\#\# Variable boundaries (no short-selling)
```

bounds = [(0, 1), (0, 1), (0, 1)]

\#\# Solve using simplex method

result_simplex = linprog(c, A_eq=A, b_eq=b, bounds=bounds, method='simplex')

print("Simplex Method Solution:", result_simplex.x)

\#\# Solve using interior-point method

result_interior = linprog(c, A_eq=A, b_eq=b, bounds=bounds, method='interior-point')

print("Interior-Point Method Solution:", result_interior.x)

` ` `

Comparing results from both methods highlights differences in performance and resource utilization—vital insights for selecting an approach based on dataset characteristics.

Algorithmic advancements also allow leveraging parallel processing power. Techniques like matrix factorization can be optimized using parallel computing frameworks such as CUDA or OpenMP. By distributing calculations across multiple processors or cores, analysts can manage larger matrices more quickly—a necessity in high-frequency trading where every millisecond counts.

Exploring these methodologies requires technical skill and strategic thinking about trade-offs between computational resources and accuracy. The choice between exact algorithms and heuristic approaches often depends on model complexity or the specific financial context. Approximation algorithms may provide sufficient precision while drastically reducing computation time—balancing performance with pragmatic needs.

Also, machine learning introduces another layer of complexity management by automating parts of the modeling process that once relied on human intuition and expertise. Algorithms trained on historical data can anticipate trends or detect anomalies beyond the reach of traditional statistical methods. This shift towards data-driven insights underscores the importance of mastering algorithmic complexity in modern finance.

Understanding complexity is not merely academic; it's about using this knowledge to craft smarter algorithms that enable better financial decision-making. Whether optimizing risk-return profiles or executing trades at lightning speed, mastering algorithmic complexity opens doors to innovative financial solutions that are both theoretically sound and practically viable.

This nuanced understanding elevates analysts from mere users of technology to architects of financial strategies—strategies that withstand market pressures while delivering optimal results with efficiency and precision.

CHAPTER 4: MATRIX ALGEBRA AND TYPES

Important Matrix Operations

Matrix operations are fundamental to linear algebra applications, especially in finance, where they enable the complex calculations that underpin trading strategies and risk assessments. Mastering these operations allows analysts to manipulate data precisely, revealing insights that drive informed decision-making.

Essentially of matrix operations is addition. When two matrices of the same dimensions are added, their corresponding elements are summed. Though simple, this operation is powerful for aggregating financial data across different datasets or time periods. Take this example, if you have matrices representing asset returns from different portfolios over the same period, adding these matrices provides combined portfolio returns—a crucial step in evaluating diversified investment strategies.

Scalar multiplication expands on this concept by multiplying each element of a matrix by a single value—a scalar. This operation is vital for adjusting datasets for variables like interest rates or scaling asset returns to reflect changes in investment size. For example, if you need to adjust a portfolio's returns for inflation, scalar multiplication allows each return value to be proportionally modified, preserving relative performance metrics while accounting for economic conditions.

Matrix multiplication is more complex and involves multiplying rows of one matrix by columns of another. This operation is foundational in financial modeling because it can transform entire datasets with a single calculation. In Markowitz's portfolio theory, for instance, matrix multiplication calculates expected portfolio returns and risks based on asset weights and covariances—tools essential for quantifying diversification benefits and risk exposure.

Here's how you can perform matrix multiplication using Python:

```python
import numpy as np

\#\# Asset returns (in percent)
returns = np.array([[0.1, 0.12], [0.15, 0.08]])

\#\# Asset weights
weights = np.array([[0.5], [0.5]])

\#\# Calculating expected portfolio returns
portfolio_returns = np.dot(returns, weights)
print("Expected Portfolio Returns:", portfolio_returns)
```

This code snippet demonstrates how matrices can efficiently

summarize financial data into actionable insights through concise calculations.

Beyond these fundamental operations lies the transpose operation—switching rows with columns. In finance, transposing matrices often simplifies complex equations or aligns data structures for comparative analysis. It facilitates easy computation of covariance matrices, crucial for analyzing risk across multiple assets.

Inversion is another pivotal operation used to solve systems of linear equations—a common task in finance when determining optimal asset allocations given constraints like budget limits or risk aversion levels. The inverse of a matrix essentially reverses its effects, akin to finding an antidote to neutralize a poison. However, not all matrices are invertible; singular matrices pose challenges that may require alternative approaches such as pseudo-inversion or regularization.

Consider inversion's practical application in portfolio optimization:

```python
from numpy.linalg import inv


\#\# Covariance matrix of asset returns

cov_matrix = np.array([[0.01, 0.002], [0.002, 0.02]])


\#\# Inverse covariance matrix

inv_cov_matrix = inv(cov_matrix)

print("Inverse Covariance Matrix:", inv_cov_matrix)
```

Inverting covariance matrices is crucial for calculating weights in minimum variance portfolios—a strategy that minimizes risk without sacrificing expected return.

These matrix operations not only simplify complex mathematical tasks but also enhance computational efficiency and accuracy in financial modeling processes. By mastering these techniques, analysts can distill vast amounts of data into succinct models that inform strategic decisions with precision and reliability.

Equipped with an arsenal of matrix operations, analysts can transform raw data into coherent narratives that guide investment choices—a testament to the profound impact these mathematical tools have on financial success and innovation.

Identity and Diagonal Matrices

In matrix theory, identity and diagonal matrices are notable for their distinctive properties and practical applications, especially in finance. Far from being mere mathematical curiosities, these matrices play crucial roles in financial computations by offering simplicity and efficiency for problem-solving.

An identity matrix is a square matrix characterized by ones on its main diagonal and zeros elsewhere. Its key feature is its role as a multiplicative identity for matrices, akin to the number one in arithmetic. Multiplying any matrix by an identity matrix leaves the original matrix unchanged. This property is invaluable in finance for simplifying computational processes, such as resetting transformation matrices without modifying the original data—a frequent requirement when recalibrating financial models.

Consider the use of identity matrices in verifying asset allocation strategies. Imagine a matrix that represents various portfolio weights across different assets. By multiplying this weight matrix by an identity matrix, we can ensure no unintended changes have occurred—crucial for maintaining the integrity of investment models.

Here's a simple demonstration using Python:

```python
import numpy as np

\#\# Portfolio weights
weights = np.array([[0.6, 0.4], [0.7, 0.3]])

\#\# Identity matrix
identity = np.eye(2)

\#\# Verifying original weights remain unchanged
verified_weights = np.dot(weights, identity)
print("Verified Portfolio Weights:", verified_weights)
```

In this example, the multiplication by the identity matrix confirms that the portfolio weights remain unaltered—providing reassurance to investors and analysts about their accuracy.

Diagonal matrices take this concept further by allowing non-zero entries along the main diagonal while maintaining zeroes elsewhere. This configuration enables diagonal matrices to efficiently scale transformations—a valuable attribute when adjusting various financial metrics simultaneously yet independently.

Take this example, in risk management, diagonal matrices can modify individual asset variances without affecting covariances between different assets. This capability is crucial when recalibrating risk exposure due to market changes or policy shifts. Selectively scaling helps maintain portfolio balance by fine-tuning specific asset risks without disturbing overall correlations.

Consider this example:

```python
\#\# Variance adjustments for assets

variance_adjustments = np.diag([1.1, 0.9])


\#\# Adjusted covariance matrix

adjusted_cov_matrix = np.dot(np.dot(variance_adjustments, cov_matrix), variance_adjustments)

print("Adjusted Covariance Matrix:", adjusted_cov_matrix)
```

By applying diagonal matrices to adjust variances directly within covariance matrices, analysts can refine risk assessments and optimize portfolios with precision.

And, both identity and diagonal matrices simplify computations involving eigenvalues—an essential component of financial modeling influencing portfolio optimization and risk assessment strategies.

As you explore linear algebra's applications in finance, appreciating the utility of these straightforward yet powerful matrices is vital. They provide foundational tools that streamline complex calculations while preserving data integrity and enhancing computational efficiency— demonstrating their lasting importance in sophisticated financial analysis.

These special matrices not only facilitate precise calculations but also highlight the elegance of mathematical solutions in addressing intricate financial challenges—seamlessly bridging theoretical concepts with practical implementation.

Inverse Matrices and Their Use

In finance, the concept of an inverse matrix holds significant importance, much like it does in mathematics. When dealing with square matrices, finding the inverse is akin to discovering a hidden counterpart capable of reversing a transformation —similar to finding an antidote for a complex potion. The inverse matrix, denoted as (A^{-1}), satisfies the condition (A A^{-1} = I), where (I) is the identity matrix. This relationship underscores its ability to revert systems back to their original state.

The utility of inverse matrices in financial applications is profound. Take this example, in scenarios involving linear equations represented by the matrix form (Ax = b), which appears in various financial models such as portfolio optimization or asset pricing, solving for (x) involves manipulating the equation to (x = $A^{-1}b$). This operation employs the inverse matrix to determine necessary solutions or conditions, which is crucial when precision is essential.

Financial analysts frequently encounter systems that require such resolution. Consider determining optimal asset allocations based on expected returns and variances; one might need to compute (x = $A^{-1}b$), where (A) reflects market covariance data and (b) captures expected returns. In this context, using inverses ensures accurate asset weightings are derived from intricate market dynamics.

Here's a practical example using Python:

```python
import numpy as np


\#\# Covariance matrix

cov_matrix = np.array([[0.04, 0.01], [0.01, 0.03]])
```

```
\#\# Expected returns
expected_returns = np.array([0.1, 0.12])

\#\# Calculate weights using inverse
inverse_cov_matrix = np.linalg.inv(cov_matrix)
weights = np.dot(inverse_cov_matrix, expected_returns)

print("Optimal Portfolio Weights:", weights)
` ` `
```

This snippet demonstrates calculating portfolio weights by applying the inverse of a covariance matrix, ensuring that investment decisions are rooted in mathematically sound principles.

And, inverse matrices play a pivotal role in risk management strategies through stress testing and scenario analysis. When evaluating potential impacts of economic shocks or policy changes on portfolios, reverse-engineered matrices help quantify exposure adjustments needed for desired outcomes.

In algorithmic trading systems and quantitative models forecasting price movements or assessing credit risk, inverses are instrumental in efficiently solving high-dimensional linear systems—a necessity given the complexity and speed of modern markets.

However, caution is warranted due to potential pitfalls like singular matrices (those without an inverse). Such situations occur when a matrix's determinant equals zero, indicating it cannot be inverted directly and necessitating alternative approaches like regularization or pseudo-inverses.

Understanding how to leverage these mathematical tools

while recognizing their limitations empowers financial professionals to model intricate relationships accurately and design strategies aligned with strategic goals under diverse conditions.

The reversibility encapsulated by inverse matrices not only enhances computational flexibility but also enriches analytical depth—enabling practitioners to dissect complex financial environments with clarity and insight.

Mastering inverse matrices opens a world where complex problems yield elegant solutions, enhancing both analytical capabilities and strategic foresight in financial contexts.

Transpose and Symmetric Matrices

The transpose operation in matrices is a fundamental and versatile concept, acting as a stepping stone to understanding more complex matrix properties, such as symmetry. Essentially, transposing a matrix involves flipping it over its diagonal, resulting in an interchange of rows and columns. If we have a matrix A with elements a_ij, its transpose, denoted as A^T, rearranges these elements so that the element in the ith row and jth column of A becomes the element in the jth row and ith column of A^T. This seemingly simple operation holds significant implications in financial computations where specific matrix structures are often necessary.

Understanding transposition is particularly important when dealing with symmetric matrices. A symmetric matrix is one that equals its transpose; formally, a square matrix A is symmetric if A = A^T. This property is common in financial contexts, especially when examining covariance matrices used to analyze portfolio risk. Covariance matrices must be symmetric because they capture how changes in one asset affect another, demonstrating reciprocal influence.

Take this example, consider a covariance matrix representing returns from three different stocks. The diagonal entries indicate variances—how much each stock's return varies from its mean—while the off-diagonal entries represent covariances between pairs of stocks. Symmetry ensures consistency: the impact of Stock 1 on Stock 2's return variability mirrors Stock 2's influence on Stock 1.

Transpose operations are also essential for tasks such as finding orthogonal vectors or calculating eigenvectors and eigenvalues for portfolios. These are critical activities in optimizing investment strategies and ensuring robust risk management. Ensuring matrices maintain necessary symmetries simplifies these calculations and guarantees accuracy.

In practical applications, tools like Excel can compute these properties effortlessly. By entering your data into an Excel spreadsheet (e.g., Matrix A), you can use the TRANSPOSE function to find its transpose. Highlight an appropriate area for the result (matching the dimensions of your transposed output), enter =TRANSPOSE(A1:C3) for data from cells A1 through C3, and press Ctrl+Shift+Enter to compute an array formula.

Similarly, Python offers straightforward manipulation of matrices using libraries like NumPy. If you have a matrix represented as 'A', NumPy's array handling capabilities allow you to quickly access its transpose by invoking 'A.T' or 'numpy.transpose(A)'. These operations become second nature as they integrate into broader analyses needed for extracting insights from financial data sets.

Symmetric matrices not only simplify computational complexity but also provide intuitive formats for finance-related problems involving correlation coefficients or credit risk assessments—reflecting equivalent relationships among variables or instruments involved.

Mastering these foundational concepts equips quantitative analysts with powerful tools for managing data representation issues effectively and leveraging them for advanced predictive modeling endeavors. The clarity provided by symmetric matrices supports both theoretical studies and enhances practical decision-making efficiency across diverse financial scenarios encountered daily.

Special Matrices in Finance

In the ever-evolving world of finance, special matrices offer indispensable solutions to complex challenges. These matrices are customized for financial modeling, providing the essential structure for precise analysis and strategic decision-making.

Take diagonal matrices, for example. They are among the simplest yet most powerful tools in finance. A diagonal matrix has zeroes for all off-diagonal elements, simplifying computations to just the diagonal values. This simplicity makes calculating powers and inverses straightforward—operations that are otherwise complicated with more general matrices. Practically speaking, diagonal matrices streamline risk assessment when evaluating portfolio return variances; each diagonal element represents individual asset risk without any cross-asset interaction.

Equally important is the identity matrix, known for its role as the multiplicative identity in matrix algebra. When any matrix A is multiplied by an identity matrix I, the result is A itself (A * I = A). This property is crucial during operations like matrix inversion or transformation in predictive modeling and simulations.

Block matrices add another layer of sophistication by allowing analysts to divide large financial datasets into smaller, manageable sections. This partitioning is especially useful for multidimensional portfolios, where each block can represent different market segments or investment categories. Structuring data in this way facilitates targeted analysis and offers a clearer view of performance across various financial instruments.

Transitioning from block matrices, triangular matrices—

either upper or lower—are frequently used in solving systems of linear equations through methods like LU decomposition. Here, a matrix is expressed as a product of an upper triangular and a lower triangular matrix. This factorization aids in efficiently solving linear problems common in quantitative analyses, such as interest rate models and derivative pricing strategies.

Orthogonal matrices offer another powerful tool. They preserve vector norms during transformations, maintaining angles and distances. This characteristic is crucial for optimizations and rotations without altering original data metrics, minimizing risks associated with high-dimensional market predictions.

Sparse matrices also deserve mention. In scenarios like network analysis or sparse data estimation—common in credit scoring models—these matrices excel due to their storage efficiency and computational advantages over dense formats.

Implementing these concepts effectively requires proficiency with tools like Python's NumPy library, which offers functions such as numpy.diag() for diagonal extraction and numpy.linalg methods for working with triangular forms.

By incorporating these special matrices into their analytical toolkit, financial professionals can enhance both accuracy and efficiency—whether simulating future asset behaviors or optimizing portfolios under market constraints.

In the end, understanding the potential of special matrices equips analysts with robust methodologies to tackle sophisticated challenges inherent in modern finance, paving the way for not just incremental improvements but transformative insights into asset management and valuation practices across sectors.

Block Matrices and Partitioning

Block matrices and partitioning play a crucial role in financial analysis, especially when working with complex, multidimensional datasets. The beauty of block matrices is their ability to break down a large matrix into smaller, more manageable submatrices or blocks, allowing each to be analyzed independently or collectively.

Take, for example, a portfolio consisting of various asset classes like equities, bonds, and commodities. A block matrix can organize this data into separate blocks for each asset class, facilitating targeted analyses. Within these blocks, covariance matrices can be used to evaluate intra-class correlations without the influence of other asset classes.

Beyond convenience, partitioning offers significant computational benefits. Operations on block matrices often require less computational power than handling an entire dataset simultaneously. In financial modeling scenarios where speed is crucial—such as in real-time trading algorithms— these efficiencies lead directly to performance improvements.

Partitioning also enables parallel processing. By distributing computations across multiple processors—each handling a different block—execution times are reduced, which is vital in high-frequency trading where every millisecond counts.

To see block matrices in action, consider their use in Python with scientific computing libraries. NumPy's slicing capabilities make it easy to manipulate submatrices within larger datasets. Take this example, if you have a large dataset stored as a NumPy array, you can extract specific blocks using slicing techniques like portfolio_matrix[0:3, 0:3] to isolate the first three rows and columns as a new matrix block.

This approach is particularly useful for assessing risk across different market segments. By analyzing smaller blocks separately, analysts gain insights into specific sectors' behaviors while retaining the ability to integrate these insights into a comprehensive overview.

In derivative pricing models used for options or futures contracts, partitioned matrices allow practitioners to model the price dynamics of underlying assets both separately and coherently. Each component's behavior can be evaluated for its impact on overall pricing strategies.

The flexibility of block matrices makes them indispensable in multi-factor models that assess various market forces simultaneously. Their modular nature allows analysts to adjust assumptions in one segment without affecting the entire model's integrity—a feature invaluable during scenario testing or stress testing exercises.

By strategically employing block matrices and partitioning techniques, financial analysts can enhance analytical clarity and improve decision-making agility across numerous applications—from portfolio management to derivative pricing—leading to more informed investment strategies and superior risk management practices.

Application in Financial Modelling

Financial modeling, a crucial tool for quantitative analysts, relies heavily on linear algebra and matrix theory to capture complex market dynamics and predict future trends with precision. These mathematical constructs enable financial professionals to build robust models that provide deeper insights into market behavior.

Central to financial modeling is the ability to represent vast amounts of data in an organized way. Matrices play a key role here, allowing analysts to efficiently arrange and manipulate data. For example, when predicting stock prices based on historical data, matrices can encapsulate various variables such as previous stock prices, trading volumes, and market indices, thus creating a comprehensive dataset ready for analysis.

The power of matrices extends beyond data storage; they

also facilitate complex calculations. Operations like matrix multiplication and inversion allow analysts to perform rapid computations essential for time-sensitive decisions. This capability is particularly valuable in high-frequency trading environments where algorithms must process extensive data in milliseconds.

In regression analysis, matrix algebra plays a practical role by revealing relationships between dependent and independent variables. Techniques such as ordinary least squares (OLS), which heavily rely on matrix calculations, enable analysts to create models that best fit historical data, providing predictive insights into future performance.

Additionally, matrices enable linear transformations critical for dimensionality reduction. Techniques like Principal Component Analysis (PCA) use these transformations to identify patterns and reduce noise, thereby enhancing model precision without losing significant information.

Matrices also excel in risk management. Covariance matrices measure how asset prices move relative to one another, offering insights into portfolio risk levels. This knowledge helps analysts optimize asset allocation strategies by identifying combinations that minimize risk while maximizing returns.

Python's powerful libraries like NumPy and Pandas streamline matrix operations in financial models. These tools efficiently handle calculations for expected returns or portfolio optimization through built-in functions that perform matrix multiplications and inversions with ease.

In derivative pricing models, such as those for options, matrix methods help compute "Greeks," which are sensitivities that assess how changes in underlying factors affect option prices. These computations are vital for hedging strategies and ensuring market positions remain balanced against potential risks.

The use of block matrices further enhances financial modeling by breaking down complex systems into manageable components. This modularity simplifies analysis and improves computational efficiency—a necessity when dealing with intricate financial instruments or large datasets.

In the end, the application of linear algebra and matrix theory in financial modeling goes beyond mere calculation; it offers a framework for understanding market behavior and making informed investment decisions. By mastering these mathematical tools, quantitative analysts can construct sophisticated models that provide strategic insights and a competitive edge in the fast-paced world of finance.

CHAPTER 5:
DETERMINANTS AND
THEIR FINANCIAL
IMPLICATIONS

Introduction to Determinants

Determinants occupy a unique niche in linear algebra, offering deep insights into the properties and behaviors of matrices. While they may initially appear as technical constructs, their practical applications, particularly in financial mathematics, are significant. Grasping the concept of determinants provides an analytical framework for tackling complex matrix-related challenges.

A determinant is a scalar value associated with square matrices that encapsulates essential information about the matrix's properties. This single number reveals whether a matrix is invertible, its volume-scaling factor during transformations, and even its eigenvalues. These attributes make determinants indispensable both theoretically and practically in various mathematical and financial contexts.

One of the most compelling features of determinants is

their ability to determine a matrix's invertibility. A non-zero determinant signifies that the matrix has an inverse—a critical aspect when solving systems of linear equations or performing matrix-based computations. In finance, this property is crucial for optimizing portfolios and conducting risk assessments, where invertible matrices are often required to balance risk with expected returns.

The calculation of determinants involves specific algebraic rules that may seem intricate but underpin more advanced operations. Techniques like cofactor expansion allow for determinant computation in larger matrices by breaking them down into smaller components, each contributing to the overall determinant value.

Determinants also have geometric implications relevant to financial modeling. When evaluating transformations represented by matrices, the determinant indicates how these transformations scale areas or volumes—vital information when analyzing market dynamics or asset interactions within a portfolio.

In multidimensional data analysis—common in financial statistics—determinants help assess whether sets of vectors (often representing assets or factors) are linearly independent. This assessment is crucial for ensuring that financial models remain stable and robust, preventing redundant data representation that could skew analyses or predictions.

And, Python libraries like NumPy provide efficient functions to compute determinants directly from matrix inputs, greatly enhancing the efficiency of financial computations involving large datasets. These tools enable quick checks on matrix properties before models are deployed in real-world scenarios.

In trading environments where swift and accurate decisions are paramount, determinants play a vital role by aiding in system consistency checks—validating assumptions before they affect investment strategies. Take this example, understanding how different parameters interact within matrices ensures effective hedging strategies and robust risk management protocols when assessing derivative products or complex trading algorithms.

Thus, while determinants might initially seem like abstract mathematical constructs, their application across financial contexts reveals their true value. They serve as gatekeepers of mathematical rigor and practical utility—enabling analysts to delve deeper into data structures while maintaining precision and strategic foresight in decision-making processes.

This understanding instills confidence among quantitative analysts who rely on these mathematical tools to navigate the unpredictable nature of markets with greater assurance and insightfulness.

Calculation Methods

Understanding how to calculate determinants is essential for anyone exploring matrix algebra, especially in fields that require precise mathematical modeling, such as finance. The method for calculating a determinant depends on the matrix size: while small matrices can be computed manually, larger ones often necessitate computational tools.

For a 2x2 matrix, the determinant calculation is straightforward. Consider a matrix with elements a, b, c, and d arranged as follows:

|a b|

|c d|

The determinant is computed as ad - bc. This simple operation offers a glimpse into the more complex calculations required for larger matrices and serves as an entry point to understanding how determinants scale with matrix size.

When dealing with 3x3 matrices, the calculation becomes more involved and introduces the concepts of minors and cofactors. A 3x3 matrix with elements structured as:

|a b c|

|d e f|

|g h i|

has its determinant determined using the formula: a(ei - fh) - b(di - fg) + c(dh - eg). Each part of this formula represents a smaller, derived determinant from submatrices within the original matrix. This approach can be extended to even larger matrices through cofactor expansion.

This expansion method applies to nxn matrices, where breaking down determinants into smaller components is crucial. Each element of a row (or column) multiplies its corresponding cofactor—a smaller determinant that excludes the row and column of that element—contributing cumulatively to the overall determinant value.

For large or complex matrices, manual calculations become impractical, necessitating the use of computational tools. Libraries such as NumPy in Python offer built-in functions like numpy.linalg.det() that efficiently compute determinants for large matrices with speed and accuracy—an invaluable resource when working with extensive financial datasets.

Consider an example using NumPy to calculate the determinant of a financial covariance matrix:

```python
import numpy as np

\#\# Define a 3x3 covariance matrix representing asset returns

covariance_matrix = np.array([[0.04, 0.002, 0.006],

[0.002, 0.03, 0.001],

[0.006, 0.001, 0.05]])
```

```
\#\# Calculate the determinant
determinant = np.linalg.det(covariance_matrix)

print("Determinant:", determinant)
` ` `
```

This quick computation provides insights into whether this covariance matrix might be invertible or stable enough for further analysis in portfolio optimization scenarios.

Beyond these methods lies Gaussian elimination— a procedural approach that transforms matrices into simpler forms (like upper triangular matrices), from which determinants are easier to compute by multiplying diagonal elements together. Although computationally intensive for manual execution, this technique underpins many algorithmic approaches found in financial software today.

The reliability of these methods is crucial in finance, where decisions hinge on data integrity and precision. Whether assessing risk through variance-covariance models or validating system equations in quantitative trading strategies, accurate determinant calculations ensure models behave predictably under market conditions.

Armed with both foundational knowledge and advanced tools, analysts can confidently engage with determinants not just as theoretical constructs but as practical instruments critical to navigating complex financial landscapes effectively.

Properties of Determinants

Determinants possess several intriguing properties that enhance our understanding of matrix behavior, particularly in financial modeling. These properties not only deepen the conceptual framework of matrix theory but also have practical applications in finance.

A fundamental property is the impact of row or column exchanges on determinants. When two rows or columns are swapped, the determinant's sign changes. This reflects an essential symmetry within matrices, offering insights into structural stability and balance—critical concepts when assessing financial risk and asset allocation strategies.

Another key property is scaling. If you multiply a row by a scalar, the determinant is multiplied by the same factor. That means scalar multiplication alters a matrix's geometric representation without affecting its proportional relationships, akin to adjusting portfolio weights without disrupting overall asset distribution.

Additivity is also crucial; adding a multiple of one row to another leaves the determinant unchanged. This invariance under elementary operations supports techniques like Gaussian elimination and LU decomposition, which are essential for solving systems of equations commonly used in regression analysis and market equilibrium models.

Determinants also indicate matrix singularity. A zero determinant signals a singular matrix with no inverse, highlighting potential vulnerabilities in financial models where such conditions might suggest ill-posed or over-fitted data sets needing reevaluation.

In block matrices composed of submatrices, determinants can be calculated from these smaller components. This understanding helps dissect complex financial structures into manageable units—vital for detailed analyses like stress testing large financial portfolios.

Practical applications of these properties include detecting linear dependence among asset returns through zero determinants or ensuring system solvability with non-zero determinants before executing large-scale portfolio optimizations. The ability to deconstruct and analyze matrices through their determinants provides analysts with a powerful tool for scrutinizing intricate financial ecosystems.

In the end, these properties highlight how determinants serve as foundational stability checks in both theoretical mathematics and applied finance. They act as diagnostic tools for model reliability, allowing analysts to identify potential issues before they lead to significant strategic errors.

Mastery of these properties transforms determinants from abstract concepts into practical tools used daily by quantitative analysts, enabling informed decision-making essential for effectively navigating today's volatile financial markets.

Application to Investment Decisions

Determinants play a crucial role in shaping investment decisions, acting as a vital link between abstract mathematical concepts and practical financial strategies. They are not just of theoretical interest; determinants provide quantitative analysts with essential tools for navigating complex investment landscapes with precision.

One key application of determinants in investment decision-making is evaluating the viability of financial models. Analysts often use systems of linear equations to model market behaviors, predict trends, and assess risk. Determinants help verify whether these systems are solvable —a non-zero determinant indicates a unique solution exists, confirming the model's robustness. This critical check prevents costly errors in portfolio management, where ill-posed models might lead to misguided allocations or inaccurate risk assessments.

In addition to solvability, determinants play a role in optimizing asset allocation. By constructing matrices from historical return data, analysts can calculate determinants to assess linear dependence among assets. A zero determinant flags redundant or highly correlated assets within a portfolio, highlighting opportunities for diversification and reduced systematic risk exposure. This insight aids in building a well-balanced portfolio that maximizes returns while minimizing risks.

Determinants also provide valuable insights into sensitivity analysis. In situations where small changes in input variables can significantly affect outcomes—such as interest rates influencing bond prices—determinants assess model stability under varying conditions. A stable model with non-zero determinants across different scenarios reassures investors of its resilience to market fluctuations and informs strategic adjustments to hedge against potential adverse effects.

In economic forecasting, determinants enhance predictive accuracy through regression analysis. Financial analysts often use regression models to forecast asset prices or economic indicators. Here, determinants ensure that the matrix of predictor variables is full rank—a prerequisite for obtaining reliable estimates and making confident predictions that guide buying or selling strategies.

Advanced applications include evaluating multivariate optimization problems, crucial for strategies like mean-variance optimization in modern portfolio theory (MPT). Determinants of covariance matrices help understand how assets co-move and interact within a portfolio context —insight that guides diversification efforts and enhances expected returns relative to risk.

Through these applications, determinants become more than mere mathematical entities; they transform into strategic instruments that facilitate informed investment decisions. Mastering this tool distinguishes adept quantitative analysts from their peers, providing an edge in crafting strategies that align closely with dynamic market conditions and investor goals.

Thus, understanding determinants equips financial

professionals with enhanced analytical capabilities necessary for devising sophisticated investment solutions tailored to today's complex economic environment.

Cramer's Rule

Cramer's Rule is a straightforward method for solving systems of linear equations using determinants, making it an invaluable tool for financial analysts who require precision in their decision-making processes. This technique is especially effective when the number of equations matches the number of unknowns, ensuring the system is square and invertible.

Imagine a financial model represented by a system of linear equations. These could model anything from asset pricing mechanisms to balance sheet optimizations. In applying Cramer's Rule, each equation corresponds to a row in a matrix, with coefficients forming a square matrix A, while the constants on the other side form a column vector b. Solving Ax = b using Cramer's Rule involves calculating the determinant of A and several related matrices.

For example, consider forecasting returns for two assets based on historical data represented by this system:

1. $ax + by = d$
2. $cx + dy = e$

Here, matrix A is [a b; c d], and vector b is [d; e]. To find x and y using Cramer's Rule, first compute the determinant of A, $det(A) = ad - bc$. This determinant must be non-zero to ensure a unique solution exists.

Next, create matrices A_x and A_y by replacing respective columns of A with vector b. For x, replace the first column with b to get A_x = [d b; e d], then calculate $det(A\_x)$ as $de - eb$. For y, replace the second column to get A_y = [a d; c e], with $det(A\_y)$ as $ae - cd$.

The solutions for x and y are then:

- $x = \det(A\_x) / \det(A)$
- $y = \det(A\_y) / \det(A)$

This method provides exact solutions without iterative approximations—an essential advantage when precision is crucial in financial forecasting or portfolio adjustments.

Beyond its theoretical clarity, Cramer's Rule offers insights into sensitivity analysis by demonstrating how changes in initial conditions or model parameters can directly affect solutions. This feature is valuable for assessing risk exposure or evaluating investment scenarios.

However, while elegant for smaller systems, Cramer's Rule becomes less efficient for larger matrices due to the complexity of calculating determinants. In such cases, alternative numerical methods might be preferred, especially when dealing with high-dimensional financial datasets.

Despite this limitation, understanding Cramer's Rule enhances an analyst's toolkit with fundamental insights into linear algebra's role in finance. It shows how mathematical concepts can be effectively used to derive actionable insights from abstract models—an essential skill in today's data-driven investment landscape.

Mastering Cramer's Rule empowers analysts to decode complex financial systems with precision and confidence.

Determinant and Matrix Inversion

The determinant of a matrix, as we've explored with Cramer's Rule, is crucial for understanding matrix behavior and solving linear systems. This concept is particularly important when discussing matrix inversion—a fundamental operation in linear algebra with wide-ranging applications, especially in finance.

Think of the determinant as a scalar that offers valuable insights into a matrix's properties. When a matrix A has a non-zero determinant, it signifies that A is invertible, meaning there exists another matrix, A^-1, such that the product of A and A^-1 is the identity matrix I. This property is highly beneficial for quantitative analysts working with systems of equations in financial models. An invertible matrix allows for efficient solutions without needing iterative methods.

Matrix inversion is essential in portfolio optimization problems. Take this example, given a covariance matrix Σ representing asset returns, finding its inverse aids in calculating the weights of an efficient portfolio by solving the equation Σw = b, where w is the vector of asset weights and b represents expected returns or constraints. The solution w = Σ^-1b illustrates how inverses streamline computations in financial models.

To compute an inverse, one method involves using the adjugate of A and its determinant. For a 2x2 matrix [a b; c d], if det(A) = ad - bc ≠ 0, then:

- A^-1 = (1/det(A)) * [d -b; -c a]

This formula underscores the relationship between determinants and inverses. However, computing inverses for larger matrices often requires sophisticated algorithms due to potential numerical instability—a crucial factor in high-frequency trading where precision is paramount.

The practical application of inverses extends into algorithmic trading systems. Traders use these calculations to dynamically adjust hedging strategies or recalibrate risk parameters in response to market changes. Accurate inverse computation can be decisive between profit and loss when executing trades at scale.

While inverses are powerful tools, they come with computational challenges. For large matrices common in big data finance environments, direct computation can be time-consuming and resource-intensive. Analysts often use techniques like LU decomposition or iterative methods to achieve efficient solutions without sacrificing accuracy, especially when real-time decisions are necessary.

Understanding determinants and matrix inversion provides analysts with essential skills to dissect complex financial models accurately. This knowledge bridges theoretical concepts with practical execution, enhancing an analyst's ability to navigate sophisticated financial landscapes confidently.

By mastering these foundational elements of linear algebra, you enhance your analytical abilities—unraveling intricate systems with clarity and precision—and prepare yourself for informed decision-making in finance's ever-evolving arena.

Interpretations in Risk Assessment

Understanding the role of determinants in risk assessment is crucial for financial analysts who aim to quantify uncertainty and manage exposure effectively. Determinants provide valuable insights into the stability and sensitivity of financial models, acting as a litmus test for potential risk factors that could impact investment strategies.

In risk assessment, the determinant of a covariance matrix is particularly significant. This matrix captures the variance and correlation among different assets within a portfolio. A non-zero determinant indicates a full-rank matrix, suggesting diverse and independent asset movements and thus reduced systemic risk. In contrast, a zero or near-zero determinant may signal multicollinearity among assets, hinting at hidden risks that could surface with shifting market conditions.

For example, consider a portfolio with assets showing correlated returns. A covariance matrix with a low determinant suggests high redundancy among these assets, making the portfolio vulnerable to collective downturns— especially critical during volatile market phases. In such cases, reevaluation and diversification are necessary to mitigate concentrated risk exposure.

Risk managers also rely on matrix determinants to assess the robustness of hedging strategies. When constructing a hedge against interest rate fluctuations using derivatives, examining the determinant of the sensitivity matrix (often called the "Greeks" matrix in options trading) reveals how well a portfolio can withstand changes in underlying rates. A well-conditioned sensitivity matrix with a significant determinant implies that minor market variable changes won't disproportionately affect the portfolio's value, boosting confidence in hedging effectiveness.

Practically speaking, if an analyst detects a small determinant in their model's sensitivity analysis, it may prompt adjustments in hedging ratios or the addition of instruments to balance exposure. This proactive approach helps prevent potential losses by leveraging mathematical insights.

The importance of determinants extends beyond static analysis to dynamic decision-making processes. In algorithmic trading platforms where rapid execution is essential, quickly assessing determinants ensures algorithms operate within predefined risk thresholds. These calculations inform traders whether strategies remain viable under current market conditions or require recalibration to avert potential risks.

Also, determinants play a critical role in stress testing financial models under hypothetical scenarios, such as economic downturns or sudden market shocks. By analyzing how determinants fluctuate across stress scenarios, analysts can identify potential vulnerabilities within their portfolios, enabling proactive rather than reactive adjustments.

Interpreting determinants within risk assessment frameworks empowers financial professionals to navigate uncertainties with heightened awareness and strategic foresight. This capability not only enhances individual decision-making but also contributes to broader financial stability by promoting informed risk management practices across markets.

With this understanding, analysts are better equipped to anticipate market movements and adjust strategies accordingly—fortifying their defenses against unexpected events while seizing emerging opportunities with precision and confidence.

Economic Implications

The economic implications of financial determinants reach far beyond risk management, significantly impacting market dynamics and strategic planning. These mathematical indicators are crucial for both micro-level portfolio adjustments and macroeconomic forecasts, informing policy decisions that can influence entire economies.

Determinants offer insights into the structural health of economic models by highlighting singularities or redundancies. In macroeconomic analysis, economists use determinants of input-output matrices to understand sector interdependencies. A determinant nearing zero may indicate inefficiencies or vulnerabilities, pointing to sectors that require reform or support to maintain economic stability.

Consider how a central bank might use determinants in monetary policy formulation. When analyzing an economy's input-output model, a high determinant can suggest strong sectoral independence and resilience against external shocks. This understanding helps in crafting growth-stimulating policies that avoid triggering inflation. Conversely, low determinants reveal systemic vulnerabilities, prompting actions like liquidity injections or fiscal stimulus.

At the corporate level, strategists use determinants in mergers and acquisitions (M&A) evaluations. During due diligence, analysts examine covariance matrices of potential targets. High determinants suggest diversified revenue streams and robust asset portfolios, increasing a target's appeal by highlighting potential synergies and mitigating risks.

In capital markets, determinants impact the cost of capital by influencing credit ratings and investor perceptions. Credit analysts rely on models where determinants indicate operational strength or weakness. Firms with high-determinant matrices often receive favorable ratings, reducing borrowing costs and enhancing access to capital—essential for growth and competitive edge.

Determinants also affect pricing strategies for complex derivatives like collateralized debt obligations (CDOs). Structures with high determinants are perceived as less risky due to their diversification benefits, commanding premium prices compared to those with lower determinants that indicate concentrated exposures.

In the venture capital landscape, startups with business plans featuring strong matrix determinants attract more investment interest. These metrics demonstrate managerial competence in building scalable operations resilient to market fluctuations, a crucial factor for investors seeking sustainable returns in volatile markets.

Globally, international trade negotiations frequently incorporate matrix analysis using country-specific input-output tables to identify comparative advantages and potential bottlenecks. Countries with favorable determinant metrics negotiate from stronger positions, pushing for trade agreements that leverage their diversified export capabilities while protecting sensitive industries.

Determinants also guide governmental resource allocation by prioritizing infrastructure investments in regions with lower matrix determinations—areas with latent economic potential hindered by current inefficiencies.

Overall, interpreting economic implications through matrix determinants enhances strategic foresight across various domains—from firms navigating competitive landscapes to national policymakers devising economic growth strategies. This analytical insight not only refines decision-making processes but also strengthens economic systems against unforeseen challenges while fostering sustainable development across interconnected financial networks.

CHAPTER 6: EIGENVALUES AND EIGENVECTORS

Characteristics and Properties

U nderstanding eigenvalues and eigenvectors is crucial for applying these mathematical tools effectively in finance. These constructs form the backbone of many advanced financial models, offering insights into system behaviors that might be overlooked through traditional analyses.

Eigenvalues, often represented by the Greek letter lambda (λ), are scalars that describe how an associated eigenvector is stretched or compressed during a linear transformation. They provide critical insights into the dynamics of financial systems, including stability and sensitivity to external factors. The real part of an eigenvalue can indicate whether a system will move towards equilibrium or instability, making them invaluable in stress-testing scenarios.

Eigenvectors, linked to these eigenvalues, point out the directions in which these transformations occur without altering direction. In financial contexts, this can relate to portfolio directionality or predicting market trends. When a matrix representing financial data acts on an eigenvector, the result is simply a scaled version of that vector—maintaining its orientation while possibly changing its magnitude.

For example, consider a covariance matrix used in risk management: the largest eigenvalue indicates the direction of maximum variance, revealing where the greatest potential for risk lies. By examining these vectors, analysts can adjust portfolios to minimize exposure to unfavorable directions while capitalizing on beneficial trends.

The relationship between eigenvalues and their corresponding vectors also supports dimensionality reduction techniques like Principal Component Analysis (PCA). In PCA, they help distill complex datasets into principal components that capture most of the variance with fewer variables—a process essential for simplifying large-scale financial models without significant information loss.

Symmetric matrices are common in finance due to properties like covariance or correlation matrices being inherently symmetric. These matrices have real eigenvalues and orthogonal eigenvectors, simplifying computations significantly—making transformations more efficient and enhancing modeling capabilities.

And, understanding these properties enables assessing matrix diagonalizability—a method where a matrix is expressed as a product involving a diagonal matrix. In finance, diagonalization simplifies complex calculations related to interest rate models or option pricing algorithms by reducing computational demands.

A practical example includes extensions of the Black-Scholes model where volatility surfaces are explored through differential equations; here, eigenvalues simplify these processes by reducing dimensionality via diagonalization. Similarly, risk management strategies often use such simplifications for calculating value-at-risk (VaR) metrics across portfolios with numerous assets.

In predictive modeling and scenario analysis, examining shifts in dominant eigenvalues over time can reveal emerging market trends or impending economic shifts—informing strategic decision-making within investment firms.

Thus, grasping the characteristics and properties of eigenvalues and eigenvectors not only demystifies complex mathematical theories but also translates into actionable insights within finance. By effectively leveraging these concepts, analysts enhance their ability to model uncertainties accurately and optimize performance across diverse market conditions—facilitating more informed strategic decisions in ever-evolving economic landscapes.

Financial Interpretation

In finance, eigenvalues and eigenvectors transcend their mathematical origins to become essential tools for analysts and traders. Grasping their financial implications can offer strategic advantages in portfolio management and risk assessment.

Consider portfolio optimization, a fundamental aspect of modern investment strategy. Here, eigenvalues and eigenvectors provide crucial insights into the correlation structure among asset returns. The largest eigenvalue of a covariance matrix pinpoints the dominant market factor influencing asset behavior, which is vital for identifying systemic risks that might otherwise go unnoticed. By aligning investments with principal eigenvectors, analysts can construct portfolios that effectively capture systematic risks while minimizing idiosyncratic volatility.

Similarly, market stability analysis benefits from these tools. Eigenvalues of Jacobian matrices derived from dynamic economic models can predict system responses to shocks, providing foresight into potential instability or downturns.

An eigenvalue with a negative real part indicates a tendency towards equilibrium, whereas positive real parts may signal explosive growth or bubbles—information crucial for managing investments during volatile periods.

In algorithmic trading and high-frequency contexts, eigenvectors help develop algorithms that detect trends and reversals by analyzing shifts in leading eigenvalues of pricing matrices over micro-intervals. This predictive capability enables traders to adjust strategies proactively to optimize returns and minimize losses.

Credit risk modeling also leverages these mathematical constructs. Within frameworks like the Merton model, firms' default probabilities are assessed using variance-covariance matrices to evaluate financial health. Eigenvalues help estimate the impact of market-wide events on credit spreads, informing decisions about loan portfolios and debt securities.

Eigenvalues also simplify derivative pricing by streamlining complex models based on stochastic processes. In interest rate modeling via frameworks like Heath-Jarrow-Morton, diagonalizing matrices related to rate movements reduces computational complexity while maintaining accuracy— facilitating valuations for options, futures, and swaps.

In stress testing across multiple financial instruments, variations in dominant eigenvalues indicate changes in underlying correlations, prompting reviews of risk management policies to adapt to evolving market conditions.

In the end, mastering the financial interpretation of eigenvalues and eigenvectors equips quantitative analysts with powerful insights into market dynamics and asset behaviors. These mathematical tools support nuanced decision-making across trading desks and investment firms, enabling strategies that are robust against uncertainties and aligned with financial goals in fluctuating economic landscapes.

Calculation Techniques

Eigenvalues and eigenvectors are fundamental components of various financial models, playing a key role in assessing system stability and behavior. Accurately calculating these values can provide deep insights, enabling analysts to optimize portfolios or forecast market trends. So, how can we compute these critical elements precisely?

Let's start with a square matrix A. To determine its eigenvalues, you need to solve the characteristic equation det(A - λI) = 0, where λ represents an eigenvalue and I is the identity matrix of the same size as A. The determinant det(A - λI) forms a polynomial in λ, known as the characteristic polynomial. Solving this polynomial yields the eigenvalues.

Consider an example with a simple 2x2 matrix:

Matrix A is given by:

[A = bmatrix 4 & 1 \ 2 & 3 bmatrix]

Subtract λ times the identity matrix from A:

[A - λI = bmatrix 4-λ & 1 \ 2 & 3-λ bmatrix]

Compute the determinant:

[det(A - λI) = (4-λ)(3-λ) - (1)(2) = λ^2 -7λ +10]

To find the eigenvalues, solve:

[λ^2 -7λ +10 = 0]

Factoring gives:

[(λ - 5)(λ - 2) = 0]

Thus, the eigenvalues are λ1=5 and λ2=2.

Next, we find the corresponding eigenvectors by solving (A - λI)x = 0 for each eigenvalue. For λ1=5:

[(A - 5I)x = bmatrix -1 & 1 \ 2 & -2 bmatrixx = 0]

This leads to x1=x2, yielding an eigenvector such as x=[1,1].

For λ2=2:

[(A - 2I)x = bmatrix 2 & 1 \ 2 & 1 bmatrixx = 0]

Here, x1 =-0.5x2 gives an eigenvector like x=[-0.5,1].

Now, let's apply this process to a financial context using a covariance matrix—a typical application in portfolio optimization. Consider a simplified covariance matrix Σ:

[Σ = bmatrix σ_1^2 & σ_12 \ σ_12 & σ_2^2 bmatrix]

By calculating its eigenvalues and eigenvectors as described above, you gain insights into the principal components of asset returns—vital inputs for portfolio construction and risk management.

While these steps may seem straightforward with small matrices, larger systems typical in real-world financial analysis often require computational software. Languages like Python or R offer robust libraries such as NumPy or Eigen for efficiently handling these calculations.

Here's an example using Python's NumPy library:

```python
import numpy as np

\#\# Define your matrix
A = np.array([[4, 1],

[2, 3]])

\#\# Calculate eigenvalues and eigenvectors
eigenvalues, eigenvectors = np.linalg.eig(A)

print("Eigenvalues:", eigenvalues)
```

print("Eigenvectors:", eigenvectors)

` ` `

Using such code allows you to process large datasets effortlessly while focusing on interpretation rather than manual computation.

Incorporating these techniques into your financial toolkit not only enhances your ability to handle complex data but also deepens your understanding of their strategic significance in market analysis.

Diagonalization and Its Use

Diagonalization is a crucial technique in linear algebra with significant applications in finance, particularly for simplifying matrix operations and analyzing complex systems. This process involves converting a given matrix into a diagonal form, which makes computations more efficient and insightful.

To grasp the concept of diagonalization, let's examine a square matrix A. If A can be represented as PDP^{-1}, where D is a diagonal matrix and P is an invertible matrix made up of A's eigenvectors, then A is considered diagonalizable. This transformation simplifies computations because operations on diagonal matrices are straightforward.

The utility of diagonalization is particularly evident when dealing with powers of matrices. In finance, this becomes vital for scenarios involving repeated matrix operations, such as calculating future states in Markov processes or optimizing asset allocation over time. For example, if you have a matrix A representing transition probabilities in a Markov chain, determining the system's state after several steps involves raising A to the power n (A^n). If A is diagonalizable:

$$A\wedge n = (PDP\wedge-1)\wedge n = PD\wedge nP\wedge-1$$

Here, computing D^n is straightforward since it involves raising each diagonal element (eigenvalue) to the power n.

Consider the following example with matrix A:

$[A = bmatrix\ 3\ \&\ 1\ \backslash\ 0\ \&\ 2\ bmatrix]$

First, we find its eigenvalues by solving the characteristic equation $\det(A - \lambda I) = 0$:

$[\det(A - \lambda I) = (3-\lambda)(2-\lambda) = \lambda^2 - 5\lambda + 6]$

This yields eigenvalues $\lambda_1 = 3$ and $\lambda_2 = 2$.

Next, calculate eigenvectors for each eigenvalue. For $\lambda_1 = 3$:

$[(A - 3I)x = bmatrix\ 0\ \&\ 1\ \backslash\ 0\ \&\ -1\ bmatrixx = 0]$

This gives $x=[1,0]$.

For $\lambda_2 = 2$:

$[(A - 2I)x = bmatrix\ 1\ \&\ 1\ \backslash\ 0\ \&\ 0\ bmatrixx = 0]$

This leads to $x=[-1,1]$.

With these eigenvectors, we form P:

$[P = bmatrix\ 1\ \&\ -1\ \backslash\ 0\ \&\ 1\ bmatrix, P^{-1} = bmatrix\ 1\ \&\ 1\ \backslash\ 0\ \&\ 1\ bmatrix]$

We can then diagonalize A as:

$[D = P^{-1}AP = bmatrix$

$3\ \&\ -3\ \backslash$

$0\ \&\ 2$

bmatrix

bmatrix

$3\ \&\ 0\backslash$

$0\ \&\ 2$

bmatrix

$]$

In practice, consider a covariance matrix Σ used in portfolio optimization:

[Σ = PDP^-1, where D contains principal variances along its diagonal. Diagonalizing Σ helps identify dominant risk factors and simplifies computing portfolio variance through calculations involving D instead of Σ.]

For handling large matrices common in financial models efficiently, tools like Python's NumPy provide functions to facilitate these transformations. Here's an implementation using Python:

```python
import numpy as np

\#\# Define your square matrix
A = np.array([[3, 1],
[0, 2]])

\#\# Calculate eigenvectors and eigenvalues
eigenvalues, eigenvectors = np.linalg.eig(A)

\#\# Form the diagonalized version
D = np.diag(eigenvalues)
P_inv = np.linalg.inv(eigenvectors)

\#\# Verify the diagonalization
A_diag = np.dot(np.dot(eigenvectors,D),P_inv)

print("Diagonal Matrix:", D)
print("Original Matrix Reconstructed:", A_diag)
```

` ` `

Transforming matrices into simpler forms via diagonalization enables more efficient computation and provides deeper insights into financial models' behavior over time. Such techniques are indispensable for analysts who aim to streamline their calculations while maintaining analytical rigor.

By mastering and applying diagonalization within your workflow effectively, you enhance both computational efficiency and strategic analysis capabilities—essential traits for success in today's fast-paced financial markets.

Risk and Eigen Analysis

In the world of finance, understanding and managing risk is essential. One key tool in this process is eigen analysis, a mathematical method rooted in linear algebra. By examining eigenvalues and eigenvectors, analysts can uncover insights into financial systems' behaviors and identify hidden risk factors.

This relationship between risk and eigen analysis is particularly significant in portfolio management. Take, for example, a covariance matrix Σ that represents the variance and covariance among different assets in a portfolio. The matrix's eigenvalues reveal the principal components of risk: larger eigenvalues suggest greater variance in certain directions, indicating which asset combinations contribute most to overall volatility.

When the covariance matrix Σ is transformed into its diagonalized form, PDP^{-1}, where D contains the eigenvalues on its diagonal, these values represent the variances linked to each principal component. This transformation simplifies identifying dominant sources of risk, with large eigenvalues highlighting significant risk factors that may require careful monitoring or hedging.

Consider a practical application: a financial analyst assessing a diversified investment portfolio's risk profile. By calculating the covariance matrix Σ for asset returns and performing an eigen decomposition, they can concentrate on principal components with high variance (large eigenvalues). This approach not only identifies critical risks but also guides strategic asset allocation decisions to minimize exposure to volatile factors.

Here's how this can be implemented using Python:

```python
import numpy as np


\#\# Simulated covariance matrix for three assets
cov_matrix = np.array([[0.05, 0.02, 0.01],
[0.02, 0.04, 0.03],
[0.01, 0.03, 0.06]])


\#\# Perform eigen decomposition
eigenvalues, eigenvectors = np.linalg.eig(cov_matrix)


\#\# Sorting eigenvalues and corresponding vectors for analysis
idx = np.argsort(eigenvalues)[::-1]
eigenvalues = eigenvalues[idx]
eigenvectors = eigenvectors[:, idx]


print("Eigenvalues (Variance Contribution):", eigenvalues)
```

```
print("Principal Components:", eigenvectors)
` ` `
```

In this example, the covariance matrix captures the relationships among three assets within a portfolio. Sorting the computed eigenvalues in descending order prioritizes components by their contribution to variance, thus enabling targeted risk assessment.

Beyond individual portfolios, eigen analysis applies to broader market models as well. In factor-based investing strategies, identifying underlying factors that influence asset returns is crucial for building robust portfolios aligned with market dynamics.

And, in stress testing scenarios—where portfolios are evaluated under hypothetical adverse conditions—understanding how these conditions impact principal components offers valuable foresight into potential vulnerabilities.

A crucial aspect of such analyses is sensitivity testing: evaluating how changes in model parameters affect outcomes ensures robustness against uncertainties inherent in financial markets.

In the end, mastering risk through eigendecomposition equips financial professionals with advanced analytical capabilities essential for informed decision-making amidst complexity and uncertainty—a vital skill set not just for success but also resilience in today's volatile economic landscape.

By effectively integrating these insights into their workflows using software tools like NumPy or MATLAB's linear algebra functions, analysts streamline complex calculations while maintaining analytical rigor—strengthening their ability to navigate dynamic markets with confidence and deeper insights into systemic risks underpinning their investment strategies globally.

Stability of Systems

Stability in financial systems is a crucial consideration, particularly when examining the complex dynamics of market interactions and portfolio management. This concept is intricately linked to eigen analysis, offering a quantitative approach for assessing the robustness of financial models.

Stability often refers to a system's ability to return to equilibrium after experiencing a disturbance. In finance, this could relate to how a portfolio reacts to market shocks or how investment returns fluctuate in response to economic changes. By analyzing the eigenvalues from a system's matrix representation—whether it's a covariance matrix for asset returns or a correlation matrix for economic indicators—financial analysts can determine if the system is stable or susceptible to volatility.

Eigenvalues are central to this analysis. The sign and magnitude of these values indicate the nature of stability: positive eigenvalues may signal growth or increased perturbations, while negative ones suggest dampening effects leading to stabilization. A practical example of this is seen in stress testing scenarios used by banks to simulate extreme market conditions and assess resilience. Through eigen decomposition, banks can simplify complex risk matrices, revealing core vulnerabilities.

Take this example, an analyst focused on maintaining an investment strategy's stability during volatile periods would break down market data into principal components using eigenvectors and eigenvalues. This process involves computing and analyzing these mathematical constructs with tools like Python:

```python
import numpy as np
```

```
\#\# Hypothetical stability matrix for an economic model
stability_matrix = np.array([[0.8, 0.1],
[0.2, 0.7]])

\#\# Calculate eigenvalues and eigenvectors
eigenvals, eigvecs = np.linalg.eig(stability_matrix)

print("Eigenvalues:", eigenvals)
print("Eigenvectors:", eigvecs)
` ` `
```

In this context, identifying any eigenvalue exceeding one in magnitude can signal potential instability within the system —prompting strategic adjustments such as rebalancing asset allocations or modifying hedging strategies.

On a broader scale, understanding systemic stability— whether within national economies or global financial networks—relies on similar analyses. Recognizing patterns through principal component analysis enables policymakers to proactively address structural weaknesses before they escalate into crises.

And, time-series analysis applies these concepts by treating temporal data as evolving systems where each time step influences subsequent states. Identifying stable versus unstable modes supports the development of effective policy interventions.

This level of insight highlights the importance of mathematical rigor in navigating uncertain environments. Practitioners who utilize these techniques not only enhance their predictive capabilities but also ensure their strategies remain resilient against unforeseen disruptions.

As technology progresses into areas like machine learning and artificial intelligence, incorporating classical linear algebra techniques becomes increasingly vital—not only enriching our understanding but also embedding robust safeguards into automated decision-making processes across industries today.

In the end, recognizing stability through analytic frameworks empowers professionals with the foresight needed for successful risk mitigation—an invaluable asset amidst ever-evolving challenges posed by interconnected global markets that rely on precision-driven analytical acumen honed over years of leveraging foundational mathematical principles in practical applications worldwide.

Portfolio Implications

Understanding the implications of portfolio management bridges the gap between theoretical stability analysis and practical financial decision-making. By analyzing system stability through eigenvalues and eigenvectors, investors gain valuable insights into constructing portfolios and managing risk. This analytical approach provides the foresight needed to optimize portfolio performance while mitigating potential volatility.

In creating a diversified portfolio, achieving an optimal balance between risk and return is paramount. Eigenvalues are crucial in identifying latent risks that might not be immediately apparent. Take this example, decomposing a covariance matrix of asset returns can uncover underlying risk factors that traditional measures might miss.

Imagine an investment manager analyzing a portfolio with equities, bonds, and alternative assets. By using principal component analysis, they can simplify complex covariance data into principal components that highlight dominant risk factors affecting portfolio variance. This analysis might reveal that much of the portfolio's risk is driven by interest rate fluctuations or market sentiment rather than individual asset performance.

Implementing these insights requires strategic action, often involving tools like Excel or Python for detailed calculations:

Excel Walkthrough:

1. Organize asset return data in a matrix format.

2. Calculate the covariance matrix using Excel's built-in functions.

3. Use Excel's 'Analysis ToolPak' for eigenvalue decomposition.

4. Analyze the output to identify significant components affecting risk.

Python Example:

```python
import numpy as np

\#\# Simulated covariance matrix for portfolio assets
cov_matrix = np.array([[0.05, 0.02],
[0.02, 0.03]])

\#\# Perform eigenvalue decomposition
eigenvalues, eigenvectors = np.linalg.eig(cov_matrix)

print("Eigenvalues:", eigenvalues)
print("Eigenvectors:", eigenvectors)
```

Here, eigenvectors indicate directions of maximum variance, while eigenvalues show the magnitude of this variance along those directions. With this information, investors can adjust their portfolios to diversify or hedge against identified risks effectively.

This analytical capability also supports stress testing by simulating extreme scenarios to assess how portfolios withstand adverse conditions. Understanding portfolio reactions to systemic shocks through their eigen-decomposed structures allows investors to preemptively adjust asset allocations or use derivatives like options and futures for protection.

Beyond traditional strategies, these mathematical concepts underpin advanced techniques like factor investing and smart beta strategies—approaches that target specific factors such as value, size, or momentum derived from eigen analysis.

Mastering these tools empowers financial professionals with enhanced prediction accuracy and tactical agility in dynamic markets. This guarantees portfolios are resilient against market fluctuations while capitalizing on growth opportunities identified through rigorous mathematical scrutiny.

Thus, appreciating the role of linear algebra in portfolio management goes beyond academic interest; it is essential for crafting sophisticated investment strategies robust against both predictable trends and unexpected market upheavals.

This ongoing integration of theory and practice highlights why professionals committed to excellence continuously refine their expertise in mathematical modeling—recognizing its transformative potential as both a shield against risk and a guide toward informed financial innovation in today's complex global landscape.

Sensitivity and Analysis

Sensitivity analysis is crucial for evaluating the robustness of financial models. By examining how variations in inputs affect outputs, investors and analysts can pinpoint vulnerabilities in their portfolios and trading strategies. This scrutiny is especially important during market volatility, enabling informed decision-making in uncertain environments.

The process often starts with analyzing eigenvalues and eigenvectors derived from asset correlation matrices. These mathematical tools help identify sensitive parameters that significantly impact model outcomes. For example, if slight changes in interest rates or currency exchange rates lead to substantial shifts in portfolio value, these factors warrant closer monitoring.

Take, for instance, an analyst reviewing a multi-asset portfolio consisting of stocks, bonds, and commodities. Sensitivity analysis might reveal that the portfolio's performance is highly sensitive to oil price fluctuations. Such insights could lead to reallocating assets to reduce reliance on oil prices or implementing hedging strategies to mitigate potential losses.

To translate this theoretical framework into practical action, we can use both Excel and Python:

Excel Approach:

1. Enter asset returns and economic factors into an Excel spreadsheet.

2. Use Excel's 'Data Analysis' tool to compute correlation matrices.

3. Conduct sensitivity testing by adjusting key variables and observing changes in model outputs.

4. Use charts to visually summarize findings and highlight key sensitivities.

Python Approach:

```python
import numpy as np

## Define sensitivity function
def sensitivity_analysis(cov_matrix, factor_variation):
## Adjust covariance matrix for variation in economic factors
adjusted_cov = cov_matrix + factor_variation
## Recalculate eigenvalues
new_eigenvalues = np.linalg.eigvals(adjusted_cov)
return new_eigenvalues

## Original covariance matrix
cov_matrix = np.array([[0.04, 0.01],
[0.01, 0.02]])

## Simulate a factor variation (e.g., interest rate change)
factor_variation = np.array([[0.005, 0],
[0, 0]])

## Perform sensitivity analysis
new_eigenvalues = sensitivity_analysis(cov_matrix, factor_variation)
print("New Eigenvalues:", new_eigenvalues)
```

This process highlights key sensitivities, showing where adjustments can mitigate risks or capitalize on opportunities.

Beyond individual portfolio assessments, sensitivity analysis is valuable for broader market evaluations and risk assessments within financial institutions. Regular application of these techniques enables firms to develop strategic foresight and bolster resilience against systemic disruptions.

Additionally, understanding sensitivities aids in stress-testing scenarios by applying hypothetical shocks to assess robustness under extreme conditions. This proactive approach is vital for risk management frameworks aiming to protect against unpredictable market dynamics.

At its core, mastering sensitivity analysis through linear algebra provides financial professionals with a detailed understanding of model behavior under various conditions. It ensures strategic decisions are based on comprehensive insights rather than speculation—empowering stakeholders to navigate the complexities of financial markets with confidence and precision.

This commitment to continuous learning and adaptation underscores the dynamic nature of finance—a field where knowledge of mathematical principles translates directly into competitive advantage and long-term success amidst ever-evolving economic landscapes.

CHAPTER 7:
DIAGONALIZATION
AND JORDAN FORM

Matrix Decomposition

Matrix decomposition, a cornerstone of linear algebra, involves breaking down a matrix into simpler components. This technique is essential for simplifying complex computations and understanding matrix structures, especially in financial applications where large datasets are prevalent.

In modeling asset returns, matrix decomposition helps quantitative analysts uncover hidden patterns and relationships within data, facilitating easier interpretation. For example, singular value decomposition (SVD) can reduce the dimensionality of financial data without significant information loss. This not only streamlines calculations but also boosts computational efficiency, critical when processing extensive financial information.

Let's explore this with an example: consider a covariance matrix representing the returns of various assets. Through decomposition, principal components that explain most of the variability in asset returns can be identified. These components aid in constructing more efficient portfolios by focusing on key factors driving returns.

Excel Approach:

1. Enter your dataset into an Excel spreadsheet.

2. Use built-in functions like MINVERSE and MMULT to perform decompositions such as LU or QR.

3. Visualize principal components using Excel charts to identify dominant factors.

Python Approach:

```python
import numpy as np

from scipy.linalg import lu


\#\# Define a matrix for decomposition

A = np.array([[1, 2, 3],

[4, 5, 6],

[7, 8, 10]])


\#\# Perform LU decomposition

P, L, U = lu(A)


print("L:", L)

print("U:", U)
```

In this Python snippet, we use LU decomposition to express matrix A as the product of a lower triangular matrix L and an upper triangular matrix U. This transformation is useful for solving systems of equations and computing inverses efficiently.

Understanding these decompositions is more than an academic exercise; it enables precise manipulation of matrices for financial modeling and forecasting. Whether used in risk assessment models or portfolio optimization, decompositions provide critical insights that inform strategic decisions.

Matrix decomposition also plays a pivotal role in risk management by isolating factors contributing to volatility. Identifying these variables allows financial institutions to develop hedging strategies that mitigate potential losses during market turbulence.

And, the ability to decompose matrices fosters innovation by enabling elegant solutions to complex problems—solutions grounded in mathematical rigor yet adaptable to real-world challenges.

In the end, mastering matrix decomposition empowers financial professionals to navigate intricate datasets with finesse and extract actionable insights that drive value creation. Breaking down complexities into manageable parts reflects a deeper understanding of the structural intricacies inherent in financial data, ensuring robust analysis and strategic foresight in decision-making processes.

Eigen Decomposition

Eigen decomposition is a powerful tool in matrix analysis, particularly valuable in finance for understanding the underlying structure of matrices. This process breaks down a matrix into its eigenvalues and eigenvectors, uncovering intrinsic properties and behaviors of financial systems.

For example, consider the covariance matrix of asset returns. Eigen decomposition helps identify the principal directions of data variation, offering insights into significant risk factors. These insights are crucial for constructing optimized portfolios, enabling analysts to allocate resources effectively by concentrating on dominant influences.

When examining a matrix representing asset correlations, eigen decomposition reveals the primary components driving these correlations. This nuanced view enhances risk assessment and improves predictive models by focusing on elements that truly matter.

Excel Example:

1. Input your correlation or covariance matrix in Excel.

2. Use the EIGENVAL function (if available) or an add-in to calculate eigenvalues and eigenvectors.

3. Visualize these components with charts to highlight significant influences on your financial data.

Python Example:

```python
import numpy as np

\#\# Define a symmetric matrix
B = np.array([[4, 1],
[1, 3]])

\#\# Perform eigen decomposition
eigenvalues, eigenvectors = np.linalg.eig(B)

print("Eigenvalues:", eigenvalues)
print("Eigenvectors:", eigenvectors)
```

In this Python example, we perform an eigen decomposition on a symmetric matrix B. The eigenvalues indicate the magnitude of each principal component's impact, while the eigenvectors define their direction within the dataset.

Applying eigen decomposition extends beyond technical mastery; it's about leveraging these insights strategically. In trading algorithms, it can refine decision-making by incorporating only relevant factors, reducing noise and enhancing accuracy.

In risk management, eigen decomposition isolates specific volatility drivers, enabling firms to develop targeted strategies that bolster resilience against market shocks. By distilling complex datasets into fundamental patterns, financial models become more interpretable and facilitate clearer communication with non-technical stakeholders.

The elegance of eigen decomposition lies in its ability to transform complexity into clarity. By dissecting matrices into elemental parts, financial professionals gain deeper understanding and predictive capabilities—an invaluable asset in a rapidly evolving market landscape.

This exploration of structural characteristics within matrices unlocks potential pathways for innovation and growth. Through a deeper comprehension of financial systems' nuances, analysts can make informed decisions and foster strategic foresight that supports sustainable success.

Application to Asset Pricing

In the complex world of finance, asset pricing is a crucial element where precision and informed judgment are key to success. One powerful tool in this domain is eigen decomposition, which provides analysts with a sophisticated means to evaluate and predict asset values accurately.

Take, for instance, the fundamental models of asset pricing like the Capital Asset Pricing Model (CAPM). While these models are foundational, they often rely on simplifying assumptions that can mask the intricate dynamics of the market. Eigen decomposition helps unravel these complexities by identifying the underlying factors that influence asset prices. By isolating these critical influences, financial analysts can refine their models to improve predictive accuracy.

Consider risk assessment within asset pricing as an example. If you have a dataset of historical returns for a portfolio, performing eigen decomposition on its covariance matrix allows you to pinpoint principal components that account for most of the variance. This insight enables adjustments in asset weights within the portfolio to better align with influential factors affecting price movements.

Excel Example:

1. Arrange your asset return data in a spreadsheet.

2. Utilize Excel's built-in functions or an add-in to perform eigen decomposition on the covariance matrix.

3. Examine principal components to identify which factors most significantly affect asset prices.

Python Example:

```python
import numpy as np


\#\# Simulate asset return data

returns = np.random.rand(100, 5) \# 100 days of returns for 5 assets


\#\# Compute covariance matrix

cov_matrix = np.cov(returns.T)
```

```
\#\# Perform eigen decomposition
eigenvalues, eigenvectors = np.linalg.eig(cov_matrix)

print("Eigenvalues:", eigenvalues)
print("Principal Components:", eigenvectors)
` ` `
```

This Python code snippet demonstrates how to use simulated return data to compute a covariance matrix and then perform eigen decomposition. The resulting eigenvalues and eigenvectors reveal principal components that can guide asset pricing decisions.

Beyond theoretical applications, using eigen decomposition in real-world scenarios requires strategic thinking. It's not just about identifying dominant factors; it's about integrating these insights into strategies that maximize returns while managing risk. By focusing on primary components identified through this process, traders can streamline their models —reducing computational demands while maintaining robustness.

In algorithmic trading, where rapid decisions are crucial, understanding and utilizing eigen decomposition enables quick adaptations based on changing market conditions. This approach equips traders with enhanced tools to anticipate price shifts influenced by underlying economic forces rather than transient noise.

In the end, applying eigen decomposition to asset pricing goes beyond mathematical elegance; it becomes a strategic enabler. Financial professionals leverage this technique to build more resilient portfolios and craft sophisticated strategies that adapt to evolving market landscapes.

This approach fosters not only technical expertise but also strategic foresight—essential traits for navigating today's dynamic financial markets. Through careful analysis and application of these mathematical principles, quantitative analysts and traders can achieve sustained financial success by aligning their strategies with fundamental market drivers.

Block Matrices in Finance

In the complex world of financial modeling, block matrices are invaluable tools that help compartmentalize and analyze intricate datasets. These matrices allow analysts to break down large systems into smaller, more manageable sub-systems—an approach particularly useful in finance, where data is often multifaceted.

Consider a portfolio comprising various asset classes, such as equities, bonds, and derivatives. Each of these classes has unique characteristics and risk profiles that necessitate distinct analytical models. Block matrices enable the separation of these components within a unified matrix structure, allowing for targeted analysis and clearer insights.

Take this example, a financial institution looking to assess its risk exposure across different sectors can benefit from block matrices. These matrices can isolate data from each sector while providing an overarching view of the entire portfolio. This setup simplifies the process of identifying correlations or dependencies between sectors without getting overwhelmed by the complexity of the full dataset.

Excel Walkthrough:

1. Data Arrangement: Organize your data into blocks for each asset class or sector.

2. Matrix Construction: Utilize Excel's matrix functions to build a block matrix.

3. Analysis: Perform operations like multiplication or

inversion on these blocks to gain sector-specific insights while understanding their collective impact.

Python Example:

```python
import numpy as np

\#\# Define blocks
equities = np.random.rand(10, 10)
bonds = np.random.rand(5, 5)
derivatives = np.random.rand(3, 3)

\#\# Create block diagonal matrix
block_matrix = np.block([
[equities, np.zeros((10, 5)), np.zeros((10, 3))],
[np.zeros((5, 10)), bonds, np.zeros((5, 3))],
[np.zeros((3, 10)), np.zeros((3, 5)), derivatives]
])

print("Block Matrix:", block_matrix)
```

This Python code demonstrates how to construct a block matrix using NumPy by combining separate matrices for each asset class into one cohesive structure. This approach provides nuanced insights crucial for comprehensive risk assessment and strategy development.

In trading strategies that involve multiple markets or products —like pairs trading—a block matrix supports simultaneous processing of different market conditions or strategies within one coherent framework. This organization can uncover arbitrage opportunities or hedging strategies that might remain hidden in traditional linear models.

As finance grows more complex with diverse product offerings and regulatory demands, block matrices ensure analyses are both scalable and adaptable. This adaptability is essential for creating models that accommodate current data while swiftly integrating new information.

By leveraging block matrices in financial modeling, analysts enhance their strategic capabilities. They can dissect complex datasets without losing sight of the bigger picture—enabling clear pathways from granular analysis to holistic strategy formation.

In the end, this method enriches the analytical toolkit of any quantitative analyst or trader aiming for precision in decision-making and execution within today's fast-paced financial environments. The ability to see both the forest and the trees through structured mathematical approaches like block matrices provides a distinct edge in successfully navigating market intricacies.

The Jordan Canonical Form

The Jordan Canonical Form is a valuable tool for quantitative analysts, providing a structured approach to handling matrices that are not easily diagonalizable. In finance, where systems often exhibit complex interdependencies and layered structures, this form simplifies analysis without losing the essential characteristics of the underlying data.

In financial applications—such as modeling credit risk or analyzing interest rate dynamics—the Jordan Canonical Form simplifies matrices while preserving their eigenvalues. This transformation facilitates easier computation and interpretation, particularly for non-diagonalizable matrices that can pose significant analytical challenges.

Consider a matrix representing a company's cash flow over time. These cash flows may be erratic, influenced by factors like market volatility or regulatory changes. The matrix capturing these flows might not be easily diagonalizable due to complex interdependencies within the cash flow streams. Transforming the matrix into its Jordan Canonical Form isolates these dependencies into manageable blocks associated with specific eigenvalues.

For example, using Python's SciPy library:

```python
import numpy as np

from scipy.linalg import jordan_form


\#\# Example matrix

A = np.array([[5, 4, 2], [0, 5, 0], [0, 0, 3]])


\#\# Compute Jordan Canonical Form

P, J = jordan_form(A)


print("Jordan Form:", J)
```

This snippet demonstrates obtaining the Jordan Canonical Form, which highlights eigenvalues and organizes them into blocks reflecting their algebraic multiplicity.

In financial contexts such as stress testing or scenario analysis, the Jordan Canonical Form is invaluable. It enables analysts to explore how small changes in one part of a system might propagate throughout, identifying potential vulnerabilities or areas needing strategic adjustment. This insight is crucial for robust risk management strategies and regulatory compliance with frameworks like Basel III.

And, in derivative pricing models where precision is key, using the Jordan Canonical Form can simplify sensitivity analysis by clarifying how small perturbations affect outcomes across different states of a financial instrument or portfolio.

Incorporating this method into routine analyses provides financial professionals with additional clarity. They can dissect complex relationships within datasets while maintaining an overarching perspective on market trends and risks. This clarity translates into practical decision-making advantages—from evaluating investment opportunities to optimizing capital allocation strategies.

In the end, mastering techniques like the Jordan Canonical Form empowers analysts and traders to convert abstract mathematical concepts into actionable financial insights. By enhancing their ability to model and interpret intricate systems accurately and efficiently, they position themselves at the forefront of innovative financial analysis—ready to tackle challenges with confidence and expertise.

Practical Considerations in Finance

In finance, quantitative analysts must not only grasp theoretical concepts like the Jordan Canonical Form but also apply them effectively in real-world scenarios. The financial landscape is dynamic and unpredictable, requiring analytical frameworks that are both flexible and robust.

Applying the Jordan Canonical Form in financial models begins with identifying areas where it can provide valuable insights. This often includes complex domains such as multi-period cash flow analysis or advanced risk management systems. In these contexts, analysts use the form to simplify matrix structures while preserving crucial system properties.

Take, for example, a portfolio of mortgage-backed securities.

These instruments involve complex layers of cash flows affected by market conditions and borrower behaviors. By transforming matrices into their Jordan Canonical Forms, analysts can pinpoint dependencies that may significantly influence future cash flows. This isolation is vital for stress testing and scenario planning, where understanding how individual shocks impact overall stability is crucial.

Another key consideration is computational efficiency. Transforming a matrix into its Jordan Canonical Form can be resource-intensive, particularly in large-scale financial systems. Analysts must weigh the depth of analysis against computational resources to ensure insights are timely without delaying critical decisions.

Data quality is also essential for effective analysis. Accurate data ensures meaningful transformations, so analysts must rigorously validate datasets before applying complex mathematical techniques to avoid skewed results that could lead to erroneous conclusions about market behavior or risk exposure.

Utilizing software tools designed for advanced matrix computations can significantly streamline these processes. Python libraries like NumPy and SciPy enable efficient calculations and allow analysts to manage large datasets with minimal manual intervention. Automating parts of the transformation process saves time and reduces human error, allowing professionals to focus on interpreting results and strategizing.

Also, communicating findings from such analyses requires clarity and precision. The outcomes of using complex forms like the Jordan Canonical need translation into actionable insights for stakeholders—whether investors, compliance officers, or strategic planners—to easily understand and apply in their decision-making.

In the end, while mastering mathematical transformations

enhances financial analysis capabilities, practical success also relies on understanding when and how to apply these tools in specific contexts. Analysts who effectively integrate theory with practice not only boost their analytical prowess but also drive meaningful change within their organizations by delivering clear insights into intricate financial phenomena.

This proficiency empowers finance professionals to navigate uncertain markets with confidence—armed with both theoretical knowledge and practical acumen to anticipate challenges and seize opportunities as they emerge.

Limitations and Computational Complexity

The Jordan Canonical Form is a powerful mathematical tool, but it presents certain limitations and challenges, particularly in the financial domain. Understanding these constraints is essential for analysts who want to use this method effectively.

Firstly, deriving the Jordan Canonical Form involves significant computational complexity. As matrix size increases, so does the demand for advanced algorithms and processing power. This can lead to longer computation times, which may not be ideal for real-time financial decision-making where time is of the essence.

Additionally, not all matrices easily reduce to their Jordan forms. The process requires precise calculations and is susceptible to numerical errors, especially with floating-point arithmetic commonly used in computations. Such errors can accumulate and lead to inaccuracies in results, posing challenges for financial models where precision is crucial.

Interpreting the Jordan Canonical Form also presents difficulties. While it theoretically simplifies matrix structures, translating these insights into actionable financial strategies requires a deep understanding of both mathematics and the specific financial context. Analysts need to discern meaningful information that can support decision-making.

Financial data further complicates matters. Data is often imperfect, subject to noise and inconsistencies that affect matrix transformation analyses. Rigorous data validation processes are necessary before using advanced mathematical forms like the Jordan Canonical.

While software tools help manage these complexities, they are not without flaws. Analysts must remain alert to potential software limitations or bugs that could distort results. Despite automation and sophisticated algorithms available in packages like NumPy or MATLAB, human oversight is crucial to ensure accuracy and reliability.

There's also a trade-off between complexity and utility. Complex models can offer deeper insights but might obscure simpler solutions that are more intuitive and equally effective for certain applications. Financial professionals need to evaluate whether the benefits of using intricate models justify their complexity and computational demands.

In addressing these challenges, analysts must weigh their desire for detailed insights against practical considerations of time, resources, and clarity. By acknowledging the constraints of computational complexity and data issues, finance professionals can make informed decisions about when and how to employ the Jordan Canonical Form in their analyses.

In the end, success depends not only on mastering advanced mathematical techniques but also on applying them judiciously within the practical confines of financial operations—enhancing analytical depth without sacrificing practicality or speed.

CHAPTER 8:
SINGULAR VALUE
DECOMPOSITION

Definition and Properties

ingular Value Decomposition (SVD) is a fundamental concept in linear algebra, providing a powerful framework for analyzing matrices and revealing their essential characteristics. Essentially, SVD breaks down a matrix into three distinct matrices, offering deeper insights that are especially useful in financial modeling.

Let's examine a matrix A with dimensions m by n. SVD decomposes A into the product of three matrices: U, Σ (Sigma), and V. In this decomposition, U is an m by m orthogonal matrix, Σ is an m by n diagonal matrix, and V is the conjugate transpose of an n by n orthogonal matrix. This specific arrangement ensures that U and V* have orthonormal columns—each column vector is both of unit length and orthogonal to others. This orthonormality is crucial as it preserves numerical stability, which is vital when working with large datasets common in finance.

The diagonal elements of Σ, known as singular values,

are noteworthy. Arranged in descending order, these non-negative numbers indicate the significance or "weight" of each corresponding singular vector within the dataset represented by matrix A. In finance, this resembles identifying dominant factors influencing market trends—providing succinct yet powerful information that can guide strategic decisions.

To illustrate SVD's practical application, consider a portfolio manager aiming to minimize risk through diversification. By applying SVD to a covariance matrix derived from historical asset returns, principal components can be identified—factors that capture most of the dataset's variance. This insight informs asset allocation decisions by distinguishing between investments that genuinely diversify risk and those with redundant risks.

Beyond this application, SVD is instrumental in data compression—a critical function when managing massive financial datasets. By retaining only the singular values and vectors that account for most data variability, significant dimensionality reduction is achieved without substantial information loss. This not only optimizes storage but also boosts computational efficiency during analysis.

And, in risk management, singular values help estimate volatility clusters or shocks within markets—a key task for stress testing financial systems against extreme but plausible events. Quickly identifying such patterns enables analysts to develop strategies capable of enduring unexpected market disruptions.

Understanding SVD's theoretical foundation is not merely academic; it leads to actionable insights for quantitative analysts eager to exploit its full potential. Through diligent exploration and application, finance professionals can use SVD not just for descriptive purposes but also as a predictive tool, accurately forecasting future market movements.

Approximating Financial Matrices

In the world of finance, where data-driven decision-making prevails, Singular Value Decomposition (SVD) emerges as an essential technique for approximating financial matrices. This method effectively distills complex datasets into their most informative components, enabling more efficient analysis and clearer insights into financial phenomena.

Imagine a large dataset of historical stock prices, where each row represents a different stock and each column corresponds to a specific time period. Although this matrix is extensive, it contains patterns and correlations that can greatly impact investment strategies. SVD helps us approximate this matrix by focusing on the most significant singular values and their corresponding vectors. This approach allows us to extract core information without getting lost in unnecessary details.

The process involves retaining only the top singular values and their associated vectors—those that contribute most to the dataset's variance. That's why, we obtain a lower-rank approximation of the original matrix that captures its essence while discarding noise. In portfolio optimization, for example, this means identifying key drivers of asset price movements and filtering out minor influences that could obscure strategic decisions.

Beyond simplification, SVD enhances computational efficiency. With reduced dimensionality, algorithms can process data more quickly, facilitating faster execution of trading strategies or risk assessments. This speed is crucial in high-frequency trading environments where milliseconds can determine profitability.

Matrix approximation through SVD also aids in predicting future market behavior. By analyzing past trends encapsulated within a few principal components—derived from singular values and vectors—analysts gain foresight into possible future movements. This predictive capability is vital for quantitative models aiming to forecast market shifts or evaluate potential investment opportunities.

Consider credit risk modeling—a domain heavily reliant on accurate data interpretation. Financial institutions must assess vast amounts of credit-related data to evaluate borrower risk profiles. SVD streamlines this process by condensing relevant variables into actionable insights, refining risk assessment models and enhancing decision-making accuracy.

Also, SVD-based matrix approximation plays a crucial role in anomaly detection within financial systems. By monitoring deviations from established patterns captured by principal components, analysts can quickly identify irregularities that may indicate fraud or systemic failures.

As you explore SVD's role in finance, recognize its power not just as a mathematical tool but as a transformative force reshaping how data informs strategy. Through careful matrix approximation, practitioners uncover hidden relationships and lay the groundwork for innovative approaches to managing complexity in today's dynamic markets.

Mastering these techniques requires more than technical skill; it demands an understanding of how they align with broader financial objectives. In the end, effectively approximating matrices equips analysts with sharper tools for navigating uncertainty and seizing opportunities in competitive financial landscapes.

SVD and Data Compression

Singular Value Decomposition (SVD) is a remarkable technique, particularly in the realm of finance, for both approximating matrices and excelling in data compression. In an industry inundated with data, the ability to distill vast amounts of information into more manageable and insightful formats is invaluable. SVD doesn't just reduce data; it transforms it, preserving essential information while eliminating redundant noise.

Consider a financial institution managing a massive database of transaction records, each containing attributes like transaction amount, time, location, and involved parties. Storing and processing such extensive data can be resource-intensive. SVD helps by identifying core patterns within these records, allowing them to be stored in a reduced form that retains crucial details.

Data compression through SVD involves truncating the original matrix to emphasize its most significant singular values, which capture the majority of the dataset's energy or information content. The resulting compressed matrix requires less storage space yet still provides insights comparable to those from the full-scale version. This efficiency is especially advantageous when dealing with high-dimensional datasets common in quantitative finance.

A notable application of SVD in finance is within risk management frameworks. Risk models often incorporate diverse datasets including market variables, historical trends, and economic indicators. By compressing these datasets with SVD, analysts streamline risk assessment processes without losing critical insights into potential exposures or vulnerabilities.

In algorithmic trading environments, quick access to relevant data is crucial. Compressed data structures enable algorithms to retrieve and analyze necessary information rapidly, allowing traders to seize fleeting market opportunities. The speed offered by SVD-driven compression directly translates into competitive advantages in fast-paced trading arenas.

Additionally, SVD facilitates collaborative efforts among teams working on large-scale financial projects. Compressed datasets are easier to share across departments or with external partners without compromising confidentiality or integrity, promoting seamless collaboration and integration of diverse analytical perspectives.

While the benefits of data compression are clear, it's essential to strike a balance. Over-compression might lead to the loss of important nuances—details that could significantly influence decision-making. Therefore, practitioners must carefully analyze singular value contributions to determine how much detail to retain.

And, compressed representations derived from SVD simplify model building and validation tasks. With fewer variables and reduced complexity, models become more interpretable and easier to validate against real-world scenarios—a significant advantage when communicating findings with stakeholders lacking technical expertise.

Harnessing SVD for data compression exemplifies a fusion of mathematical elegance and practical utility in finance. This synergy empowers analysts to extract maximum value from their data resources efficiently and effectively. By thoughtfully leveraging these techniques, financial professionals position themselves at the forefront of innovation in an increasingly data-driven landscape.

Through continuous refinement and application of such methodologies, quantitative analysts enhance their ability to discern meaningful patterns amidst complexity—a skill indispensable for navigating contemporary financial markets with acumen and agility.

Covariance and Correlation

Covariance and correlation are essential tools for financial analysts, providing insight into how variables move in relation to one another. Grasping these concepts is key in quantitative finance, where the relationships between variables can shape investment strategies and risk evaluations.

Let's start with covariance, a statistical measure that shows the degree to which two variables change together. A positive covariance means that as one variable increases, the other tends to increase too. On the other hand, a negative covariance suggests an inverse relationship. For example, if two stock prices rise and fall in tandem, their covariance is positive.

In practice, covariance helps assess asset pairs within a portfolio. By evaluating covariances among various assets, traders can understand how their combined fluctuations might influence portfolio performance. This knowledge is vital for building diversified portfolios aimed at minimizing risk and maximizing returns.

Despite its usefulness, covariance has its drawbacks. It is scale-dependent, meaning changes in units can alter its magnitude without changing the underlying relationship. This is where correlation comes in—a normalized version of covariance that adjusts for differences in units and scales.

Correlation measures the strength and direction of a linear relationship between two variables on a standardized scale from -1 to 1. A correlation close to 1 indicates a strong positive relationship; -1 denotes a strong negative relationship; and 0 suggests no linear relationship.

In finance, correlation is crucial for strategies like hedging and diversification. Selecting assets with low or negative correlations can reduce overall portfolio volatility—a key consideration when managing risk amid uncertain market conditions.

Understanding these metrics enables analysts to delve deeper into market dynamics. Take this example, if economic indicators like interest rates and inflation have a high positive correlation, it could signal synchronized policy impacts on economic growth forecasts—valuable insights for macroeconomic analysis.

And, algorithmic trading systems utilize correlations to optimize decision-making processes. Algorithms designed to capitalize on correlated price movements can execute trades quickly based on expected co-movements across markets or instruments.

However, reliance on historical correlations requires caution as they may not hold during market disruptions or structural changes—known as regime shifts. Correlations are sensitive to sample periods; what was true historically may not apply under new conditions.

Analyzing rolling correlations offers dynamic insights into evolving relationships over time rather than static snapshots. This perspective allows for more adaptive strategies capable of responding swiftly to emerging trends or anomalies—a critical advantage in rapidly changing markets.

For practical application, consider two technology stocks: Company A and Company B. By calculating both covariance and correlation for their returns over a specific timeframe using Python libraries like NumPy or pandas, analysts can determine whether investing in both would enhance or mitigate risk compared to investing independently.

```python
import numpy as np

import pandas as pd


\#\# Simulated stock returns

returns = 'Company_A': [0.01, 0.02, -0.01], 'Company_B': [0.02, 0.01, 0]

df = pd.DataFrame(returns)


\#\# Covariance calculation

cov_matrix = df.cov()

print("Covariance Matrix:")
```

```
print(cov_matrix)

\#\# Correlation calculation
corr_matrix = df.corr()
print(" Matrix:")
print(corr_matrix)
` ` `
```

These calculations reveal underlying relationships that might not be immediately apparent through casual observation alone—empowering traders with actionable intelligence for informed decision-making amid uncertainty.

The interplay between covariance and correlation extends beyond traditional finance into fields like machine learning, where they inform model training processes through feature selection techniques that ensure models capture relevant dependencies without redundancy—demonstrating their versatility across diverse analytical contexts within financial landscapes enriched by continuous innovation powered by mathematical rigor and real-world applicability.

Applications in Credit Risk Models

Credit risk models heavily rely on the mathematical principles of linear algebra to assess and predict the likelihood of a borrower defaulting on their financial obligations. These models utilize matrices and vectors to quantify various risk factors and probabilities, providing a framework for understanding a borrower's ability to meet financial commitments.

At the heart of credit risk modeling is the probability of default (PD), which estimates the likelihood that a borrower will fail to meet debt obligations. Matrices represent large datasets containing borrower-specific information, such as credit scores, income levels, and payment histories. In these matrices, each row corresponds to a borrower, while each column represents a different attribute or feature.

Calculating PD involves applying statistical techniques, with correlation matrices being particularly important. These matrices help identify how different risk factors relate to one another and influence the overall risk profile. For example, a strong correlation between unemployment rates and default rates might reveal economic vulnerabilities affecting borrowers' repayment abilities.

Stress testing is another critical aspect of credit risk models. It simulates extreme economic scenarios to evaluate how resilient financial institutions are against potential defaults. Covariance matrices are used to assess how assets might behave under stress by examining their historical co-movements. Such analyses are essential for regulatory compliance and ensuring capital adequacy during financial downturns.

Consider an analyst tasked with determining how sensitive a bank's loan portfolio is to interest rate changes—a common stress factor. Using Python's NumPy library, one can construct covariance matrices from historical loan performance data to predict potential outcomes under different interest rate scenarios:

```python
import numpy as np

\#\# Simulated loan performance data (in percent returns)

loan_data = np.array([

[0.02, 0.01], \# Scenario 1: Interest rate increase

[0.01, -0.02], \# Scenario 2: Economic downturn
```

])

\#\# Covariance matrix calculation

cov_matrix = np.cov(loan_data.T)

print("Covariance Matrix:")

print(cov_matrix)

` ` `

These computations provide insights into potential risks associated with each scenario, enabling banks to devise strategies for mitigating losses.

The integration of machine learning techniques into credit risk models has become increasingly common, enhancing predictive accuracy through advanced algorithms grounded in linear algebra principles. Techniques like logistic regression and support vector machines use vector spaces to classify borrowers into different risk categories based on historical patterns.

Take this example, logistic regression can be employed using Python's scikit-learn library to predict binary outcomes—such as whether a borrower will default—based on their attributes:

` ` `python

from sklearn.linear_model import LogisticRegression

\#\# Example feature matrix (borrower attributes) and target variable (default status)

features = np.array([[750, 50], [680, 70]]) \# Credit score, Debt-to-income ratio

default_status = np.array([0, 1])   \# Non-defaulted = 0; Defaulted = 1

```
\#\# Logistic regression model training

model = LogisticRegression()

model.fit(features, default_status)


\#\# Prediction on new data

new_borrower = np.array([[700, 60]])

prediction = model.predict(new_borrower)

print("Default Prediction:", prediction)
` ` `
```

This approach demonstrates how blending statistical methods with computational tools creates robust frameworks for credit evaluation—offering comprehensive insights into borrower reliability and supporting informed decision-making.

Given the dynamic nature of financial markets, these models must be continually refined to adapt to emerging trends and risks within evolving economic landscapes—a process that depends on rigorous mathematical foundations and innovative technological advancements driving modern finance forward with precision and foresight.

Stability and Predictive Applications

Stability in financial models is crucial, particularly when forecasting outcomes influenced by economic conditions and market behaviors. Linear algebra offers a solid framework for evaluating model stability through the analysis of eigenvalues and eigenvectors. These mathematical tools are essential for understanding how minor input changes can significantly affect outputs, a concept known as sensitivity.

In linear algebra, stability refers to how systems respond to disturbances. For financial models, this involves examining how slight variations in economic indicators or model parameters might impact forecasts or valuations. Eigenvalues are key in this context; they indicate whether a system will return to equilibrium after a disruption. A system is considered stable if all the eigenvalues of its matrix have negative real parts, meaning any perturbations will gradually diminish.

Take this example, an investment firm might use a predictive model to forecast stock prices based on various economic indicators. By constructing a matrix that represents the relationships between these indicators and calculating its eigenvalues, the model's stability can be assessed:

```python
import numpy as np


\#\# Example matrix representing relationships between economic indicators

economic_matrix = np.array([

[0.9, 0.1],

[0.2, 0.8]

])


\#\# Compute eigenvalues

eigenvalues = np.linalg.eigvals(economic_matrix)

print("Eigenvalues:", eigenvalues)
```

A financial model with stable eigenvalues ensures reliable forecasts despite minor fluctuations in underlying data.

Predictive modeling and stability analysis are closely linked. Forecasting models rely on historical data to predict future trends, necessitating accuracy and resilience against unpredictable market dynamics. Linear regression models often employ matrix operations to derive coefficients that best fit historical patterns.

Implementing linear regression in Python is straightforward with libraries like NumPy and scikit-learn, which support the necessary matrix manipulations:

```python
from sklearn.linear_model import LinearRegression


\#\# Historical data: Economic indicator (X) vs Stock price (Y)

X = np.array([[1], [2], [3], [4]])

Y = np.array([2.5, 3.5, 4.5, 6])


\#\# Train linear regression model

regression_model – LinearRegression()

regression_model.fit(X, Y)


\#\# Predict future stock prices based on new economic data

future_data = np.array([[5]])

prediction = regression_model.predict(future_data)

print("Predicted Stock Price:", prediction)
```

This example demonstrates how predictive accuracy can be achieved through robust mathematical principles. As markets evolve, maintaining model stability is essential for consistent performance.

The interplay between stability analysis and predictive modeling highlights the need for strategies that adapt to new information—a dynamic process supported by rigorous computational techniques rooted in linear algebra. As technological advancements and global events reshape financial landscapes, the ability to foresee changes with stable models becomes invaluable.

In this ever-changing environment, financial professionals must possess both technical skills and an understanding of how these mathematical tools apply in real-world contexts. By cultivating an adaptable mindset grounded in precise calculations and strategic foresight, analysts and traders can confidently navigate uncertainties, driving sustainable success through informed decision-making based on stable predictive frameworks.

Financial modeling extends beyond formula application; it involves developing insights that guide prudent actions amidst complexity—a pursuit made possible by mastering the intricate dance of numbers and algorithms within the expansive realm of linear algebra.

Numerical Stability

Numerical stability in financial computations is crucial, especially when handling large datasets and complex algorithms. The goal is to ensure that minor errors in data or calculations do not lead to significant deviations in results. This is vital in finance, where even small errors can have substantial consequences.

Take matrix inversion, for instance—a common task in financial modeling. If the matrix is ill-conditioned, even slight disturbances can cause large variations in the inverse matrix. An ill-conditioned matrix, characterized by a high condition number, is sensitive to numerical errors. Therefore, understanding and managing these conditions is essential for reliable computations.

To achieve numerical stability, it's often necessary to use algorithms designed to minimize error propagation. For example, LU decomposition is preferred over direct inversion when dealing with systems of linear equations:

```python
import numpy as np

from scipy.linalg import lu


\#\# Example matrix for LU decomposition

A = np.array([

[2, 3],

[5, 4]

])


\#\# Perform LU decomposition

P, L, U = lu(A)

print("L (Lower triangular matrix):", L)

print("U (Upper triangular matrix):", U)
```

This method breaks down a matrix into lower and upper triangular matrices, offering more stability for solving equations than direct inversion.

Stability also plays a key role in financial models using iterative methods. In optimization algorithms like gradient descent, step sizes must be chosen carefully to ensure convergence without overshooting the solution space. A solid grasp of linear algebra enables analysts to adjust these parameters effectively.

Consider using gradient descent on a simple quadratic function—commonly seen in portfolio optimization:

```python
def gradient_descent(starting_point):
learning_rate = 0.01
tolerance = 1e-6
max_iterations = 1000

x = starting_point
iteration = 0

while iteration < max_iterations:
gradient = 2 * x \# Derivative of x^2 function
next_x = x - learning_rate * gradient

if abs(next_x - x) < tolerance:
break

x = next_x
iteration += 1

return x

\#\# Starting point for the descent
```

```
result = gradient_descent(10)

print("Minimum found at:", result)
```
` ` `

Choosing an appropriate learning rate ensures the algorithm converges smoothly without oscillating or diverging—demonstrating numerical stability.

Floating-point arithmetic adds another layer of complexity. The limited precision of digital computers means calculations may not exactly reflect theoretical mathematics. To mitigate errors, carefully arranging operations—like avoiding subtraction between nearly equal numbers—can prevent loss of significance.

Using libraries that address these issues is advisable. Take this example, relying on numpy's built-in functions rather than manual calculations ensures optimizations and precautions are automatically applied:

` ` `python

```
import numpy as np


\#\# Computing square root using numpy's stable method

result_stable = np.sqrt(16)

print("Stable square root calculation:", result_stable)
```
` ` `

Understanding numerical stability extends beyond technical skills; it involves strategic foresight and planning in financial computations.

In the end, mastering numerical stability isn't just about preventing errors—it's about building models that inspire confidence through their resilience and reliability under various conditions. In the fast-paced world of finance, where precision reigns supreme, ensuring stable computations forms the foundation upon which successful analytical endeavors are built. Such expertise empowers financial professionals to tackle today's challenges and anticipate tomorrow's evolving landscapes with clarity and precision.

Practical Examples in Finance

Practical examples in finance highlight the crucial role of linear algebra and matrix theory in real-world applications. These mathematical tools are indispensable in tasks ranging from constructing diversified investment portfolios to optimizing trading algorithms. Let's explore some scenarios where their application significantly impacts financial outcomes.

One fundamental model in modern portfolio theory is the Markowitz Mean-Variance Optimization model. This model uses covariance matrices to evaluate risk and return trade-offs, helping investors determine the most efficient asset allocation. By representing assets and their relationships through matrices, investors can identify the portfolio with the highest expected return for a specified level of risk.

To calculate this, one typically forms a covariance matrix from historical asset returns and uses it to derive efficient frontiers. With Python and numpy, this computation becomes straightforward:

```python
import numpy as np

\#\# Historical returns for three assets

returns = np.array([

[0.05, 0.07, 0.1],
```

[0.02, 0.04, 0.05],

[0.03, 0.06, 0.08]

])

\#\# Calculate covariance matrix

cov_matrix = np.cov(returns.T)

print("Covariance Matrix:", cov_matrix)

\#\# Portfolio weights example

weights = np.array([0.4, 0.3, 0.3])

\#\# Portfolio variance

portfolio_variance = np.dot(weights.T, np.dot(cov_matrix, weights))

print("Portfolio Variance:", portfolio_variance)

` ` `

In this example, matrix multiplication is used to capture complex relationships between assets succinctly —demonstrating how linear algebra simplifies financial decision-making.

Linear algebra also plays a key role in risk management through Value at Risk (VaR) calculations. VaR estimates potential portfolio losses over a specific time frame under normal market conditions and often employs linear algebraic methods to model price changes and correlations between financial instruments.

Monte Carlo simulations provide another application by generating random price paths based on volatility and correlation matrices to forecast potential outcomes:

```python
import numpy as np

\#\# Simulating correlated price paths for two assets
correlation_matrix = np.array([[1, 0.8], [0.8, 1]])
chol_decomp = np.linalg.cholesky(correlation_matrix)

\#\# Random normal variables
random_shocks = np.random.normal(size=(2, 10000))

\#\# Correlated shocks
correlated_shocks = chol_decomp @ random_shocks

print("Sample Correlated Shocks:", correlated_shocks[:5])
```

Here, linear algebra provides a framework for simulating thousands of possible future states of a portfolio—a task that would be cumbersome without such mathematical structures.

In algorithmic trading, matrix theory is also essential. High-frequency trading algorithms rely on efficient data processing and pattern recognition facilitated by matrix computations. Techniques like Singular Value Decomposition (SVD) help reduce data dimensionality while retaining crucial information—key for quickly identifying trends in vast datasets.

And, matrices are vital in derivative pricing models like Black-Scholes or binomial trees, where they discretize continuous processes or handle large systems of equations describing option pricing dynamics across various scenarios.

These examples clearly illustrate how linear algebra and matrix theory underpin critical financial operations—from optimizing investment strategies to managing risks and enhancing computational efficiency in trading systems.

The integration of these tools into financial practices is not just an academic exercise but a strategic necessity that enhances analytical capabilities and improves decision-making under uncertainty. This emphasizes their significance in shaping modern finance's analytical landscape. As we explore these practical implementations further, remember that each example refines skills that translate directly into superior financial performance and competitive advantage in the marketplace.

CHAPTER 9: MATRIX FACTORIZATIONS

LU Decomposition

L U Decomposition is a fundamental concept in numerical linear algebra, playing a crucial role in finance. By decomposing a matrix into a lower triangular matrix and an upper triangular matrix, LU Decomposition simplifies complex computations. This makes it an invaluable tool for solving linear systems, a common requirement in financial modeling.

Take this example, consider a system of equations that represents the interactions or constraints of various financial assets within an investment portfolio. Such a system can be expressed as (Ax = b), where (A) is the coefficient matrix, (x) is the vector of unknowns (such as asset weights), and (b) is the outcome vector. Efficiently solving these systems is essential, especially when handling the large datasets typical in finance.

LU Decomposition proves particularly useful in portfolio optimization. Imagine an investment model that requires frequent recalibrations due to changing market conditions. Continuously inverting matrices can be computationally expensive. However, by decomposing the matrix, one can achieve more efficient recalibrations, thereby reducing computational overhead.

Here's a practical example in Python using numpy to perform LU Decomposition:

```python
import numpy as np

from scipy.linalg import lu


\#\# Coefficient matrix A

A = np.array([

[2, 1, 1],

[4, -6, 0],

[-2, 7, 2]

])


\#\# Perform LU decomposition

P, L, U = lu(A)


print("Lower Triangular Matrix L:", L)

print("Upper Triangular Matrix U:", U)
```

This code demonstrates how to decompose matrix (A) into lower (L) and upper (U) triangular matrices using scipy's lu function. This decomposition breaks down the original problem into two simpler systems: (Ly = Pb) and (Ux = y), which can be solved sequentially with forward and backward substitution techniques.

In practice, LU Decomposition aids not only in direct solutions but also in portfolio stability analysis—a critical component when managing risk amid fluctuating market conditions. Understanding how slight changes in inputs affect outcomes helps determine sensitivity levels in financial models.

And, LU Decomposition boosts computational efficiency in high-frequency trading environments where speed is crucial. Trading strategies often depend on rapidly recalculating optimal positions as new data arrives—here LU Decomposition is vital for enabling quick updates without reconstructing entire systems.

Beyond individual asset allocations or trading tactics, this technique has broader applications across various financial analyses, such as stress testing banks' capital adequacy or optimizing derivatives pricing models involving large-scale simulations.

As computational power advances and data complexity grows, methods like LU Decomposition remain essential for handling sophisticated calculations efficiently without excessive resource use. This balance between accuracy and efficiency characterizes modern quantitative finance practices.

Additionally, LU Decomposition supports robust risk management frameworks by facilitating scenario analyses under different economic conditions. Whether simulating interest rate shocks or assessing the impact of credit defaults on portfolios, this tool streamlines these processes and enhances strategic decision-making.

In summary, mastering LU Decomposition equips analysts with the ability to navigate complex financial landscapes confidently—enabling quicker responses to market signals while maintaining precision across diverse operations from portfolio management to algorithmic trading strategies. As data volumes and market volatility increase, such techniques are integral not only for competitive advantage but also for ensuring long-term stability and growth within the sector.

Cholesky Decomposition

Cholesky Decomposition is a crucial tool in quantitative finance, offering an efficient way to handle positive definite matrices. This decomposition method is particularly beneficial in financial models, especially those involving covariance matrices used in portfolio optimization and risk management.

Consider an analyst tasked with optimizing an investment portfolio. The covariance matrix, which represents the variances and covariances of asset returns, becomes increasingly complex as the number of assets grows. Cholesky Decomposition simplifies this complexity by breaking down the covariance matrix into the product of a lower triangular matrix and its transpose. This not only reduces computational load but also maintains precision—critical when processing large volumes of market data.

To illustrate, let's look at how this works in Python:

```python
import numpy as np


\#\# Sample positive definite matrix (covariance matrix example)

cov_matrix = np.array([

[4, 2, 2],

[2, 3, 1],

[2, 1, 3]

])
```

```
\#\# Perform Cholesky Decomposition

L = np.linalg.cholesky(cov_matrix)


print("Lower Triangular Matrix L:", L)
` ` `
```

In this example, np.linalg.cholesky effectively decomposes the covariance matrix into its lower triangular form. This transformation is especially useful when solving systems like (Ax = b) through forward and backward substitution.

Cholesky Decomposition's benefits extend beyond efficiency—it enhances numerical stability by reducing round-off errors that can occur with other methods like LU Decomposition. This precision is vital in areas such as high-frequency trading or derivative pricing models, where minimizing errors leads to more reliable outputs and better-informed decisions.

And, Cholesky Decomposition is invaluable in Monte Carlo simulations for risk assessment and derivative pricing. By applying it to the covariance matrix of asset returns, analysts can generate correlated random variables more accurately, leading to simulations that effectively capture market dynamics.

In econometric modeling, Cholesky aids in estimating large vector autoregressions (VARs), offering a computationally efficient approach to model selection and estimation processes that are otherwise resource-intensive.

Additionally, Cholesky plays a key role in stress testing—a critical process for financial institutions managing systemic risks. By using this decomposition technique, firms can rapidly simulate various economic scenarios and evaluate their capital buffers against potential crises. This proactive approach strengthens financial resilience amidst market uncertainties.

In the end, Cholesky Decomposition goes beyond solving linear equations; it refines analytical approaches within finance by merging mathematical rigor with practical application. It enables analysts to navigate complex datasets with ease and precision.

As financial markets evolve with technological advancements driving data growth, methods like Cholesky become increasingly relevant. They offer scalable solutions that adapt to rising analytical demands without compromising computational efficiency or accuracy—essential for maintaining a competitive edge in finance.

Mastering Cholesky Decomposition provides professionals with a deeper understanding of the mathematical frameworks underlying risk analysis and portfolio management strategies. It transforms abstract concepts into actionable insights that guide impactful financial decisions.

Such expertise not only enhances immediate analytical capabilities but also positions analysts at the forefront of innovative finance practices—highlighting the importance of continuous learning and adaptation in an ever-changing landscape.

QR Factorization

QR Factorization is a key technique in linear algebra, highly valued in financial computations for its ability to efficiently manage systems of linear equations and optimization problems. Essentially, it breaks down a matrix into two components: an orthogonal matrix (Q) and an upper triangular matrix (R). This decomposition is crucial for numerical methods that enhance stability and accuracy in financial modeling.

Imagine optimizing a complex trading strategy that relies on massive datasets to predict asset returns. QR Factorization becomes invaluable here, enabling the efficient resolution of least squares problems where traditional methods may struggle with computational demands. By simplifying matrices into more manageable forms, analysts can perform calculations more efficiently without losing precision.

Here's how you might apply this technique using Python:

```python
import numpy as np
from scipy.linalg import qr

## Sample matrix (e.g., regression design matrix)
A = np.array([
[12, -51, 4],
[6, 167, -68],
[-4, 24, -41]
])

## Perform QR Factorization
Q, R = qr(A)

print("Orthogonal Matrix Q:", Q)
print("Upper Triangular Matrix R:", R)
```

The qr function from SciPy performs this factorization efficiently. The orthogonal matrix (Q) retains the column space characteristics of the original matrix while ensuring numerical stability—critical when handling overdetermined systems common in regression analyses.

In finance, QR Factorization is also useful for calculating interest rate models and calibrating financial instruments, where robust statistical inference is necessary. It simplifies complex calculations without compromising accuracy— essential in high-stakes environments.

And, QR Factorization minimizes errors in iterative processes like those used in algorithmic trading and risk assessment simulations. Its ability to maintain data integrity through successive computations ensures reliable convergence towards precise outcomes.

In portfolio management, where diversification strategies depend on historical return data across numerous assets, QR Factorization facilitates effective dimensionality reduction. It preserves essential information while reducing complexity, enabling timely and informed investment decisions.

Beyond computational efficiency, QR Factorization supports the development of predictive financial models that anticipate market movements. It integrates seamlessly into machine learning workflows where model training involves large matrices with high variance and dynamic inputs.

Additionally, this decomposition aids in sensitivity analysis by illuminating how changes in one part of the financial system can affect interconnected networks—a critical aspect of assessing systemic risks and implementing robust hedging strategies.

Mastering QR Factorization provides financial analysts with a refined skill set to tackle diverse analytical challenges. Whether reducing computational burdens or enhancing model reliability, this technique exemplifies precision-driven financial analysis—a cornerstone for success in ever-evolving market landscapes.

Implications for Regression Analysis

Regression analysis is a cornerstone of financial data analysis, leveraging advanced mathematical techniques to derive valuable insights. At the heart of this process, QR Factorization plays a crucial role by ensuring both stability and accuracy in computations. When a regression model involves multiple predictors, QR Factorization simplifies finding the best fit line, reducing computational complexity and enhancing numerical precision.

Imagine an analyst exploring the relationship between various economic indicators and stock market performance. The dataset at hand is extensive, with numerous variables potentially influencing outcomes. By applying QR Factorization, the analyst can break down the regression matrix into orthogonal components, streamlining the complex calculations required.

Here's a practical example using Python:

```python
import numpy as np

from scipy.linalg import qr


\#\# Simulated dataset: economic indicators (X) and market performance (y)

X = np.array([

[1, 2104, 5],

[1, 1416, 3],

[1, 1534, 3],

[1, 852, 2]

])
```

```
y = np.array([460, 232, 315, 178])


\#\# Perform QR Factorization on X

Q, R = qr(X)


\#\# Solve for coefficients using R and Q.T

coefficients = np.linalg.solve(R[:3], np.dot(Q.T[:3], y))


print("Regression Coefficients:", coefficients)
` ` `
```

In this script, (X) represents the economic indicators matrix with an added intercept term as the first column, while (y) indicates market performance. Through QR Factorization, (X) is decomposed into (Q) and (R), facilitating efficient calculation of regression coefficients.

The advantage of this approach is its ability to tackle multicollinearity—a frequent issue in financial datasets where predictors often correlate. By decomposing the original matrix into orthogonal components, QR Factorization reduces dependencies among variables, yielding more reliable coefficient estimates.

This method also enhances model interpretability by highlighting each predictor's independent contribution to the response variable. Analysts can pinpoint the most significant factors driving market performance changes and tailor their strategies accordingly.

Additionally, QR Factorization supports model fit assessment through residual analysis. By analyzing deviations from predicted values, analysts can refine models to better capture underlying trends—a vital step in developing predictive financial models.

In scenario testing and stress analysis, QR Factorization proves invaluable. Given the inherent volatility of financial markets, models must withstand varying conditions. QR Factorization supports robust statistical inference, maintaining numerical stability even when input data is highly variable or noisy.

And, when integrated with machine learning algorithms for forecasting asset prices or assessing credit risk, QR Factorization ensures that models remain accurate and scalable. It empowers analysts to efficiently handle large datasets without losing detail or precision.

In the end, mastering QR Factorization within regression analysis equips financial professionals with a powerful methodology to effectively navigate complex data landscapes. This approach underscores a commitment to precision and reliability—essential elements for insightful financial decision-making that drive strategic success in ever-evolving market dynamics.

Solving Financial Problems

Financial problem-solving often relies on mathematical frameworks, particularly linear algebra and matrix theory, which are foundational to many analytical approaches. Matrix factorization techniques such as LU and QR Factorization are especially notable, as they empower analysts to solve a variety of financial challenges with precision.

In portfolio optimization, for example, the objective is to allocate assets to maximize returns while minimizing risk. This involves solving linear equations based on historical data on asset performance and correlations, a task that requires both accuracy and efficiency—achievable through matrix factorization.

Consider an analyst optimizing a portfolio with multiple stocks. The goal is to assign optimal weights to each stock to meet return targets without exceeding risk limits. The process begins by forming a matrix of past stock performances and their covariances. Here, LU Decomposition is invaluable, as it simplifies this matrix into lower and upper triangular matrices, making it easier to compute inverses for determining optimal weights.

Here's a Python example illustrating this approach:

```python
import numpy as np

from scipy.linalg import lu


\#\# Simulated covariance matrix for a portfolio

cov_matrix = np.array([

[0.1, 0.02, 0.04],

[0.02, 0.08, 0.01],

[0.04, 0.01, 0.06]

])


\#\# Perform LU Decomposition

P, L, U = lu(cov_matrix)


print("Lower Triangular Matrix L:", L)

print("Upper Triangular Matrix U:", U)
```

In this code snippet, cov_matrix captures asset covariances in a portfolio context. LU Decomposition breaks it into L and U, facilitating subsequent calculations for optimal asset weights under various market conditions.

Beyond optimization, these techniques are crucial in risk management, where understanding the interplay of market variables is key. Matrix decompositions can highlight significant patterns within complex datasets.

Take this example, in credit risk modeling, banks evaluate borrowers' default probabilities using vast datasets of borrower characteristics and economic indicators—a task made feasible by Singular Value Decomposition (SVD), which reduces dimensionality while preserving key patterns.

Predictive modeling also benefits from these techniques when forecasting price movements or interest rate changes based on historical trends. Accuracy here depends not only on selecting relevant predictors but also on maintaining numerical stability during computations—a benefit provided by robust factorizations like QR.

Also, algorithmic trading strategies require real-time decision-making supported by efficient computational methods such as Cholesky Decomposition for positive-definite matrices typical in trading algorithms involving asset return covariances. This enhances the speed and reliability of trading systems.

Mastery of advanced linear algebra tools in financial problem-solving enhances analytical capabilities and empowers decision-makers across finance sectors—from portfolio managers optimizing asset allocations to traders crafting high-frequency strategies and risk analysts safeguarding against market uncertainties.

As we explore the nuanced applications of these methodologies across diverse financial landscapes, it's clear that mastering them equips professionals with strategic leverage—enabling informed decisions grounded in mathematical rigor amidst evolving economic challenges and opportunities alike—ensuring robust outcomes tailored toward achieving specific financial goals efficiently and effectively at every step along this analytical journey.

Accuracy and Efficiency Trade-offs

In the realm of matrix factorizations, achieving a balance between accuracy and efficiency is a crucial aspect that significantly impacts financial modeling. The precision of mathematical calculations is directly linked to the reliability of predictive models, but if not managed wisely, computational costs can become prohibitive. Let's explore how this balance influences the practical application of matrix theory in finance.

Take, for instance, a hedge fund using LU decomposition for asset allocation. The analysts must ensure high precision in matrix decompositions to prevent discrepancies during optimization. However, exact calculations can demand substantial computational resources, especially when handling large datasets typical in finance. Here, efficiency becomes key. Efficient algorithms can significantly cut processing time while maintaining acceptable precision levels, enabling financial analysts to make timely decisions without compromising accuracy.

Cholesky decomposition offers another angle on this trade-off. It's particularly suitable for positive definite matrices often found in covariance and correlation matrices used in portfolio risk assessments. By reducing computational complexity compared to methods like LU decomposition, Cholesky decomposition is especially advantageous for high-frequency trading strategies that require quick execution and real-time processing.

Despite the need for efficiency, model prediction integrity must not be compromised. Financial decisions based on inaccurate models can lead to significant losses. To mitigate this risk, quantitative analysts often use software packages that optimize matrix operations—such as LAPACK or BLAS libraries—which balance speed and precision with sophisticated algorithms designed for large-scale computations.

Consider an example involving QR factorization in linear regression models for econometric analysis. Here, both accuracy and efficiency are vital for determining model reliability and execution speed. When applied to real-world data—particularly during volatile market conditions—the ability to perform accurate QR factorizations swiftly enables robust predictive analytics essential for strategic decision-making.

Trade-offs extend beyond computational aspects to include hardware capabilities and software design choices. High-performance computing environments can handle complex calculations more efficiently but often at a higher cost. Analysts must assess whether investing in advanced computing infrastructure aligns with their strategic goals.

In the end, understanding the interplay between accuracy and efficiency requires a thorough grasp of both theoretical constructs and their practical implications in finance. Analysts must continually refine their approaches to remain competitive in an industry where decisions based on milliseconds can dictate success or failure.

This intricate balancing act highlights the importance of continuous learning and adaptability in financial analytics —skills crucial for navigating a constantly evolving landscape where mathematical expertise meets technological innovation.

Applications in Derivative Pricing

In the intricate realm of finance, derivative pricing is among the most complex applications of matrix factorizations. Derivatives, whose values are based on underlying assets, demand sophisticated mathematical models for accurate valuation. By employing matrix techniques, analysts can enhance precision and better navigate the nuances of these financial instruments.

Take the Black-Scholes model, a foundational approach to options pricing. Though initially rooted in partial differential equations, its application often benefits from matrix algebra, especially when adapted to real-world scenarios with multiple uncertainties. Matrix decomposition is invaluable here, simplifying complex systems into manageable forms and facilitating efficient computations.

One practical use of matrix techniques is Singular Value Decomposition (SVD) in option pricing models. SVD aids in reducing dimensionality without significant information loss, which is particularly useful when handling large datasets. This includes evaluating extensive arrays of correlated options or managing hedging strategies across various markets. By concentrating on principal components that capture essential data variance, SVD streamlines calculations.

Consider Monte Carlo simulations for pricing exotic options like barrier options. Matrix factorizations enhance these simulations by improving the stability and speed of convergence in random walks modeling asset price paths. Techniques such as LU or Cholesky decompositions optimize matrix operations within simulation algorithms, expediting computations and reducing errors.

Portfolio managers frequently encounter challenges in aligning their pricing models with market realities. QR factorization proves useful here, refining econometric models that account for varying interest rates or currency fluctuations—critical factors in derivative pricing strategies. Such precise adjustments allow for more accurate estimation of option Greeks, which measure risk sensitivities in financial derivatives.

In environments where computational efficiency is key, like high-frequency trading, matrix theory provides robust solutions for real-time derivative pricing. Algorithms utilizing factorization techniques swiftly process information and adapt to market changes with minimal delay. This agility is crucial for seizing arbitrage opportunities or fine-tuning risk management strategies amid rapid market shifts.

And, advanced software tools like MATLAB and R offer built-in functions that simplify implementing matrix factorizations in derivative pricing models. These platforms enable analysts to seamlessly integrate complex mathematical constructs into their workflows, fostering innovation and enhancing analytical capabilities.

The use of matrix factorizations in derivative pricing exemplifies how mathematics can transform financial analysis into a discipline marked by precision and foresight. As quantitative analysts refine their expertise in these methodologies, they unlock new strategic dimensions, driving advancements across the financial landscape with each calculated decision.

In this dynamic interplay between theory and practice, matrix techniques serve as catalysts for evolution within the field —paving pathways for future innovations that will redefine possibilities in derivative markets.

Matrix Factorization Tools

MATLAB leads the way with its powerful computational capabilities and user-friendly interface. It excels at matrix operations, offering built-in functions for various factorizations like LU, QR, and Cholesky. Its intuitive scripting language allows users to execute complex algorithms seamlessly. For example, the lu function decomposes a matrix A into lower and upper triangular matrices L and U effortlessly, enabling tasks from solving linear systems to optimizing portfolio models with simple inputs like L, U = lu(A).

R is another key player in statistical computing and data analysis. With robust packages such as 'Matrix' and 'lme4', it simplifies tasks like Singular Value Decomposition (SVD), crucial for data reduction and exploratory analysis in large financial datasets. Using svd(matrix), users can efficiently perform SVD, identifying principal components that capture significant variance—an essential step for reducing dimensionality without losing data integrity.

Python has gained prominence with libraries like NumPy and SciPy due to its versatility and open-source nature. NumPy's numpy.linalg module includes functions for essential matrix operations such as inversion and factorization. Take this example, numpy.linalg.qr(A) performs QR decomposition on matrix A, aiding regression analysis by resolving multicollinearity issues in financial models. Additionally, Python's Pandas library offers excellent data manipulation capabilities, facilitating seamless integration of financial datasets into analytical workflows.

For high-frequency trading or real-time analytics, Julia shines with both speed and simplicity. Its ability to handle high-performance computations makes it ideal for implementing complex algorithms necessary for real-time decision-making processes. Julia's LinearAlgebra package supports various factorizations like LU and Cholesky with concise syntax that minimizes execution time—a critical advantage in volatile markets where timing is crucial.

Excel remains a staple for many finance professionals due to its accessibility and ease of use. While not as powerful computationally as specialized software, Excel's Solver add-in allows users to perform optimization tasks and solve systems of linear equations through GUI-based interactions—perfect for rapid prototyping or initial analyses before moving on to more sophisticated tools.

These tools empower analysts to effectively bridge the gap between theory and practice. By leveraging software that enhances computational efficiency and accuracy, financial analysts can concentrate more on strategic decision-making rather than computational overhead. This synergy between mathematics and technology not only optimizes current models but also fosters innovation—driving advancements that will continue to shape the future of finance.

Mastering these matrix factorization tools equips professionals with the analytical prowess needed to thrive in today's complex financial environment—a vital skill for turning theoretical constructs into actionable insights.

CHAPTER 10: NORMS AND METRICS

Vector Norms

U nderstanding vector norms is essential for grasping the magnitude and direction of vectors, which are foundational concepts in quantitative finance. In this field, vector norms offer a way to measure vector sizes, aiding analysts in interpreting data sets, modeling financial risks, and optimizing portfolios.

Let's begin with the most familiar type: the Euclidean norm, also known as the L2 norm. It is calculated as the square root of the sum of the squares of a vector's components. Take this example, for a vector v with components (3, 4), the Euclidean norm is the square root of $(3^2 + 4^2)$, resulting in 5. This measure resembles finding the hypotenuse in a right triangle, making it especially intuitive when visualizing vectors in two or three dimensions.

In practical financial applications, the Euclidean norm helps quantify risk through distance metrics. In portfolio optimization, for example, it serves as a gauge for how much a portfolio's performance deviates from an optimal set of returns. This scalar representation simplifies comparisons between different portfolio configurations.

Beyond Euclidean norms, there are other norms like the L1 norm—the sum of absolute values—and the infinity norm—the maximum absolute value—each offering distinct advantages in specific contexts. The L1 norm is useful for handling sparse data sets or highlighting individual component contributions. In finance, it becomes valuable when analyzing transaction cost models or constructing portfolios with liquidity constraints that emphasize certain asset allocations.

The infinity norm is crucial for robustness analysis. By concentrating on the largest component of a vector, it helps analysts identify and address outliers or extreme values in financial datasets. This is particularly important when assessing market volatility or stress testing financial models under adverse conditions.

Calculating these norms can be seamlessly integrated into analytical workflows using software tools like Python's NumPy library. For example, numpy.linalg.norm(v) computes various norms depending on specified parameters—ord=2 for Euclidean, ord=1 for L1 norm, and ord=inf for infinity norm—allowing flexible adaptation to different analytical needs.

Understanding these mathematical constructs enables financial analysts to accurately assess scenarios and make informed decisions based on quantitative metrics rather than qualitative judgments alone. Norms act as foundational tools supporting rigorous analysis across numerous financial applications—from risk management and algorithmic trading strategies to compliance monitoring and beyond.

By incorporating vector norms into routine analysis, professionals are better equipped to navigate complex financial landscapes with precision and confidence, leveraging these powerful metrics to drive performance improvements and strategic advancements within their organizations.

Matrix Norms

Matrix norms, which extend the concept of vector norms to matrices, provide a quantitative measure of a matrix's size or length. In finance, understanding these norms is crucial for assessing the stability and sensitivity of numerical solutions in problems involving large datasets or complex models. For financial analysts aiming to ensure robustness and accuracy in their analyses under varying conditions, a grasp of matrix norms is essential.

Among the various types of matrix norms, the Frobenius norm is particularly common. It calculates the square root of the sum of the absolute squares of a matrix's elements. Consider a matrix A with components [[1, 2], [3, 4]]; its Frobenius norm would be $\sqrt{(1^2 + 2^2 + 3^2 + 4^2)}$, resulting in $\sqrt{30}$. This norm extends the Euclidean norm for vectors to matrices and is especially useful when overall variability needs to be understood rather than focusing on individual elements.

Another significant type of matrix norm in financial applications is the operator norm, specifically when using L2. This norm, linked to the largest singular value of the matrix, assesses how much a matrix can stretch a vector. It becomes invaluable when examining an investment portfolio's sensitivity to market conditions or estimating potential maximum losses under stress scenarios. That's why, operator norms are crucial for calculating risk metrics like Value-at-Risk (VaR) or Conditional Value-at-Risk (CVaR).

Though these mathematical formulations may appear abstract initially, they are practically significant when analyzing financial data using computational tools such as Python. With libraries like NumPy and SciPy, analysts can efficiently compute various norms. The function numpy.linalg.norm(A) provides different results depending on whether you're considering element-wise (Frobenius) or spectral (operator) approaches by setting parameters like ord='fro' or ord=2.

The decision between different norms depends largely on specific analytical requirements and contexts within finance. While Frobenius norms offer a comprehensive view by equally aggregating all elements, operator norms focus on worst-case scenarios by emphasizing maximal amplification effects caused by particular market dynamics or rare events.

Incorporating these tools into daily financial analysis enables professionals to verify model consistency and predict changing conditions with greater foresight and agility. Matrix norms thus become indispensable allies in navigating complex datasets and ensuring that strategic decisions are based on rigorous quantitative assessments rather than conjecture.

By adeptly leveraging matrix norms, analysts gain the precision needed for tasks ranging from regulatory compliance assessments to algorithmic trading optimizations. This guarantees their strategies remain robust against unforeseen shifts while capitalizing on opportunities for innovation and growth within constantly evolving financial landscapes.

Measuring Financial Data

Matrix norms are essential for understanding the stability and behavior of matrices across various operations. In financial contexts, these concepts are crucial for analyzing datasets, especially in high-stakes environments like stock markets or investment portfolios. Accurate measurement is vital for making informed decisions that can significantly impact financial outcomes.

In financial analysis, measuring data involves grasping both its scale and intrinsic characteristics. Take, for instance, a covariance matrix derived from asset returns; its dimensions indicate the correlation level between assets. Matrix norms help analysts determine how closely aligned assets are within a portfolio, which is key for assessing diversification levels and managing systemic risk.

Financial analysts often use the L1 norm, or Manhattan norm, to measure datasets with sparse data points or extreme values —common in economic time series that include outliers. This norm focuses on the sum of absolute values of matrix entries, making it ideal for highlighting deviations that may signal market anomalies or arbitrage opportunities. For example, an analyst might apply the L1 norm to bond yield spreads to identify bonds that deviate significantly from expected yields, flagging them for further investigation.

In large-scale financial datasets, computational efficiency is crucial. Tools like Python's pandas library provide robust solutions for managing such data. Functions such as pandas.DataFrame.corr() to compute correlation matrices and numpy.linalg.norm() for calculating various norms help analysts streamline their workflow while maintaining precision. This integration allows for quick analysis without sacrificing the depth needed for strategic decision-making.

Ensuring data integrity is also critical for accurate measurement and analysis. Analysts must address missing or incomplete data points—issues that can skew results if not properly managed. Techniques like imputation or normalization maintain dataset reliability, enabling meaningful comparisons across time periods or between asset classes.

Consider constructing an optimal portfolio through mean-variance optimization, where accurately measuring expected returns and covariances is essential. Using matrix norms ensures that risk assessments reflect true market conditions rather than being distorted by noise or volatility spikes often present in raw financial data.

In the end, leveraging these mathematical tools allows analysts to extract valuable insights and enhance model robustness and predictive accuracy across diverse financial scenarios. With precise measurements forming the backbone of their analytical processes, finance professionals are better equipped to navigate uncertainties in ever-evolving markets.

By integrating rigorous quantitative methods into their practice, analysts can transform raw data into actionable intelligence, ensuring their strategies are well-informed and adaptable to future challenges in the financial world.

Errors and Approximations

In financial analysis, errors and approximations are inevitable, yet effectively managing them is crucial for maintaining the integrity of analytical models. Financial decisions—from asset pricing to risk assessment—rely heavily on data accuracy and the ability to predict outcomes within an acceptable margin of error.

Consider numerical precision: in financial modeling, small inaccuracies can accumulate through complex calculations, leading to significant discrepancies over time. This is especially true with iterative processes or large datasets. For example, a minor error in estimating interest rates could significantly alter projected investment returns over several years.

To mitigate these risks, analysts use various approximation techniques. Taylor series expansions allow for the approximation of complex functions by breaking down intricate equations into simpler components. This approach provides insights without compromising computational efficiency. Take this example, when modeling an exotic option's payoff structure, Taylor approximations offer a practical yet precise representation.

Linearization is another valuable tool. By assuming linear relationships within certain intervals or conditions, complex nonlinear systems become more manageable. This technique is particularly useful in scenario analysis during sudden market shifts when swift decisions are necessary.

Errors also stem from assumptions embedded in models themselves. Take the Capital Asset Pricing Model (CAPM), which assumes a linear relationship between expected return and risk via beta coefficients. However, real-world data often deviate from these assumptions due to factors like changing market sentiments or unexpected geopolitical events. Recognizing these limitations allows analysts to adjust their models dynamically, incorporating additional variables or constraints as needed.

Software tools such as Python and R enhance error management with built-in functions designed for statistical analysis and numerical methods. Python's scipy.optimize library provides optimization algorithms that help fine-tune model parameters, effectively reducing approximation errors. Meanwhile, R's lm() function supports robust regression analysis that addresses issues like multicollinearity or heteroscedasticity prevalent in financial datasets.

And, backtesting is essential for validating model accuracy against historical data before live market deployment. By simulating strategies across different timeframes and conditions, analysts can identify potential pitfalls and refine their approaches accordingly.

In the end, viewing errors as learning opportunities rather than setbacks enriches the analytical process. Through careful management of approximations and continuous model refinement, finance professionals can better navigate market uncertainties while capitalizing on emerging opportunities with confidence and precision.

This proactive approach not only ensures robust analyses but also empowers decision-makers to act decisively amidst the complexities of global finance—transforming potential pitfalls into pathways for innovation and growth.

Conditioning of Financial Models

In financial modeling, ensuring that models are well-conditioned is key to achieving accurate and reliable predictions. Model conditioning refers to how sensitive a model's output is to changes or errors in its input data. This is particularly important in financial markets, where even small fluctuations can significantly impact investment decisions and market forecasts.

The idea of model condition is often quantified by the condition number, which measures how much the output value can change with slight variations in input values. A model with a low condition number is considered well-conditioned, meaning it is robust against small perturbations. In contrast, a high condition number indicates a poorly conditioned model that is more susceptible to inaccuracies.

Consider the valuation of complex derivatives, which involves intricate calculations based on asset prices and volatility measures. Poorly conditioned models in this context can lead to significant pricing errors from minor misestimations in volatility, affecting trading strategies and risk assessments.

Improving model conditioning can be achieved through several methods. One practical approach is preprocessing data before inputting it into the model. Normalizing data so that input features have similar scales reduces discrepancies caused by large numerical differences among variables. Standardizing financial metrics like asset returns or volatility indices ensures that no single input disproportionately influences outcomes due to its magnitude.

Another method involves refining algorithmic choices during model development. For example, using regularization methods such as Ridge or Lasso regression can mitigate overfitting by penalizing overly complex models. This not only improves conditioning but also enhances the model's ability to generalize across varying market conditions.

Software solutions also play an instrumental role in managing model conditioning effectively. Python libraries like NumPy provide functions for computing condition numbers, helping analysts assess their models' stability before deployment. These tools also offer advanced matrix operations that facilitate early error detection during development.

Iterative refinement through backtesting further strengthens a model's resilience against unforeseen market movements. By continuously evaluating performance against historical scenarios and adapting parameters accordingly, financial professionals can ensure their models remain robust over time.

Portfolio optimization is a domain where well-conditioned models are crucial, relying heavily on linear algebra techniques like covariance matrices for risk assessment and return projections. Ensuring these matrices are well-conditioned significantly reduces estimation error impacts, leading to more reliable portfolio allocations.

The pursuit of well-conditioned financial models is ongoing and iterative, requiring vigilance and adaptability as markets evolve and new data becomes available. By prioritizing model conditioning as an integral part of analytical workflows, finance professionals are better equipped to tackle complex challenges with precision, safeguarding investments while capitalizing on strategic opportunities within dynamic markets.

This focus not only supports robust decision-making but also fosters an environment where innovation thrives—transforming uncertainty into strategic advantage through meticulous craftsmanship grounded in mathematical rigor.

Stability of Algorithms

In financial modeling, algorithm stability is a cornerstone for generating reliable and accurate outputs. Stability here refers to an algorithm's capacity to produce consistent results despite minor variations or errors in input data. This is vital in finance, where precise calculations can differentiate between profit and loss.

Take, for example, high-frequency trading algorithms that execute numerous trades in milliseconds. An unstable algorithm might react unpredictably to small market fluctuations, leading to erroneous trades and potential financial losses. Thus, ensuring algorithm stability is crucial for maintaining trust and effectiveness in automated trading systems.

To enhance stability, selecting numerical techniques appropriate to the specific problem is essential. When handling large datasets or matrices common in financial computations, choosing numerically stable algorithms—like QR decomposition for solving linear equations—can prevent error propagation that might otherwise magnify through calculations.

Understanding and mitigating round-off errors inherent in computer-based calculations is another critical aspect. These small discrepancies can accumulate over time or across multiple operations. Implementing algorithms designed to minimize such errors is vital for maintaining accuracy in complex financial models.

Testing algorithms under various scenarios also plays a key role in assessing stability. By simulating diverse market conditions—including extreme events—and observing algorithm performance, analysts can pinpoint potential weaknesses and refine models accordingly. This rigorous approach ensures models remain robust across different environments.

The choice of programming language and software influences algorithm stability as well. Languages like Python, with robust libraries such as NumPy and SciPy, offer functions optimized for numerical stability, providing financial analysts with a reliable foundation for building stable computational models.

Documentation and peer reviews significantly contribute to stability assurance processes. Comprehensive records of model assumptions, parameter choices, and testing outcomes ensure transparency and facilitate collaborative evaluation of model reliability.

Regular updates based on new research or technological advancements further bolster algorithmic stability over time. Staying informed about emerging techniques allows practitioners to integrate innovative approaches into existing frameworks, adapting swiftly to evolving market dynamics without sacrificing precision or dependability.

In the end, adopting a mindset of continuous improvement is paramount—seeing each iteration not as an endpoint but as a stepping stone toward greater accuracy and resilience within the ever-changing financial landscape.

By incorporating these strategies into their practice, finance professionals not only strengthen their analytical capabilities but also contribute to fostering an industry culture rooted in excellence—where meticulous attention to detail turns complex challenges into opportunities for strategic growth amidst uncertainty.

Portfolio Optimization Strategies

Portfolio optimization combines the art and science of selecting the optimal mix of assets to maximize returns while minimizing risk. This skill is crucial for financial analysts, especially in today's volatile and complex markets. The strategies used in portfolio optimization are diverse, yet they all rely on the effective application of linear algebra concepts to achieve precise and profitable outcomes.

At the heart of portfolio optimization lies the mean-variance framework, developed by Harry Markowitz. This approach uses matrices to represent asset returns and covariances, forming the foundation for calculating efficient frontiers

—portfolios that offer the highest expected return for a given level of risk. By constructing and manipulating these matrices, analysts can visually map potential portfolios and strategically select those that align with their risk tolerance and investment goals.

For example, consider an investor managing a diversified portfolio. The covariance matrix quantifies how different assets within this portfolio move relative to each other. This information allows analysts to identify combinations that yield optimal diversification benefits, effectively reducing unsystematic risk through careful asset selection. Pairing stocks with low correlation coefficients, for instance, reduces overall portfolio volatility—a principle well understood in quantitative finance.

Adding constraints introduces another layer of complexity to optimization strategies. Investors may impose restrictions based on ethical considerations or regulatory requirements, such as limiting investments in certain industries or maintaining minimum liquidity levels. Linear programming techniques help incorporate these constraints into optimization models, ensuring portfolios remain compliant without sacrificing performance.

Technology significantly enhances portfolio optimization processes. Python libraries like Pandas for data manipulation and PyPortfolioOpt for optimization offer powerful tools for implementing advanced models efficiently. Analysts leverage these technologies to process large datasets and quickly simulate various market scenarios—enabling them to adjust strategies dynamically in response to changing market conditions.

Real-world applications often involve rebalancing portfolios by periodically adjusting asset weights to maintain desired risk-return profiles amid shifting market landscapes. This requires continuous analysis of current positions against strategic objectives using updated data inputs—a task well-suited for algorithmic solutions capable of executing trades swiftly across global markets.

Risk management is closely tied to optimization strategies. Through stress testing techniques that simulate adverse market events, analysts assess potential impacts on portfolio performance under extreme conditions—allowing for preemptive adjustments that mitigate downside risks while capitalizing on emerging opportunities.

And, sensitivity analysis provides insight into how changes in key assumptions affect outcomes, guiding decision-making processes with clarity and foresight. Understanding how variations in input variables influence results empowers investors to make informed choices grounded in robust quantitative analyses.

In the end, successful portfolio optimization balances scientific rigor with intuitive judgment—a delicate interplay where mathematical precision meets human insight. As finance professionals refine their expertise through practice and ongoing education, they contribute not only to their personal success but also advance collective knowledge within an ever-evolving field at the intersection of mathematics, technology, and strategic investment management.

CHAPTER 11: ORTHOGONALITY AND ORTHOGONAL MATRICES

Concepts of Orthogonality

O rthogonality, a fundamental concept in linear algebra, is vital in many financial applications due to its ability to simplify models and enhance computational efficiency. It involves the idea of perpendicularity between vectors within a given space, which helps in understanding complex relationships in data sets. In finance, orthogonality becomes particularly important as it allows analysts to deal with multiple financial variables more effectively.

When financial variables are represented as vectors, orthogonality means they are uncorrelated—each variable stands independently without influencing the others. This property is crucial for constructing predictive models or performing regression analysis because it enables a clearer separation of influences among variables. Achieving orthogonality often involves transforming data sets into new bases where the variables exhibit this independence.

A practical example is the Gram-Schmidt process, which converts any set of vectors into an orthogonal set while retaining their span. In finance, this process can help construct orthogonal risk factors from correlated market indicators. By breaking down correlated data into uncorrelated components, analysts can better isolate individual risk contributions and refine their investment strategies.

Orthogonality also plays a significant role in matrix theory through orthogonal matrices—square matrices whose rows and columns are mutually orthogonal unit vectors. These matrices have special properties that preserve distances and angles during transformations. Financial analysts use these features to maintain data integrity during complex computations, such as rotating coordinate systems or reducing dimensionality.

In portfolio management, understanding orthogonality aids in diversifying investments effectively. A well-diversified portfolio often comprises assets that do not move in tandem; mathematically speaking, their returns should be as close to orthogonal as possible. This minimizes overall portfolio volatility by ensuring that losses in some assets do not significantly impact the entire portfolio's performance.

Additionally, projecting high-dimensional financial data onto lower-dimensional subspaces using techniques like Principal Component Analysis (PCA) leverages orthogonality principles to retain essential information while discarding noise. PCA identifies principal components—orthogonal directions capturing maximum variance—thus simplifying data analysis without substantial loss of information.

The utility of orthogonality is further highlighted in signal processing within algorithmic trading systems. Separating noise from true market signals requires distinguishing independent sources from composite observations—a task facilitated by recognizing orthogonal relationships among underlying factors.

Mastering these concepts equips quantitative analysts with tools necessary for rigorous analysis across various domains—from risk assessment and asset pricing models to developing robust trading algorithms grounded in sound mathematical principles.

As you explore finance's mathematical underpinnings, embracing the utility of orthogonality fosters both precision and creativity within your analytical endeavors. It bridges abstract theory with tangible results through its elegant capacity to simplify complex interactions into manageable components—a testament to its enduring relevance in advancing both individual expertise and broader financial innovation initiatives globally.

Transition to Orthogonal Finance

In finance, the shift to orthogonal finance represents a move towards methodologies that emphasize independence and clarity in data analysis. This involves adopting strategies that apply the principles of orthogonality to untangle complex financial relationships, leading to more robust and transparent models.

Consider portfolio construction as an example of this transition. The aim is to build a portfolio where asset returns are as uncorrelated as possible. This requires adjusting asset weights so the portfolio aligns along orthogonal axes in return space. Such alignment is achieved through careful analysis and strategic selection, ensuring diversification maximizes risk-adjusted returns. Here, orthogonality is not just a mathematical concept but a practical tool for achieving investment goals.

Incorporating orthogonal finance into risk management highlights its significance further. Risk factors often show correlations that obscure their individual impacts on asset returns. By using techniques like factor analysis, analysts can break down these risk factors into orthogonal components, clarifying each factor's distinct contributions. This clarity enables more targeted hedging strategies and efficient capital allocation.

Orthogonal methods also transform regression analysis in financial modeling. Traditional regression may struggle with multicollinearity, where predictor variables are interdependent, leading to unreliable coefficient estimates. Orthogonalizing these variables—through methods like principal component regression—addresses multicollinearity by ensuring input variables contribute independently to the model's output.

In computational finance, algorithmic trading systems gain significantly from orthogonal techniques. These systems process vast amounts of market data to execute trades swiftly and accurately. By leveraging orthogonal transformations such as Singular Value Decomposition (SVD), traders can extract meaningful signals from noisy datasets. SVD breaks down data matrices into orthogonal components, simplifying complex patterns into actionable insights—a crucial step in developing adaptive trading algorithms.

And, machine learning in finance highlights the role of orthogonality even further. Machine learning models thrive on high-dimensional data but suffer when features are correlated or redundant. Orthogonal feature selection helps streamline model training by focusing on independent predictors that enhance predictive accuracy while reducing overfitting risks.

Exploring these applications makes it clear that transitioning to orthogonal finance is not just about using advanced mathematical techniques; it's about fostering an analytical mindset that values simplicity amid complexity. This mindset encourages professionals to seek clarity and precision in their analyses—transforming data intricacies into comprehensible narratives that drive informed decision-making.

This transition requires a commitment to continuous learning and adaptation, as the financial landscape rapidly evolves with technological advancements and market dynamics. Analysts equipped with a strong understanding of orthogonality are better positioned to anticipate changes and innovate solutions for emerging challenges.

In the end, the journey towards orthogonal finance enriches both individual expertise and collective financial wisdom. It facilitates a paradigm shift where mathematical elegance meets practical application—a synergy poised to redefine success across diverse financial sectors.

Application in Minimizing Risks

Minimizing risk is a cornerstone of financial strategy, and orthogonality plays a crucial role in achieving this goal. By breaking down complex risk structures into simpler, uncorrelated components, financial analysts can develop more precise models, offering clarity and reducing exposure to unexpected market shifts.

In portfolio management, orthogonalization aims to create portfolios with asset returns that show minimal correlation. This approach not only enhances diversification but also stabilizes returns amidst market volatility. Techniques like principal component analysis (PCA) transform correlated asset returns into orthogonal factors, simplifying the market landscape and providing clearer insights into how each factor independently influences portfolio performance.

In risk management, orthogonalization dissects and analyzes various sources of risk. It is essential to isolate and address each component separately to avoid overlooking subtle yet critical influences on asset behavior. Take this example, interest rate risk and credit risk often intertwine, obscuring their individual impacts on financial instruments. By decomposing these risks orthogonally, analysts can allocate resources more effectively to mitigate each distinct threat.

Orthogonal methods also enhance precision in derivative pricing and hedging strategies. Derivatives are sensitive to multiple underlying variables whose interactions complicate pricing models. Orthogonal techniques segregate these variables into independent entities, facilitating more accurate hedging strategies that account for each variable's unique influence on derivative values.

In quantitative risk modeling, multicollinearity among predictor variables can lead to misleading model outputs. Orthogonal transformations ensure predictors contribute independently to the model's predictions, crucial for developing robust models that withstand scrutiny and deliver reliable forecasts under varied market conditions.

Orthogonality enriches machine learning applications in finance as well. Selecting features that are orthogonal— or independent—enhances model performance by reducing redundancy and overfitting. These streamlined models are faster and more adaptable to new data inputs, offering real-time insights critical for timely decision-making.

And, integrating orthogonal techniques into algorithmic trading systems amplifies efficiency. By distilling complex data streams into orthogonal components, traders can identify unique signals for buy or sell decisions with greater accuracy. This ability to extract actionable insights from vast data is essential for maintaining a competitive edge in fast-paced markets.

In the end, applying orthogonality in risk minimization results in models and strategies characterized by clarity and resilience. These methods provide a solid foundation for building defenses against unforeseen market events and optimizing financial outcomes.

The integration of these techniques underscores a broader commitment within the finance industry to embrace innovation while safeguarding stability. Analysts adept at employing orthogonal strategies are well-equipped to navigate an ever-evolving landscape, ensuring sustained success in managing both traditional and emergent risks.

Economic Insights Possibilities

In finance, orthogonality transcends its mathematical roots to offer profound economic insights. By studying orthogonal matrices, financial analysts can unravel the complex interactions of seemingly unrelated variables within financial systems. This analytical prowess is essential for decoding the intricate web of market behaviors and trends.

Take, for instance, two financial assets exhibiting orthogonal behavior, such as stocks from companies in distinct sectors. Here, the correlation between these assets is near zero, indicating minimal interaction. This finding is significant as it allows for the creation of diversified portfolios that aim to maximize returns while minimizing risk. By leveraging these orthogonal relationships, traders can enhance their strategic planning with precision and foresight.

Implementing orthogonality in practice often involves sophisticated mathematical modeling techniques like principal component analysis (PCA). PCA simplifies datasets by reducing their dimensions while preserving key characteristics. This technique is particularly beneficial in high-dimensional financial markets, allowing analysts to isolate significant patterns amidst the noise and make clearer decisions.

In risk management, understanding the orthogonal components of asset returns helps identify systemic risks and hidden vulnerabilities within portfolios. This insight is crucial for developing robust hedging strategies that safeguard against unforeseen market shocks.

Orthogonality also plays a critical role in econometrics, especially in regression models. When predictor variables are orthogonalized, or transformed to be uncorrelated, model estimation becomes more stable and reliable, enhancing the predictive accuracy of economic forecasts and investment strategies.

In macroeconomic analysis, identifying orthogonal shocks can illuminate the underlying economic forces driving changes in metrics such as GDP, inflation rates, or employment levels. These insights are invaluable for policymakers seeking to implement informed economic interventions.

For practical applications, software tools like R or Python facilitate the computation and visualization of orthogonal matrices in financial contexts. For example, using PCA in Python with libraries like NumPy or Scikit-learn enables analysts to swiftly transform raw data into meaningful insights:

```python
from sklearn.decomposition import PCA

import numpy as np


\#\# Simulated dataset with asset returns

data = np.array([[0.01, 0.02], [0.02, 0.03], [0.03, 0.01]])


\#\# Apply PCA

pca = PCA(n_components=2)

principalComponents = pca.fit_transform(data)


print("Principal Components:", principalComponents)
```

\` \` \`

This code snippet demonstrates a straightforward application of PCA on asset returns to uncover their principal components —identifying a new basis where these returns are expressed as linear combinations of uncorrelated factors.

By embracing the possibilities offered by orthogonality, quantitative analysts are equipped with both tools and enhanced intuition to navigate financial landscapes marked by complexity and volatility. These insights empower them to develop strategies grounded in both theoretical soundness and practical effectiveness—a synthesis crucial for thriving in dynamic market conditions.

Gram-Schmidt Process

The Gram-Schmidt process is a fundamental technique in linear algebra, used to transform a set of linearly independent vectors into an orthogonal set, which can then be normalized to create an orthonormal basis. This transformation is particularly valuable in financial mathematics, where simplifying complex datasets into an efficient analytical basis is crucial.

Consider dealing with multiple financial indicators, each representing distinct economic variables. In their raw form, these indicators might be linearly independent but not orthogonal. The Gram-Schmidt process refines these indicators into an orthogonal set, eliminating overlap or redundancy in information. This transformation clarifies each indicator's unique contribution to a portfolio's behavior.

The Gram-Schmidt process works by starting with an initial vector from your dataset and adjusting each subsequent vector by subtracting its projection onto the previously processed vectors. This subtraction ensures that each new vector is orthogonal to all prior ones. In financial data analysis, this means extracting distinct components that do not share variance, effectively reducing multicollinearity issues in econometric models.

Mathematically, given a set of vectors v1, v2, ..., vn, the orthogonal set u1, u2, ..., un is derived as follows:

1. Set u1 = v1.

2. For each k from 2 to n:

3. Compute the projection of vk onto each uj (for j < k).

4. Subtract these projections from vk to form uk.

In practice, tools like Python simplify this process significantly. Here's an example:

```python
import numpy as np

\#\# Original set of vectors

v1 = np.array([1, 0])

v2 = np.array([1, 1])


\#\# &Step 1: Normalize v1

u1 = v1 / np.linalg.norm(v1)


\#\# &Step 2: Subtract the projection of v2 onto u1

proj_v2_on_u1 = np.dot(v2, u1) * u1

u2 = v2 - proj_v2_on_u1


\#\# Normalize u2

u2 /= np.linalg.norm(u2)
```

```
print("Orthogonal Vectors:", u1, "", u2)
` ` `
```

This code snippet demonstrates transforming a simple two-vector system into an orthogonal basis using the Gram-Schmidt process. Such transformations are essential for constructing financial models that require uncorrelated variables for accurate predictions and analysis.

The elegance of the Gram-Schmidt process lies in its ability to reshape financial data into more analyzable forms while preserving essential characteristics. It serves as a practical tool for econometricians and quantitative analysts managing high-dimensional data efficiently.

Insights gleaned from these transformations can lead to more robust investment strategies and clearer interpretations of market trends. By adopting these techniques, professionals are better equipped to handle the complexities inherent in financial modeling and decision-making processes.

In the end, the power of the Gram-Schmidt process lies in its capacity to distill complexity into clarity—transforming tangled financial narratives into straightforward analytical paths that enhance understanding and strategic action within markets.

The Role of Least Squares

In the realm of financial analysis, the least squares method is a foundational tool for data approximation, providing precise modeling and prediction capabilities. It originates from the need to derive the best fit line through a series of data points, an essential task for any quantitative analyst aiming to extract clarity from market chaos.

This approach works by minimizing the sum of the squared differences between observed values and those predicted by a model. Despite its mathematical simplicity, it has a profound impact: it transforms raw, noisy data into coherent trends, enabling analysts to draw informed conclusions about financial phenomena.

For example, consider an analyst trying to predict stock prices using historical data. Least squares regression becomes invaluable here. By fitting a line that minimizes discrepancies between past values and their projections, one can construct a model offering insights into future price movements.

To implement this method, analysts construct equations representing these relationships. Given a dataset with pairs (xi, yi)—where xi is an independent variable (such as time) and yi is a dependent variable (like stock price)—the goal is to determine coefficients m and c for the linear equation yi = mxi + c that best fits this data.

Python, with libraries like NumPy and SciPy, simplifies these calculations:

```python
import numpy as np


\#\# Sample data points

x = np.array([1, 2, 3, 4])

y = np.array([2.2, 2.8, 3.6, 4.5])


\#\# Fit line using least squares

A = np.vstack([x, np.ones(len(x))]).T

m, c = np.linalg.lstsq(A, y, rcond=None)[0]


print(f"Slope: m, Intercept: c")
```

` ` `

This script illustrates how to fit a linear model to data points using least squares regression. The calculated slope and intercept provide parameters to forecast future values or assess trends over time.

Beyond simple linear regression, least squares extend into multiple dimensions—essential for multifactor financial models involving numerous variables. This extension allows analysts to consider complex interactions among diverse factors influencing market behavior.

The technique's versatility extends beyond prediction; it also supports robust econometric testing and hypothesis validation, such as evaluating asset pricing models or assessing investment performance against market indices.

Least squares empower financial professionals to distill vast datasets into actionable insights—enabling precise risk assessments or identifying undervalued opportunities in markets. As applications evolve alongside advancements in big data analytics and machine learning integration, least squares remain pivotal within contemporary quantitative finance frameworks.

By blending numerical precision with analytical acumen through least squares methods, analysts can confidently navigate the vast sea of financial information—transforming complexity into actionable intelligence while upholding rigorous standards crucial for sound decision-making in dynamic economic landscapes.

Efficiency in Computations

Efficiency in computational tasks is crucial for financial analysts, especially when managing vast datasets and complex models. The least squares method, despite its power, can become computationally demanding in high-dimensional spaces or during real-time data processing. Achieving streamlined calculations without losing accuracy requires both algorithmic expertise and advanced technology.

One effective way to enhance computational efficiency is by leveraging the properties of matrix algebra. Matrix operations are foundational to many least squares computations; thus, optimizing these processes can lead to significant time savings. Take this example, using preconditioning techniques can improve convergence rates in iterative methods, making them more suitable for large-scale problems where direct methods might struggle.

Python's libraries offer powerful tools for these optimizations. Libraries such as NumPy and SciPy not only include efficient linear algebra routines but also support sparse matrices, which are essential when dealing with datasets containing many zero entries. Sparse matrices help reduce memory usage and speed up computations by focusing only on non-zero elements.

```python
from scipy.sparse import csc_matrix

from scipy.sparse.linalg import lsqr


\#\# Sparse matrix representation

A_sparse = csc_matrix(A)


\#\# Efficient least squares solution

result = lsqr(A_sparse, y)

slope_sparse = result[0][0]

intercept_sparse = result[0][1]


print(f"Slope (Sparse): slope_sparse, Intercept (Sparse):
```

intercept_sparse")

``` ` ` ` ```

This code snippet illustrates how sparse matrix techniques can streamline least squares regression computations. Converting dense data structures into sparse ones allows analysts to handle larger datasets more efficiently—a critical capability in high-frequency trading or when analyzing vast asset classes.

Parallel computing further boosts efficiency by distributing computational loads across multiple processors. By implementing parallelization strategies, financial models can scale seamlessly with data size, enabling rapid processing that keeps pace with volatile markets. Tools like Dask offer a Python interface for parallel computing without requiring extensive rewrites of existing codebases.

For example, distributed arrays allow large datasets to be partitioned across multiple cores:

``` ```python
import dask.array as da

\#\# Create a Dask array from a NumPy array

x_dask = da.from_array(x, chunks=(2,))

y_dask = da.from_array(y, chunks=(2,))

\#\# Perform computation on Dask arrays

m_dask, c_dask = da.linalg.lstsq(da.vstack([x_dask, da.ones(len(x_dask))]).T, y_dask)

print(f"Slope (Dask): m_dask.compute(), Intercept (Dask): c_dask.compute()")
```
```

` ` `

This example demonstrates how Dask facilitates handling data across multiple processors or even clusters, enhancing both the speed and scalability of financial computations.

In addition to software solutions, hardware advancements significantly contribute to increased efficiency. The rise of GPUs has transformed numerical computations by offering massive parallel processing capabilities that surpass traditional CPUs in certain tasks. Financial institutions now use GPU acceleration for various applications, from option pricing to risk management simulations.

Incorporating these computational strategies ensures that financial analysts remain agile amid growing data volumes and increasingly complex market models. By optimizing their tools through advanced algorithms and cutting-edge technology, they maintain the precision necessary for accurate decision-making while minimizing computational overhead —a balance essential for success in today's fast-paced financial landscape.

In the end, the pursuit of efficiency underscores a commitment to excellence in quantitative finance— a field where every millisecond matters and each calculation can provide a strategic advantage in the marketplace.

Practical Applications

Practical applications of linear algebra and matrix theory in finance are both diverse and profound, playing a crucial role in decision-making processes across the sector. These mathematical tools are essential for tasks ranging from optimizing portfolios to pricing complex derivatives, and their effective use often sets successful analysts apart from their peers.

Take portfolio optimization, a fundamental aspect of modern finance. This process involves selecting the optimal asset distribution to maximize returns while minimizing risk. Matrix operations simplify the complexity of handling numerous variables and constraints, with the covariance matrix being central to this endeavor. This matrix captures asset return variances and covariances, facilitating the quantification of portfolio risk through efficient frontier analysis—a graphical tool that highlights the portfolios offering the highest expected return for a specified level of risk.

Implementing these concepts requires robust computation. Take this example, using Python's NumPy library, analysts can quickly calculate the covariance matrix:

```python
import numpy as np

\#\# Sample returns data for assets

returns = np.array([[0.05, 0.1, 0.02], [0.04, 0.12, 0.01], [0.03, 0.08, 0]])

\#\# Calculate covariance matrix

cov_matrix = np.cov(returns.T)

print("Covariance Matrix:")

print(cov_matrix)
```

This straightforward operation enables analysts to pursue Markowitz portfolio optimization or explore advanced strategies like Black-Litterman models—both heavily dependent on precise covariance estimations.

Beyond portfolio management, matrix theory is vital

in derivative pricing and risk management. Given the complexities and sensitivities of financial instruments to market conditions, precision is crucial. Methods such as finite difference and Monte Carlo simulations benefit from efficient matrix computations to calculate Greeks or simulate paths under stochastic processes.

Algorithmic trading platforms also leverage matrix manipulations for real-time data analysis, identifying arbitrage opportunities or executing trades based on statistical patterns in historical price movements.

In risk management, linear algebra's versatility shines through Value at Risk (VaR) calculations and stress testing scenarios. These methods use matrices to track potential losses over time or incorporate extreme market events into simulations. Credit risk assessment further employs singular value decomposition (SVD) to evaluate large datasets like loan portfolios or client credit histories, transforming raw data into insights about potential defaults or credit rating downgrades.

Linear algebra's applications extend into econometrics and macroeconomic forecasting models, where regressions and time series analyses rely on matrices to estimate relationships between economic indicators—offering crucial foresight for policy-making and strategic planning within financial institutions.

Real-world application demands overcoming challenges such as ill-conditioned matrices or ensuring numerical stability in computations. Fortunately, modern computational resources and refined algorithms make these tasks manageable.

In the end, these practical applications highlight the importance of not just theoretical knowledge but also the strategic acumen needed to apply mathematical insights effectively in the fast-paced financial markets. This emphasizes linear algebra's power and relevance in driving industry innovation.

Mastery of these practical aspects equips financial professionals with a formidable toolkit—enabling them to navigate complex landscapes confidently and contribute meaningfully to their organizations' success stories.

CHAPTER 12: LINEAR TRANSFORMATIONS

Fundamental Definitions

L inear algebra is the mathematical language that allows us to express complex relationships within financial systems with clarity and precision. It bridges theoretical concepts with actionable insights, primarily through its core elements: vectors and matrices. These structures encode financial information in a form that is conducive to analysis and transformation.

To begin, let's define some fundamental concepts that will serve as the building blocks for our exploration. At the most basic level, a scalar is a single numerical value that represents magnitude without direction. Scalars are ubiquitous in finance, representing quantities such as interest rates, stock prices, or exchange rates—crucial for everyday decision-making.

Moving beyond scalars, we encounter vectors, which are ordered lists of numbers. These lists can represent various data points, such as the returns of different assets in a portfolio or changes in economic indicators over time. The direction and magnitude of a vector provide valuable information about trends and patterns, enabling analysts to discern meaningful relationships within datasets.

Vectors are often part of vector spaces—a collection of vectors characterized by operations like addition and scalar multiplication. For example, if two portfolio return vectors exist within the same space, their sum or any scaled version should also reside in that space. This property underpins many financial models that rely on linear combinations of asset returns to forecast outcomes.

Next, we have matrices: arrays of numbers organized in rows and columns. Matrices extend vectors into multiple dimensions, representing data from complex systems like multiple portfolios or economic variables across countries. In finance, matrices facilitate large-scale computations needed for risk assessments or derivative pricing.

Consider a matrix A with m rows and n columns (m x n). This structure enables operations such as matrix addition—where matrices of the same order are combined element by element —or scalar multiplication, which adjusts each element by a constant factor. These operations reflect practical tasks like adjusting risk metrics or reallocating capital across sectors.

Another pivotal concept is the transpose of a matrix—an operation that flips its rows with columns, offering a change in perspective. This proves instrumental when analyzing cross-sectional data or creating models that must accommodate diverse data orientations without losing coherence.

The identity matrix is another cornerstone: a square matrix with ones on the diagonal and zeros elsewhere. It acts like the number one in scalar arithmetic; multiplying any matrix by an identity matrix leaves it unchanged, highlighting notions of equivalence and preservation in financial transformations.

Matrix inversion extends these ideas further. For a non-singular square matrix A, an inverse matrix $A^{(-1)}$ exists such that $A * A^{(-1)}$ yields the identity matrix. Inversion is crucial for solving systems of linear equations—a task frequently encountered when optimizing portfolios or calibrating models under various constraints.

While these constructs may initially seem abstract, their relevance becomes apparent when applied to real-world finance problems. Understanding these definitions provides a strong foundation from which more complex theories can be built—preparing us to delve deeper into how linear algebra facilitates problem-solving within dynamic markets.

As we explore this intricate field, remember that each concept logically connects to those before it—a testament to linear algebra's cohesive nature. Mastery of these basics ensures readiness for exploring applications essential for thriving in today's sophisticated financial environments.

Matrices as Transformations

In the realm of finance, matrices serve as powerful tools for transforming data, seamlessly connecting theoretical concepts with practical applications. By representing linear transformations, matrices offer a structured approach to manipulating and interpreting complex financial datasets. This helps analysts to uncover patterns and insights that might otherwise remain hidden.

Think of a matrix as a function that maps input vectors to output vectors through a series of linear operations. This mapping is particularly valuable in finance, where it can illustrate changes in market conditions, shifts in economic indicators, or adjustments in investment strategies. By applying matrices to vectors of financial data, analysts can model these changes both efficiently and predictively.

For example, consider a matrix A that reflects the influence of various economic factors on a set of assets. When this matrix multiplies a vector representing asset returns, the resulting vector reveals how these returns are transformed by external conditions. This not only forecasts potential outcomes but also helps identify which factors have the most significant impact—essential for risk management and strategic planning.

Matrix transformations also enable dimensional reduction, simplifying complex datasets into more manageable forms without losing critical information. Techniques like Principal Component Analysis (PCA) employ matrices to distill large volumes of data into principal components, highlighting underlying trends while minimizing noise. In portfolio management, this aids in constructing optimized portfolios aligned with an investor's risk tolerance and return expectations.

Additionally, matrices facilitate the rotation and scaling of financial data—key concepts for adjusting portfolios amid changing market dynamics. Rotation alters data orientation to align with desired axes or benchmarks, while scaling adjusts the magnitude of data points to reflect shifts in market volatility or investor preferences. These transformations allow for dynamic asset reallocation in response to market movements.

A practical example is found in the transformation matrix used in arbitrage pricing theory (APT), where factor loadings —a type of transformation matrix—model factors affecting asset prices. This approach quantifies the sensitivity of asset prices to underlying economic variables, offering insights into potential mispricings and opportunities for arbitrage.

Matrices also simplify solving systems of linear equations commonly encountered in finance, such as those from multi-factor models or equilibrium equations. Methods like Gaussian elimination or LU decomposition rely on matrix operations to efficiently derive solutions critical for pricing derivatives or managing portfolio constraints.

Finally, transformation matrices support financial modeling by laying the groundwork for scenario analysis and stress testing. By systematically altering inputs and observing the resultant transformations on output vectors, analysts can simulate various economic conditions and their potential impacts on portfolios or balance sheets. This capability enhances decision-making under uncertainty and supports robust risk mitigation strategies.

Understanding matrices as transformations provides financial professionals with a versatile framework for navigating complex markets. Mastering these concepts allows one to translate abstract mathematical ideas into concrete solutions tailored to real-world challenges—ensuring preparedness for the ever-evolving landscape of modern finance.

Financial Transform Models

In the ever-evolving world of finance, matrix transformation models have become indispensable tools for predicting market movements and assessing risks. These models blend mathematical precision with economic theory, offering a robust framework for analyzing complex financial data.

At the heart of these models is the capability to structure and manipulate vast datasets. Matrices play a crucial role by converting raw financial data into interpretable and analyzable formats. Take this example, a covariance matrix captures the relationships between multiple financial variables, providing insights into how asset returns co-vary. This information is vital for identifying potential hedging strategies or opportunities for portfolio diversification.

Linear transformations in finance go beyond simple mappings; they enable sophisticated modeling of asset behaviors under various conditions. Models like the Capital Asset Pricing Model (CAPM) and Arbitrage Pricing Theory (APT) use transformation matrices to quantify how different factors influence asset returns. This allows analysts to break down an asset's return into components driven by market-wide phenomena and unique events.

Consider a scenario where an analyst wants to understand the impact of macroeconomic indicators on equity prices. By constructing a model with transformation matrices that represent each economic factor's influence, the analyst can simulate various economic environments. Such simulations help determine equity price sensitivity to changes in inflation rates, interest rates, or GDP growth—critical information for informed investment decisions.

And, financial transform models are essential in risk management practices. Value at Risk (VaR), a widely used risk measure, uses transformation techniques to estimate potential portfolio losses over a specified period under normal market conditions. This process considers historical volatility and correlation patterns among assets, providing a quantifiable measure of risk exposure.

Another application is stress testing, where financial institutions evaluate their resilience against hypothetical adverse scenarios. By applying matrices that represent extreme economic shocks to balance sheets and income statements, organizations can assess their vulnerability to crises such as market crashes or sudden interest rate hikes.

Matrix transformations also enhance forecasting capabilities. Time series models use these techniques to accurately capture trends and seasonal patterns within financial data, allowing analysts to predict future values based on past behaviors and adjust strategies accordingly.

These concepts find practical application in algorithmic trading, where transformation models drive real-time decision-making processes. Algorithms analyze streaming data through matrices that encapsulate current market conditions, executing trades based on predefined criteria to maximize profit potential while minimizing risk exposure.

Incorporating matrix transformations into financial modeling empowers professionals to navigate uncertainty with confidence and precision. Whether dissecting complex datasets or simulating hypothetical scenarios, these models provide invaluable tools for understanding market dynamics and crafting strategic responses tailored to shifting financial landscapes. Mastery of these techniques enables analysts to extract meaningful insights from data—turning theoretical constructs into actionable intelligence that informs critical decisions across various sectors of finance.

Application in Forecasting

Navigating the unpredictable waters of finance is much like steering with a well-calibrated compass. Matrix transformation models are indispensable in this endeavor, offering precision and adaptability to financial analysts as they decode complex data patterns. These tools enable analysts to make informed predictions about future market behaviors.

An important part of effective forecasting is identifying and quantifying trends within financial data. Matrices excel here, providing a structured method to manage vast information and organize it into meaningful sequences through time series analysis. This approach helps capture fluctuations over time, allowing analysts to discern cyclical patterns and seasonal variations, ultimately crafting forecasts that anticipate future movements.

Consider, for instance, an analyst predicting next quarter's stock prices. By organizing historical price data into a time series matrix, the analyst can apply linear transformations to identify trends. Incorporating factors such as historical volatility and trading volume allows for refined predictions through iterative adjustments based on new data inputs.

The use of autoregressive integrated moving average (ARIMA) models exemplifies the power of matrices in advanced forecasting techniques. ARIMA leverages past values

—arranged in matrices—to predict future points while accounting for seasonality and noise. This helps financial professionals to generate reliable forecasts, crucial for strategic investment decisions and risk assessments.

In more complex scenarios, vector autoregression (VAR) expands these capabilities by simultaneously considering multiple interdependent variables. Analysts construct matrices to encapsulate interactions between economic indicators—like interest rates, inflation rates, and currency exchange rates—modeling how changes in one variable influence others over time. This interconnected view offers a comprehensive perspective on economic dynamics, aiding in crafting robust forecasts.

Forecasting goes beyond equity markets into areas such as credit risk assessment and macroeconomic projections. Transformation matrices in credit risk models help predict default probabilities by analyzing past repayment behaviors and current economic conditions. These insights guide lending decisions, helping institutions maintain healthy credit portfolios.

In macroeconomic forecasting, matrices model GDP growth or inflation trends based on various economic indicators. Central banks and government agencies rely on these forecasts to set monetary policies or develop fiscal strategies that effectively address emerging challenges.

Algorithmic trading systems further illustrate the impact of matrix-based forecasting models. Equipped with predictive capabilities, these algorithms execute trades automatically when forecasted conditions align—capitalizing on fleeting opportunities while minimizing human error.

Effective utilization of these forecasting applications requires technical proficiency and an understanding of the underlying assumptions and limitations of each model type used. Financial professionals must continuously refine their methodologies as new data emerges or market conditions evolve, ensuring forecasts remain accurate in an ever-changing financial landscape.

Matrix transformations distill complex datasets into actionable insights that drive strategic decision-making across diverse financial domains—from equities trading to macroeconomic policy planning. By mastering these techniques, analysts gain foresight rooted in analytical rigor —a crucial asset for achieving precision-driven results amidst the challenges of uncertainty.

Impact on Market Models

Market models are essential in financial analysis, serving as dynamic frameworks that capture the complex interactions between economic variables. Linear algebra plays a pivotal role in revolutionizing the construction and analysis of these models. Its robust tools provide a lens through which market behaviors can be interpreted and predicted more accurately.

Central to these models is the representation of multifaceted data interactions. By using matrices, analysts can cohesively organize various market factors—such as supply and demand dynamics, investor sentiment indices, and regulatory impacts. This method allows for the simultaneous analysis of multiple variables, offering a comprehensive snapshot of market conditions at any point in time.

Take this example, take a model designed to forecast bond yields based on economic indicators like inflation rates and unemployment statistics. Within a matrix framework, these variables can be organized to reveal their interrelationships, each contributing to a nuanced understanding of yield fluctuations. The predictive power of the model is further enhanced by applying transformations that isolate specific effects or assess hypothetical scenarios.

The use of eigenvalues and eigenvectors enriches analysis within these market models by decomposing matrices into their core components. This decomposition identifies principal components—the key factors driving market changes. Such an approach reduces dimensionality, enabling analysts to focus on the most influential variables without losing sight of the system's complexity.

Risk assessment models also benefit significantly from matrix algebra techniques. By constructing covariance matrices, analysts can thoroughly examine asset correlations within a portfolio. This process helps quantify systemic risks and uncover diversification benefits, providing critical insights for portfolio managers aiming to optimize asset allocation in line with risk tolerance levels.

With technological advancements, algorithmic trading systems increasingly rely on sophisticated market models powered by linear algebra. These systems use transformation matrices to process real-time data streams and execute trades based on predictive indicators—enhancing reaction times to market movements and optimizing trading strategies.

Matrix applications extend further into project valuation models through real options analysis. By structuring potential decision pathways as matrix representations, analysts can evaluate different investment scenarios under varying conditions—ultimately developing strategies that maximize returns while mitigating risks.

The influence of linear algebra on market models extends beyond enhancing existing techniques; it drives innovation by facilitating new model development. As financial markets become more interconnected and data-rich, traditional modeling approaches must adapt. Leveraging matrix theory accommodates increased complexity and uncertainty.

By harnessing linear algebraic methods, financial professionals transform raw data into actionable insights that shape strategic decisions across various sectors. This toolkit empowers analysts to uncover patterns within vast datasets, driving progress in predictive analytics and fostering a deeper understanding of global market forces.

In the end, matrix-based approaches redefine how market models are conceptualized and utilized—enabling analysts to navigate complexity with precision and agility. The ongoing refinement of these methodologies ensures they remain at the forefront of financial innovation, providing a critical edge in an industry where success depends on anticipating and swiftly adapting to change.

Transformation Properties

Understanding the properties of linear transformations is essential for applying matrix theory in finance, where precision and adaptability are crucial. Linear transformations form the backbone of many financial applications, providing a structured way to manipulate data while preserving key characteristics such as linearity and dimensional integrity.

A fundamental property of linear transformations is their ability to maintain vector addition and scalar multiplication. This guarantees that when a transformation matrix is applied to financial data—like returns or cash flows—the mathematical relationships between these vectors remain consistent. Take this example, if we consider two portfolios represented by vectors in a multidimensional space, applying a transformation yields a new set of vectors that still adheres to the original combination rules.

Commutativity and associativity further enhance computational efficiency. Practically, this means that the order of applying multiple transformations does not affect the outcome—an important aspect when designing complex financial models that require iterative adjustments and recalibrations. Consider adjusting risk models daily based on fluctuating market conditions; these properties allow seamless integration of new data without computational redundancy.

The idea of invertibility plays a vital role in assessing market scenarios. An invertible transformation implies a one-to-one correspondence between input and output data, enabling analysts to accurately reconstruct original datasets from transformed versions. In portfolio management, this resembles backtracking from observed performance metrics to determine initial asset allocations—a task facilitated by applying inverse matrices to gain insights into past decision impacts.

Determinants are also critical in analyzing transformation properties. A non-zero determinant indicates an invertible transformation with full rank, which is desirable for ensuring no loss of information during transformations. Conversely, a zero determinant signals potential issues like dependent variables or overfitting within models—a warning for analysts seeking robust and reliable model constructions.

Eigen-decomposition is another significant property that simplifies complex transformations by breaking them down into components—specifically eigenvalues and eigenvectors. In finance, this approach is useful in stress-testing scenarios where models face extreme market conditions. By analyzing how individual components react under stress, financial professionals gain insights into systemic vulnerabilities and resilience.

Scaling is another leveraged property in financial contexts, particularly when normalizing datasets or adjusting asset weights within portfolios. Scaling transforms inputs proportionally, allowing consistent comparisons across diverse datasets without distorting inherent relationships between variables—a key consideration when harmonizing international data sources for global risk assessments.

Symmetry in transformations provides analytical advantages by simplifying calculations while maintaining interpretability —a valuable feature when constructing balanced scorecards or performance metrics aligned with strategic objectives. Symmetric matrices ensure analyses focus on intrinsic qualities rather than extraneous computational complexities.

Orthogonality complements symmetry by facilitating efficient computation through reduced dimensionality—beneficial for high-frequency trading algorithms that rely on rapid execution speeds without sacrificing accuracy. Orthogonal transformations preserve distances and angles between vectors, critical attributes when evaluating correlation structures within multi-asset portfolios or determining optimal hedging strategies against volatility spikes.

In the end, understanding these transformation properties empowers financial analysts to design adaptive models capable of navigating evolving market landscapes with confidence and foresight. This knowledge allows them not only to predict future trends but also to proactively adjust strategies in response to emerging risks or opportunities.

In summary, mastering transformation properties equips quantitative analysts with robust tools for interpreting financial phenomena through the lens of linear algebra, enabling them to transform raw market data into actionable intelligence with unparalleled precision and clarity compared to traditional approaches.

The Financial Analyst's Toolkit

In the intricate world of finance, having a robust toolkit is essential for any analyst looking to navigate the complex web of data, predictions, and decision-making. This toolkit goes beyond just being a collection of instruments; it's an integrated system that significantly enhances an analyst's ability to interpret and influence market dynamics effectively.

At the heart of this toolkit is matrix theory—a powerful framework that simplifies handling large datasets common in financial analysis. Matrices help organize and manipulate information, allowing analysts to succinctly model relationships between variables. Take this example, when evaluating the performance of multiple assets within a portfolio, matrices enable simultaneous computation of returns and risks, providing a comprehensive perspective for strategic decision-making.

Central to this analytical arsenal are linear transformations. These offer a structured approach to data manipulation, maintaining consistency while enabling complex adjustments. With these transformations, analysts can project market trends and adjust variables to simulate various economic scenarios—crucial for constructing predictive models or stress-testing financial systems under hypothetical conditions.

The role of software in enhancing these analytical capabilities cannot be overstated. Tools like Excel, Python, and R are staples in quantitative finance, each offering unique advantages. Excel provides intuitive interfaces for matrix operations and visualizations, perfect for quick calculations or presentations. Python excels with rich libraries like NumPy and Pandas that streamline matrix manipulations and data analysis. R offers statistical robustness with packages such as 'ggplot2' for advanced data visualization, each enhancing an analyst's ability to extract insights from raw data.

Consider Python's NumPy library for matrix computations:

```python
import numpy as np

\#\# Define two matrices
A = np.array([[1, 2], [3, 4]])
B = np.array([[5, 6], [7, 8]])
```

\#\# Perform matrix multiplication

result = np.dot(A, B)

print("Matrix Multiplication Result:", result)

` ` `

This code snippet illustrates how Python effortlessly handles operations that would be cumbersome manually, freeing analysts to focus on interpretation rather than calculation.

Beyond technical tools, theoretical concepts like eigenvalues and eigenvectors are crucial in risk management and portfolio optimization. They offer insights into asset behavior through variance decomposition, enabling analysts to identify factors driving market volatility. By dissecting these components, analysts can design strategies that mitigate risk while maximizing returns.

Linear regression models also form a cornerstone of an analyst's toolkit, predicting future outcomes based on historical data. Regression coefficients enhance this process by quantifying variable impacts on outcomes like stock prices or economic indicators.

Here's how R can implement linear regression:

` ` `r

\#\# Sample linear regression in R

data <- read.csv("financial_data.csv")

model <- lm(dependent_var ~ independent_var1 + independent_var2, data = data)

summary(model)

` ` `

This script demonstrates how R facilitates robust statistical analysis, enabling analysts to derive actionable conclusions from complex datasets efficiently.

Complementing these quantitative methods, visualization remains critical for effectively conveying findings. Charts and graphs translate complex numerical results into accessible visuals that stakeholders can easily understand—an essential skill when presenting investment recommendations or market forecasts.

In the end, a financial analyst's toolkit is not static; it evolves with technological advancements and market demands. Continuous learning and adaptation ensure analysts remain equipped to tackle emerging challenges with dexterity and insight—turning mathematical theories into strategic actions that drive financial success.

Armed with foundational knowledge and cutting-edge tools, financial analysts are well-positioned to transform their understanding into impactful decisions—ensuring they not only keep pace with market changes but also lead with foresight and innovation in an ever-evolving financial landscape.

CHAPTER 13:
VECTOR SPACES
AND SUBSPACES

Foundations and Definitions

I n mathematics, understanding the fundamental concepts of vector spaces is a key step for anyone delving into linear algebra, especially when applying it to finance. This comprehension forms the foundation upon which more complex theories and applications are built, enabling analysts to decode intricate market data with precision.

A vector space is a set of vectors that can be added together or multiplied by scalars to produce another vector within the same space. These operations follow specific rules that ensure mathematical consistency. For example, in a financial context, vectors can represent different asset returns. The ability to sum these vectors allows for the calculation of a portfolio's overall return, while scalar multiplication might adjust portfolio weights.

These operations are governed by properties such as closure under addition and scalar multiplication, associativity, commutativity, identity elements, and inverses. Each property ensures that calculations remain stable and predictable, which is essential when modeling economic phenomena or assessing financial risks.

Within vector spaces are subspaces—smaller collections of vectors that themselves form a vector space. Identifying subspaces in financial datasets allows analysts to focus on relevant factors or trends, minimizing extraneous noise. Subspaces can represent specific market sectors or asset classes, simplifying complex analyses by narrowing the focus to pertinent data.

Central to these spaces is the concept of a basis—a set of vectors from which all other vectors in the space can be constructed. In finance, selecting an appropriate basis might involve choosing key economic indicators or market drivers that encapsulate broader trends. The dimensionality of a vector space corresponds to the number of vectors in its basis, capturing its complexity and richness.

For practical applications, Python offers powerful tools for handling vector operations:

```python
import numpy as np


\#\# Define a vector

v = np.array([2, 3])


\#\# Scalar multiplication

scaled_v = 3 * v


\#\# Vector addition

w = np.array([1, 4])
```

```
sum_vw = v + w


print("Scaled Vector:", scaled_v)

print("Sum of Vectors:", sum_vw)
```

This script demonstrates how basic vector operations can model financial scenarios such as scaling investment returns or combining portfolio strategies.

The elegance of linear combinations arises from these foundational ideas, allowing for diverse yet structured combinations of assets or strategies in financial models. Through linear combinations, analysts create new vectors— or portfolios—tailored to specific investment goals or risk appetites.

Understanding these elements leads naturally into exploring more complex constructs like spans and null spaces. The span of a set of vectors encompasses all possible linear combinations within a vector space—a crucial concept for building robust financial models that reflect market dynamics accurately.

Conversely, null spaces help identify solutions where certain constraints (like zero risk) must be met. They assist analysts in pinpointing redundancies or dependencies within datasets, offering insights into areas such as multi-factor model validation or stress testing for risk management.

Balancing theoretical understanding with practical application is essential for effective data interpretation and decision-making amidst evolving financial landscapes. Analysts must continually refine their grasp of these concepts to transform raw numerical data into strategic insights that influence markets and decisions.

The journey through vector spaces requires mastery of both mathematical principles and creative application; this dual proficiency empowers analysts to achieve impactful results in finance, turning data into valuable insights that shape the future of markets and decision-making processes.

Financial Vectors

Financial vectors are a fundamental concept in quantitative finance, serving as an essential tool for summarizing complex financial data efficiently. These vectors transform abstract numbers into actionable insights, helping analysts understand and manipulate data for practical applications. The inherent nature of a vector—a collection of elements arranged in a specific order—makes it ideal for representing multidimensional financial information, such as asset returns, risk factors, or economic indicators.

To illustrate, consider analyzing a portfolio's performance. Each asset's return over time can be captured as a vector. Suppose we have three assets: stocks, bonds, and commodities. Their monthly returns over the last year can be represented as vectors: R_stocks = [0.02, 0.015, ..., 0.03], R_bonds = [0.01, 0.012, ..., 0.008], and R_commodities = [0.025, 0.03,..., 0.022]. These vectors provide a clear picture of each asset's performance over different periods.

The strength of vectors lies in their ability to facilitate operations that uncover deeper insights into portfolio dynamics. Take this example, calculating the average return across assets is straightforward by adding these vectors element-wise and dividing by the number of periods analyzed. Additionally, understanding correlations between assets involves evaluating the dot product of these return vectors—a measure that reveals how closely their movements align over time.

Vectors are also crucial in risk assessment through covariance matrices, where each element captures how two assets vary together—an invaluable insight for constructing diversified portfolios aimed at minimizing risk while maximizing returns. A vector representing weights assigned to each asset in a portfolio enables efficient computation of expected returns and variances.

Incorporating financial vectors into quantitative models goes beyond mere computation; they enable precise optimization techniques like Markowitz's mean-variance optimization framework, which relies heavily on vector mathematics to identify optimal asset allocations based on expected returns and risk tolerances.

A practical application is evident when using Excel for financial modeling with vectors. By inputting return data into columns or rows within spreadsheets and applying built-in functions like SUMPRODUCT for dot products or COVAR for covariance calculations, analysts can derive critical insights without extensive programming knowledge.

In programming languages like Python or R—commonly used in quantitative finance—vectors are handled effortlessly using libraries such as NumPy or pandas in Python or base functions in R. These tools provide robust capabilities for manipulating and analyzing financial datasets efficiently with concise code.

As we explore this topic further throughout this book, remember that understanding financial vectors is not just an academic exercise. It represents the transformation of data into actionable strategies that empower decision-making in complex environments characterized by uncertainty. This knowledge ultimately drives successful outcomes across various sectors, from investment management firms to hedge funds striving to achieve superior performance benchmarks against competitive peers globally.

Understanding financial vectors is about more than mastering matrix theory; it involves leveraging advanced analytical techniques necessary for addressing modern-day challenges faced by traders worldwide seeking alpha-generation opportunities amidst ever-evolving market conditions. The practical application of this knowledge results in transforming theoretical constructs into profitable ventures that yield tangible results over time, showcasing the potential for long-term sustainability achieved through strategic foresight coupled with disciplined execution.

Span and Basis Concepts

The concepts of span and basis are fundamental to understanding vector spaces, providing deep insights into the structure and dimensionality of financial data. The idea of a span involves capturing the range of possibilities generated by a set of vectors through linear combinations. In finance, this concept is particularly useful for analyzing the potential outcomes or scenarios that result from varying asset behaviors within a portfolio.

Imagine a set of vectors representing different financial indicators, such as interest rates, stock returns, and currency fluctuations. The span of these vectors includes every possible linear combination that can be formed from them, illustrating the myriad ways these factors can interact to influence overall financial performance. This notion becomes especially relevant when constructing scenarios for stress testing or modeling economic environments that could impact investment portfolios.

To illustrate this practically, consider creating a model in Python using NumPy. Suppose we have three vectors: A = [0.1, 0.2], B = [0.3, 0.4], and C = [0.5, 0.6]. The span would include any vector that can be expressed as c1A + c2B + c3*C for some scalars c1, c2, and c3. By adjusting these coefficients, analysts can simulate diverse market conditions to understand how a portfolio might react under different circumstances.

Building on this foundation, the concept of basis helps streamline our understanding of vector spaces by identifying the minimal set of vectors required to generate every element within a space. In financial terms, establishing a basis allows for efficient representation and analysis of datasets without redundancy, ensuring each basis vector contributes uniquely to spanning the space.

In practice, selecting an optimal basis is akin to identifying key performance drivers in an investment strategy—those crucial factors that encapsulate the majority of information needed for decision-making without overwhelming with unnecessary data points. Take this example, in risk management practices within trading firms or asset management companies where multiple risk factors are at play simultaneously (e.g., credit risk versus market risk), defining an appropriate basis enables streamlined calculations that enhance both clarity and operational efficiency.

For example, in Excel, working with several correlated stock indices represented as column vectors—such as the Dow Jones Industrial Average (DJIA), S&P 500 Index (SPX), and Nasdaq Composite Index (IXIC)—might involve conducting principal component analysis (PCA) to identify which index serves best as part of your basis. This can be achieved through built-in tools like XLStat or VBA scripting methods tailored specifically towards eigen-decomposition techniques integrated directly within Microsoft Excel's environment.

In computational settings like R programming language environments utilizing libraries such as 'Matrix', determining whether given sets form bases involves rigorous matrix algebra operations, including determinant checks and orthogonality assessments. Specialized functions available in these libraries simplify complex tasks considerably while maintaining the precision necessary during execution stages encountered routinely across quantitative disciplines worldwide. These advanced mathematical constructs are applied pervasively across numerous industry verticals, driving impactful change progressively forward more rapidly than ever before.

Examining Financial Portfolio Space

When exploring financial portfolios, we examine how different assets combine to form a comprehensive and dynamic investment landscape. Essentially, this involves using vector spaces to model potential portfolio compositions, helping investors grasp the variety of achievable outcomes based on asset selection and allocation. This approach embodies the principles of portfolio diversification and strategic asset management.

A financial portfolio can be envisioned as a collection of vectors, with each vector representing an asset characterized by attributes such as expected return, risk level, and correlation with other assets. The sum of these vectors plots a point in a multidimensional portfolio space. This geometric perspective enables quantitative analysts to visualize how changes in asset composition can influence overall portfolio characteristics.

Let's delve into a practical example using Python and NumPy to construct portfolios. Imagine three assets: stocks, bonds, and commodities. Each asset is depicted by a vector that details its expected return and risk—such as A = [0.12, 0.3], B = [0.04, 0.1], C = [0.08, 0.2]. These vectors can be combined in varying proportions to create different portfolios, each reflecting unique risk-return profiles. By coding this in Python, you would create arrays for each asset and employ linear combinations to simulate different allocations.

The analysis extends beyond mere combination; it includes optimization—identifying the efficient frontier where returns are maximized for a given level of risk. Techniques like quadratic programming can pinpoint these optimal points within the portfolio space, transforming mathematical precision into strategic financial decisions.

In finance, understanding both individual asset behavior

and their interdependencies is vital. Covariance matrices play a crucial role here by quantifying how asset returns move together. Analyzing these matrices using R or similar statistical software helps in assessing how diversification impacts risk across portfolios.

Further visualization of this concept using Excel could involve plotting efficient frontiers with scatter plots mapping expected returns against risks (standard deviations). Excel's solver add-in allows users to dynamically manipulate data, enabling interactive exploration of optimal asset mixes under various constraints such as capital limits or regulatory requirements.

And, examining portfolio space requires considering the complexities of real-world markets—like liquidity constraints or transaction costs—which can alter theoretical models when applied practically in settings such as hedge funds or pension schemes managing large capital flows daily.

In advanced institutional contexts, proprietary software developed by quantitative hedge funds often uses sophisticated algorithms that leverage extensive market data sets alongside cutting-edge computational techniques from advanced matrix theory disciplines covered earlier in this book. This integration allows for continued exploration of future sections that naturally progress from previously established foundations, offering a seamless transition into further discussions without interruption.

Null Spaces and Their Significance

In the realm of linear algebra, the concept of null spaces is both intriguing and essential, particularly when applied to financial analysis. Null spaces offer insights into the solutions of homogeneous linear equations, enhancing our understanding of constraints and dependencies within a system. In finance, this means analyzing scenarios where certain combinations of variables yield zero output, which is crucial for identifying redundancies or inefficiencies in portfolio management.

Consider a financial model represented by a matrix equation Ax = 0, where A is a matrix depicting various factors influencing an investment strategy, and x is a vector of decision variables. The null space of A includes all vectors x that satisfy this equation, representing all possible interactions of these factors without affecting the outcome. This understanding is vital when simplifying complex models or designing systems that are robust against certain perturbations.

Take this example, in risk assessment across multiple portfolios, examining the null space can reveal potential hedging strategies that offset risks without altering expected returns. If changes in one asset's risk are counterbalanced by changes in another within the null space configuration, this balance can be strategically advantageous.

Let's explore this with Python. Suppose we have a matrix A representing correlations between four assets:

```python
import numpy as np


A = np.array([
[1, 0.8, 0.5, 0],
[0.8, 1, 0.3, 0],
[0.5, 0.3, 1, -0.2],
[0, 0, -0.2, 1]
])


null_space = np.linalg.null_space(A)
```

```
print(null_space)
` ` `
```

This code calculates the null space of matrix A using NumPy's linear algebra module. The result provides vectors indicating how changes in asset correlations might lead to no net impact on portfolio variance—a powerful insight for constructing portfolios that minimize risk through internal offsets.

Similarly, in Excel, analyses can be conducted using matrix functions like MMULT and MINVERSE to explore dependency patterns within financial datasets. By identifying and leveraging these null space vectors in Excel models or solver applications, investors can build portfolios tailored to specific risk-neutralizing characteristics.

The significance of null spaces also extends to optimizing resource allocation within financial institutions. When banks or hedge funds analyze trading algorithms or capital distribution strategies that rely on complex linear models, understanding null spaces can reveal hidden efficiencies or suggest areas for reallocation to enhance performance without additional risk exposure.

Also, insights from null spaces are invaluable for regulatory compliance and stress testing requirements where maintaining certain ratios or thresholds must not inadvertently affect other parameters due to unforeseen dependencies in modeled systems.

In the end, understanding the role and significance of null spaces transforms abstract mathematical constructs into practical tools for real-world financial challenges. This helps analysts and traders to navigate uncertainties with greater confidence and precision in decision-making processes.

Exploring null spaces lays the groundwork for examining broader implications within vector spaces and beyond—each layer offering further clarity on navigating complex financial landscapes while upholding rigorous quantitative standards essential for sustainable success in today's competitive markets.

Rank and Financial Applications

Understanding the rank of a matrix is a fundamental concept in linear algebra with numerous applications in finance. The rank, which represents the dimension of the column space or row space of a matrix, provides insight into the number of linearly independent columns or rows. This property is crucial for analyzing financial datasets, as it helps determine the degrees of freedom available and identify which variables truly drive changes in financial outcomes.

Imagine a dataset containing historical prices of various assets over time, structured as a matrix where each column corresponds to an asset and each row to an observation. The rank of this matrix indicates how many unique price movements exist among these assets. If the rank matches the number of columns, it suggests that each asset's price movement is distinct. Conversely, a lower rank implies that some assets move in tandem due to underlying correlations or dependencies.

Such insights are invaluable in financial modeling. For example, when constructing investment portfolios, identifying linearly dependent assets allows analysts to avoid redundancy and enhance diversification. By selecting assets that contribute unique variance to the portfolio—signified by their inclusion in an independent column set—investors can optimize risk-adjusted returns.

To illustrate this concept, let's use Python and NumPy to determine a matrix's rank:

```python
import numpy as np
```

```
\#\# A matrix representing asset returns over different periods
asset_returns = np.array([
[0.05, 0.07, 0.04],
[0.06, 0.08, 0.03],
[0.07, 0.07, 0.05],
[0.08, 0.09, 0.06]
])

rank = np.linalg.matrix_rank(asset_returns)
print(f"The rank of the asset returns matrix is: rank")
```

The output reveals the number of independent sources of return within this set of assets, guiding portfolio construction by highlighting combinations that offer unique exposure.

In Excel, similar analyses can be conducted using functions like RANK.EQ for individual data points or array formulas for broader dataset insights. By sorting and ranking financial metrics or ratios, decision-makers can prioritize investments based on criteria such as performance consistency or risk-adjusted returns.

Understanding matrix rank is also pivotal in developing predictive models for financial markets. Models with full-rank matrices are typically more robust as they incorporate all relevant variables without multicollinearity issues that could skew predictions or lead to unstable estimates.

Also, matrix rank plays a crucial role in stress testing and scenario analysis frameworks used by financial institutions to ensure resilience under adverse conditions. By employing matrices representing various economic indicators and examining their ranks under different stress scenarios, analysts can pinpoint vulnerabilities within portfolios or operational structures and take preemptive measures to mitigate potential impacts.

The importance of matrix rank extends to algorithmic trading as well, where high-frequency strategies often rely on vast matrices encoding market data across timeframes and securities. Understanding which features truly influence trade signals helps streamline computational processes while maintaining efficacy.

In summary, appreciating the significance of rank not only enhances comprehension of mathematical structures but also empowers financial professionals with actionable insights tailored to real-world challenges. This transformation of abstract numerical concepts into strategic advantages is evident across diverse applications in finance, underscoring the power of mathematics when wielded with precision and creativity in today's dynamic markets.

Industry-Based Case Studies

Real-world applications of linear algebra in finance are vividly demonstrated through industry-based case studies, offering practical insights into how theoretical concepts drive significant outcomes. In the asset management sector, portfolio optimization is a primary focus. Here, linear algebra is invaluable for balancing risk and return through techniques like mean-variance optimization.

This process involves constructing a covariance matrix of asset returns, which represents their variances and covariances. This matrix informs investment decisions by revealing asset interactions, enabling managers to minimize portfolio risk for a given expected return. Take this example, when allocating assets in a diversified fund, managers can use quadratic programming—rooted in matrix operations—to achieve optimal weight distributions that align with investor preferences.

Consider a fund manager handling a diversified portfolio. They might analyze past returns using Python libraries like NumPy and pandas to calculate the covariance matrix:

```python
import numpy as np

import pandas as pd


\#\# Example asset returns data

data =

'Asset A': [0.02, 0.03, 0.01],

'Asset B': [0.01, 0.02, 0.03],

'Asset C': [0.03, 0.02, 0.01]


returns_df = pd.DataFrame(data)


\#\# Calculate the covariance matrix

cov_matrix = returns_df.cov()

print(cov_matrix)
```

This output provides insights into asset interdependencies, which are critical for constructing efficient frontiers that define optimal portfolios.

Beyond asset management, linear algebra plays a crucial role in credit risk assessment within banks and financial institutions. Banks use it to model credit exposure and predict default probabilities with factor models that decompose complex datasets into interpretable components.

A prominent example is principal component analysis (PCA), which reduces dimensionality while preserving essential variance information by performing eigenvalue decomposition on correlation matrices. This method helps risk managers identify factors driving creditworthiness among borrowers.

In algorithmic trading platforms, linear algebraic methods are indispensable for rapidly analyzing vast datasets to identify profitable opportunities. High-frequency trading firms employ singular value decomposition (SVD) to filter out noise from data streams and extract significant signals—a testament to the efficacy of mathematical tools in optimizing trading algorithms.

Whether in Excel or Python environments, these techniques streamline decision-making and enhance predictive accuracy within trading systems:

```python
from sklearn.decomposition import PCA


\#\# Applying PCA on sample market data

pca = PCA(n_components=2)

principal_components = pca.fit_transform(returns_df)

print(principal_components)
```

These principal components offer reduced-dimension views that retain critical patterns necessary for informed trade execution strategies.

Also, fintech innovations showcase startups leveraging

machine learning models underpinned by linear algebra concepts for real-time data analytics solutions in payment processing and fraud detection services.

These examples highlight how financial professionals use mathematical frameworks as integral elements shaping strategic imperatives—where understanding matrices directly translates into tangible business value.

The interplay between academic principles and industry applications underscores a pivotal message: mastery of these tools offers competitive advantages that resonate throughout financial ecosystems—enabling organizations to navigate complexities with agility and foresight.

As we explore vector spaces' implications on modeling accuracy in subsequent discussions, these case studies remind us of the profound impact well-applied mathematical strategies have on advancing financial frontiers—from fostering innovation to ensuring institutional stability amidst evolving landscapes.

Impacts on Model Accuracy

The accuracy of financial models significantly depends on the robust application of linear algebra concepts, forming the backbone of quantitative analysis across various domains. This precision is not merely theoretical; it is crucial for predicting market behaviors and assessing risks effectively. A well-tuned model transcends a mere collection of data points and equations; it resembles an intricate symphony where each note must be precisely calibrated to reflect the reality it seeks to simulate.

The relationship between vector spaces and financial modeling vividly illustrates this precision. In constructing a model, each variable can be viewed as a vector within a space, where interactions with other variables are expressed through operations like addition and scalar multiplication. These operations allow analysts to capture complex relationships within financial data, enabling more nuanced interpretations that inform strategic decision-making.

A key factor in model accuracy is orthogonality, ensuring that vectors—representing different financial indicators—are statistically independent. This property reduces redundancy and overfitting, common issues that can distort predictions. By maintaining orthogonality, analysts ensure that each vector contributes unique information to the model, enhancing its predictive power.

Take regression analysis in Excel as an example. Ensuring orthogonality between predictors strengthens the model's stability:

1. Data Preparation: Compile historical data for variables such as interest rates and stock returns.

2. Checking Orthogonality: Use matrix multiplication to verify if the dot product between different predictor vectors equals zero, indicating statistical independence.

3. Model Application: Apply these insights to refine regression models and improve forecasting accuracy.

Achieving such precision requires effectively leveraging computational tools. Software like R or Python streamlines these processes with built-in functions that automate complex calculations while minimizing human error.

Take this example, conducting linear regression analysis in R:

```r
``` `r
\#\# Example dataset

dataset <- data.frame(

InterestRate = c(2.5, 3.0, 2.8),

StockReturn = c(5.0, 4.5, 4.7)
```
```

)

\#\# Running linear regression

model <- lm(StockReturn ~ InterestRate, data = dataset)

summary(model)

` ` `

This analysis yields coefficients quantifying the relationship between interest rates and stock returns—crucial insights for investment strategies.

And, covariance matrices expose dependencies among assets —a critical element in portfolio construction where risk requires careful quantification and management:

` ` `r

\#\# Calculating covariance matrix

cov_matrix <- cov(dataset)

print(cov_matrix)

` ` `

This matrix informs asset allocation strategies by clarifying inter-asset correlations essential for optimizing portfolios according to investor risk profiles.

Beyond regression analysis, eigenvalue decomposition provides another layer of accuracy refinement by facilitating dimensionality reduction while preserving essential variance within datasets—a process integral to principal component analysis (PCA). When correctly executed via algorithms like singular value decomposition (SVD), it helps filter out noise from market data streams, ensuring signals used for trading decisions remain sharp and reliable.

In the end, precise mathematical representations underpin

every successful financial model's foundation—underscoring their role not merely as numerical abstractions but as instruments driving real-world profitability outcomes.

By diligently applying these mathematical frameworks across industry applications—from banking risk assessments to hedge fund strategies—financial analysts derive insights that foster innovation while reinforcing institutional resilience against market volatility's unpredictabilities.

As we explore how these advancements influence broader economic landscapes in subsequent sections, we recognize the enduring impact of model accuracy on shaping global financial narratives—transforming abstract mathematics into tangible results that resonate throughout markets with unparalleled clarity and foresight.

CHAPTER 14: INNER PRODUCT SPACES

Introduction to Inner Products

Inner products are fundamental to linear algebra, acting as the link between geometric intuition and algebraic operations. They provide a way to measure angles and lengths in vector spaces, revealing the structural relationships between vectors. For quantitative analysts, understanding inner products is essential for accurately assessing correlations and variances in financial data.

An inner product can be thought of as a function that takes two vectors and returns a scalar, capturing the projection of one vector onto another. This projection isn't just a mathematical curiosity; it quantifies the similarity between two financial indicators. In finance, such similarity often translates to correlation, which is crucial for risk management and portfolio optimization.

For example, consider two vectors representing daily returns of different stocks. Calculating their inner product can reveal how these returns move relative to each other. A high inner product indicates strong correlation, suggesting that the stocks tend to move together—an insight vital for constructing diversified portfolios.

In practical terms, implementing inner products in Python can help clarify these relationships:

```python
import numpy as np

\#\# Vectors representing daily returns of two stocks
returns_stock1 = np.array([0.01, 0.02, 0.015])
returns_stock2 = np.array([0.011, 0.019, 0.016])

\#\# Calculate inner product
inner_product = np.dot(returns_stock1, returns_stock2)
print("Inner Product:", inner_product)
```

This simple computation shows how aligned the stocks' performances are over time.

Inner products also form the basis for defining orthogonality in vector spaces—a property where vectors are perpendicular if their inner product is zero. This concept extends beyond geometry into financial applications like principal component analysis (PCA), where it helps identify independent directions of variance within datasets.

To understand PCA's application, imagine a dataset with variables representing financial metrics—such as GDP growth rates or inflation trends across countries. By applying PCA and focusing on orthogonal components that capture maximum variance without overlap, analysts can reduce dimensionality while preserving essential data features.

Here's how Python facilitates PCA analysis:

```python
from sklearn.decomposition import PCA

\#\# Sample data matrix (each row: observation; each column: financial metric)
data_matrix = np.array([[1.2, 2.3], [1.8, 2.5], [1.3, 2.4]])

\#\# Apply PCA to identify orthogonal components
pca_model = PCA(n_components=2)
principal_components = pca_model.fit_transform(data_matrix)

print("Principal Components:", principal_components)
```

The output reveals transformed coordinates in terms of significant orthogonal components, uncovering patterns hidden in complex datasets.

These computations are not merely theoretical exercises; they guide real-world decisions—from risk assessment frameworks that rely on diverse market signals to asset allocation strategies that exploit uncorrelated investments for optimal performance.

Mastering inner products is indispensable for navigating the complex landscapes of financial markets. They enable analysts to not only interpret existing data but also predict future trends with greater precision.

As we delve deeper into financial mathematics throughout this book, remember that each mathematical tool is more than an equation—it's a lens through which we view and interpret market dynamics with clarity and insight.

Every scalar from an inner product calculation reveals underlying relationships within market systems— transforming abstract numbers into actionable intelligence that drives strategic decision-making in global finance landscapes.

Financial Contexts

In the realm of finance, inner products transcend mere mathematical abstractions to become central tools in quantitative analysis. Financial markets thrive on data, and inner products provide a powerful method for distilling this information into meaningful correlations and dependencies. By understanding the mechanics of inner products, analysts can uncover insights hidden within complex datasets, leading to more precise predictions and informed decision-making.

Consider the vast array of financial instruments: stocks, bonds, commodities, and derivatives. Each is influenced by various factors—market trends, economic indicators, and geopolitical events. The challenge lies in identifying how these elements interrelate. Inner products quantify these relationships by measuring the alignment between different financial vectors. For example, calculating the inner product of vectors representing commodity prices over time can reveal how closely their valuations move together, highlighting potential arbitrage opportunities.

Take exchange rates as another illustration. If you are interested in the relationship between two currencies, such as the US dollar and the euro, analyzing historical exchange rate data through an inner product calculation can determine how their fluctuations correlate. This insight is crucial for international investment strategies or hedging currency risk in multinational portfolios.

Here's a practical demonstration using Python to analyze exchange rate correlations:

```python
import numpy as np

\#\# Historical daily changes in exchange rates (USD/EUR and USD/GBP)
usd_eur_changes = np.array([0.0012, -0.0005, 0.0007])
usd_gbp_changes = np.array([0.0015, -0.0006, 0.0009])

\#\# Compute inner product to assess correlation
exchange_rate_correlation = np.dot(usd_eur_changes, usd_gbp_changes)
print("Exchange Rate Correlation (Inner Product):", exchange_rate_correlation)
```

This calculation yields a numerical value that represents how changes in USD/EUR align with those in USD/GBP—a vital metric for currency traders who need to predict how shifts might affect international trade.

Beyond assessing correlations, inner products also help evaluate asset volatility and manage risk across portfolios. A well-diversified portfolio ideally contains assets with low or near-zero inner products, minimizing exposure to systematic risks that could simultaneously impact multiple assets.

In practice, financial professionals rely on these calculations daily—whether through sophisticated software or custom models—to guide investment choices and assess market dynamics efficiently.

The importance of mastering these concepts is underscored by their broad applicability across various financial scenarios—

from shaping macroeconomic policies through cross-country comparisons to making micro-level trade decisions within specific market segments.

While mathematical rigor underlies every computation involving inner products, their practical applications offer tangible benefits to those navigating complex financial environments. Analysts armed with this knowledge can transform raw data into strategic insights—insights that drive profitability and secure a competitive edge in today's rapidly evolving financial landscape.

Engaging with these foundational ideas lays a solid groundwork for exploring deeper aspects of linear algebra and its application in finance throughout our journey together. The ability to discern subtle patterns and connections within data empowers analysts not only to react to current market conditions but also to anticipate future shifts—reinforcing their role as pivotal contributors to strategic financial planning and execution.

With an appreciation for both the theoretical underpinnings and practical contexts of inner products, you are now poised to delve further into the intersection of mathematics and finance—unraveling more intricate layers of meaning from numbers that narrate the story of global economic currents.

Angles and Orthogonality

Angles and orthogonality are crucial concepts in financial analysis, acting as powerful tools for interpreting data relationships and optimizing portfolio strategies. Grasping these ideas empowers quantitative analysts to break down complex datasets and identify critical market signals.

Visualize vectors as arrows pointing in a multidimensional space, with each dimension representing a specific financial indicator. The angle between these vectors indicates the degree of correlation, where smaller angles suggest stronger relationships. This understanding translates into actionable insights for asset managers aiming to optimize investment portfolios or design risk mitigation strategies.

Consider two investment strategies represented by vectors. By calculating the cosine of the angle between them, analysts can quantify their relationship. A cosine value near one suggests the strategies move in tandem, while a value near zero indicates orthogonality, or independence. This distinction is crucial when constructing diversified portfolios, as it enables analysts to select non-correlated assets, thus reducing overall risk.

Here's a practical example using Python to calculate the cosine of angles between investment strategy returns:

```python
import numpy as np

\#\# Hypothetical returns of two investment strategies
strategy_A_returns = np.array([0.02, 0.03, 0.01])
strategy_B_returns = np.array([0.01, 0.04, -0.01])

\#\# Compute cosine of angle between the strategies
cosine_similarity = np.dot(strategy_A_returns, strategy_B_returns) / (np.linalg.norm(strategy_A_returns) * np.linalg.norm(strategy_B_returns))

print("Cosine of Angle Between Strategies:", cosine_similarity)
```

This calculation provides a measure of similarity that guides portfolio managers in assembling robust asset combinations that balance potential returns with risk exposure.

Orthogonality not only helps in identifying independent

variables but also simplifies computations in multivariate analyses by reducing dimensionality while preserving relevant data structures. In regression analysis, for example, orthogonal projections minimize estimation errors by aligning model parameters with observed data directions.

Also, orthogonality plays a pivotal role in signal processing within financial contexts—such as filtering noise from price fluctuations or extracting meaningful trends from vast datasets. Techniques like the Gram-Schmidt process enable analysts to transform correlated data into an orthogonal set, facilitating clearer interpretations and more accurate forecasting.

In practice, achieving orthogonality can be demonstrated through matrix operations that convert correlated data series into independent components—a method frequently used in principal component analysis (PCA) for identifying underlying factors affecting asset prices.

The geometric interpretation of angles and orthogonality lays the groundwork for more advanced topics such as eigenvalues and eigenvectors, which further elucidate market dynamics and stability considerations. Mastering these concepts equips analysts with a nuanced understanding of data interrelations —enabling them to craft strategies that thrive under diverse market conditions.

As we delve deeper into linear algebra's application in finance, remember how angles and orthogonality uncover hidden layers within financial datasets—each angle representing an opportunity to enhance analytical precision and elevate decision-making efficacy amidst ever-evolving economic landscapes.

Applications in Correlation Analysis

In finance, correlation analysis is an essential tool that sheds light on the relationships between various financial variables. These insights enable analysts to make informed decisions about asset selection and portfolio diversification. Correlation quantifies how two variables move in relation to each other, with values ranging from -1 (a perfect inverse relationship) to +1 (a perfect direct relationship). At its foundation, this analysis utilizes linear algebra concepts like vectors and matrices to efficiently compute and interpret these relationships.

Imagine a portfolio manager needing to evaluate the relationships between asset returns to mitigate risk and maximize gains. By employing correlation matrices, they can easily visualize and quantify these relationships. The matrix offers a compact representation of pairwise correlations among multiple assets, facilitating quick assessments of diversification strategies.

Take this example, if you have returns data for four different assets over a specific period, you can calculate their correlation matrix using Python:

```python
import numpy as np


\#\# Sample returns data for four assets
returns_data = np.array([

[0.01, 0.02, -0.01, 0.03],

[0.02, 0.01, 0.00, -0.02],

[0.03, 0.03, -0.02, 0.01],

[0.01, 0.02, 0.01, 0.02]

])


\#\# Compute the correlation matrix
```

```
correlation_matrix = np.corrcoef(returns_data)

print("Correlation Matrix:", correlation_matrix)
```
` ` `

This matrix becomes a powerful decision-making tool: by examining it, a manager can identify assets with low or negative correlations and adjust the portfolio accordingly to achieve the desired balance of risk and return.

Beyond simple correlation coefficients, eigenvalue decomposition of the correlation matrix can offer deeper insights into market dynamics by identifying principal components or latent factors driving asset movements. This dimensional reduction technique helps highlight which factors most influence a given set of financial instruments.

Correlation analysis plays a critical role in models for risk assessment such as Value at Risk (VaR) and Conditional Value at Risk (CVaR), which rely heavily on accurate correlation measurements to forecast potential losses under varying market conditions.

Understanding correlations is also crucial in arbitrage strategies, where small pricing inefficiencies between related securities can be exploited for profit. Quantitative analysts use this understanding to develop sophisticated trading algorithms that capitalize on these temporary disparities.

Also, the integration of correlation analysis with machine learning techniques has opened new possibilities in predictive modeling and anomaly detection within trading systems. Machine learning algorithms can now process large datasets and dynamically update their assessments of asset correlations in real-time.

As technology advances, so does our ability to measure and interpret these relationships with greater granularity— transforming raw data into actionable intelligence that aligns with strategic financial goals.

The applications of correlation analysis are extensive and varied—impacting every facet of financial decision-making from risk management to strategic planning and beyond. A thorough understanding of how linear algebra underpins these analyses not only enhances accuracy but also enriches the analytical toolkit available to financial professionals in today's data-driven marketplace.

Grasping these intricate correlations equips analysts with foresight into potential market shifts—enabling them to navigate uncertainty with confidence and precision amidst complex financial environments.

Implications for Financial Data

In the realm of finance, data transcends mere numbers; it serves as the vital force that guides strategic decisions and shapes market dynamics. Linear algebra plays a crucial role in this context by providing tools that convert raw data into meaningful insights. This transformation hinges on the ability to model, analyze, and predict outcomes with precision and confidence.

Financial data is often characterized by its large volume and complex structure. Here, linear algebra offers a framework for managing such complexity through matrix representation and manipulation. Organizing data into matrices streamlines operations like calculating returns, assessing risks, and optimizing portfolios. This structured approach not only simplifies analysis but also enhances computational efficiency —essential in high-frequency trading environments where split-second decisions are necessary.

Take, for instance, the task of optimizing a portfolio to maximize returns while minimizing risk, a fundamental challenge in asset management. Linear algebra aids this process through covariance matrices, which capture interactions between different assets. These matrices enable analysts to calculate the variance of portfolio returns and determine the optimal asset allocation within specified risk parameters.

The utility of linear algebra extends beyond static analysis; it is instrumental in crafting dynamic models that respond to evolving market conditions. Time-series models, for example, use linear transformations to predict future values based on historical trends. Techniques like eigenvalue decomposition or singular value decomposition (SVD) distill complex datasets into essential components driving financial behavior, thereby enhancing market forecasts' accuracy.

And, linear algebra underpins machine learning algorithms increasingly utilized in finance for tasks such as credit scoring, fraud detection, and algorithmic trading. These algorithms depend heavily on matrix operations like multiplication and inversion to discern patterns and make predictions from vast datasets.

To illustrate with a practical example using Python's NumPy library to calculate the covariance matrix for a set of asset returns:

```python
import numpy as np

\#\# Sample returns data for three assets
returns_data = np.array([
[0.05, 0.02, -0.01],
[0.04, 0.03, 0.00],
[0.06, 0.01, -0.02]
])
```

```
\#\# Compute the covariance matrix

covariance_matrix = np.cov(returns_data.T)

print("Covariance Matrix:", covariance_matrix)
` ` `
```

This covariance matrix lays the groundwork for constructing efficient frontiers and exploring various risk-return trade-offs within a portfolio context.

The significance of linear algebra for financial data is also evident in stress testing scenarios where institutions assess their resilience against adverse market events. By using matrix simulations that incorporate correlations and covariances across asset classes, firms can identify vulnerabilities and formulate strategies to mitigate them.

As financial markets grow more interconnected and complex, the demand for advanced analytical tools rises—spurring innovation in quantitative finance practices. Linear algebra remains at the forefront of this evolution by providing the mathematical rigor needed to navigate these challenges effectively.

In the end, leveraging linear algebra not only enhances analytical capabilities but also enriches decision-making processes by providing clarity amidst uncertainty. This empowers financial professionals to fully harness data's potential in developing strategies that are both robust and adaptive in an ever-evolving market landscape.

The seamless integration of mathematical theory with practical application enables financial analysts to transform abstract data into actionable insights—paving the way for informed decisions that align with both short-term objectives and long-term strategic goals in today's fast-paced financial world.

Orthogonal Projections

Orthogonal projections are a powerful technique in linear algebra, particularly valuable in finance for simplifying complex problems through dimensionality reduction. By projecting data points onto a subspace, analysts can focus on the most relevant aspects, filtering out noise and uncovering the underlying structures that drive financial insights.

In the context of multivariate data, such as asset returns over time, complexity can be daunting. Orthogonal projections help by concentrating analysis on a subspace that captures the primary variance in the data, typically defined by orthonormal basis vectors. These vectors maintain their independence and scale across dimensions, ensuring a clear view of the essential data features.

Take this example, in portfolio optimization, reducing dimensions without losing significant information is crucial. Imagine a dataset of returns from multiple assets. By projecting these returns onto a lower-dimensional space defined by principal components, analysts can isolate factors accounting for most of the variance, often reflecting market trends or sector-specific movements.

Here's a practical demonstration using Python and NumPy to calculate an orthogonal projection onto a principal component:

```python
import numpy as np

\#\# Returns data for three assets

returns_data = np.array([

[0.05, 0.02, -0.01],

[0.04, 0.03, 0.00],
```

[0.06, 0.01, -0.02]

])

```
\#\# Mean normalization
mean_returns = np.mean(returns_data, axis=0)
normalized_data = returns_data - mean_returns

\#\# Calculate covariance matrix
cov_matrix = np.cov(normalized_data.T)

\#\# Perform eigen decomposition
eig_vals, eig_vecs = np.linalg.eig(cov_matrix)

\#\# Choose principal component (e.g., the one with max eigenvalue)
principal_component = eig_vecs[:, np.argmax(eig_vals)]

\#\# Project original data onto this component
projected_data = normalized_data @ principal_component

print("Projected Data:", projected_data)
```
` ` `

This approach captures key patterns in asset returns by focusing on principal components derived from the covariance matrix's eigenvectors, providing streamlined insights into portfolio dynamics.

In finance, orthogonal projections also enhance model robustness and interpretability by minimizing multicollinearity issues common in regression analyses with correlated variables. Projecting predictors onto an orthogonal subspace before estimation results in more stable models and reliable predictions.

And, these projections support machine learning applications like factor models used to quantify risk exposure or derive alpha signals from large datasets. When factors are orthogonally projected from raw features, they offer clearer interpretations and better control over model complexity.

Incorporating orthogonal projections into stress testing allows financial institutions to effectively evaluate asset correlations under extreme conditions—providing critical insights into systemic risks and aiding strategic decision-making during market turmoil.

By distilling vast amounts of data to its core components through orthogonal projections, financial analysts gain enriched perspectives that drive informed decision-making—a crucial advantage when navigating volatile markets.

This capability to focus on essential information makes orthogonal projections indispensable for modern finance professionals seeking clarity amidst complexity, transforming theoretical concepts into practical tools that enhance analytical prowess across diverse financial domains.

Case Studies in Finance

Exploring the practical applications of inner product spaces in the financial sector reveals their significant impact on decision-making processes. These mathematical constructs, when applied effectively, enhance the precision and foresight required in finance. Case studies bridge the gap between theory and practice, demonstrating the tangible benefits of these abstract concepts. Understanding inner product spaces can significantly improve the efficiency and reliability of financial models.

Take, for example, a hedge fund manager who uses correlation matrices to manage risk. By leveraging inner products, they can more accurately quantify relationships between different assets. This method uncovers patterns and correlations that might not be immediately apparent, helping to construct portfolios that maximize returns while minimizing risk. In a multi-asset portfolio, calculating the inner product of vectors representing asset returns allows managers to identify combinations that yield optimal outcomes under various market conditions.

Algorithmic trading firms also benefit from inner product spaces, particularly through machine learning models that predict market trends. These spaces are fundamental to principal component analysis (PCA), crucial for dimensionality reduction. PCA transforms complex datasets into simpler forms without losing essential information, relying on eigenvectors and eigenvalues within these spaces. Firms using this technique can process massive data sets quickly, enhancing prediction accuracy and decision-making speed.

In credit risk assessment, banks use similar techniques to evaluate borrower profiles against default probabilities. Inner products help measure similarities between current applicants and historical data, allowing analysts to assess creditworthiness more confidently. This approach reduces default rates and optimizes lending processes.

The insurance industry provides another compelling example: insurers use inner product spaces to model the impact of catastrophic events on portfolios. By analyzing historical loss data against current exposures, these models predict potential losses, enabling insurers to set premiums more accurately.

These examples illustrate how the integration of

mathematical precision with financial strategy leads to superior outcomes. Inner products play a crucial role in transforming vast amounts of data into actionable insights, bridging numerical analyses and strategic decisions that directly affect financial health.

Successful implementation requires not only technical expertise but also creativity and adaptability in rapidly changing markets. Financial professionals who master these tools position themselves at the forefront of their field—capable of not only responding to market changes but also anticipating them with mathematical foresight.

Overall, these applications underscore the indispensable role of theoretical concepts like inner products in real-world finance, serving as catalysts for innovation and driving efficiency in an industry where every decision counts.

Real-World Applications in Trading

In the fast-paced world of trading, inner product spaces emerge as crucial tools for gaining a competitive edge. Traders navigating volatile markets depend on precise mathematical frameworks to make informed decisions, and inner products form the backbone of many quantitative strategies, providing clarity and efficiency when it matters most.

For high-frequency trading firms, where speed is essential, inner product calculations are indispensable. These firms use them to swiftly assess and execute trades, processing market data at lightning speed. By employing vectorized computations, they streamline operations, minimizing latency and maximizing the execution of profitable trades. This mathematical precision allows traders to react instantly to market shifts, ensuring they capitalize on fleeting opportunities.

Similarly, portfolio managers apply inner products in risk management. When constructing diversified portfolios, managers evaluate potential asset combinations by calculating the covariance between returns—a process directly tied to inner product spaces. This analysis helps them strike an optimal balance between risk and return, aligning investment strategies with clients' financial goals.

In derivative pricing, understanding the interplay of various financial instruments is crucial. Traders use models based on inner product spaces to simulate different scenarios and assess pricing under varying conditions. This helps them to identify arbitrage opportunities or effectively hedge against adverse price movements.

And, sentiment analysis in trading benefits from these mathematical concepts as well. By analyzing textual data from news articles or social media feeds using vector representations, traders can quantify market sentiment —transforming qualitative information into quantitative signals that inform their strategies.

The integration of these techniques into trading platforms underscores their practical significance. Advanced algorithms built on inner product spaces offer traders unparalleled insight into complex financial landscapes. These tools enhance analytical capabilities and foster a deeper understanding of market dynamics.

In the end, the successful application of inner product spaces in trading illustrates how mathematics empowers professionals to transcend traditional boundaries. By bridging theoretical knowledge with practical implementation, traders unlock new possibilities for innovation and strategic foresight in an industry characterized by rapid change and relentless competition.

Computational Considerations

Computational considerations are crucial when effectively utilizing inner product spaces in trading environments. As financial markets become increasingly complex, the demand for precise and efficient computation intensifies. This requires a deep understanding of both the mathematical principles and the technological frameworks that underpin these processes.

One of the main challenges is balancing speed with accuracy. Trading algorithms must process vast amounts of data in real-time, necessitating optimized computational methods to ensure that inner product calculations do not create bottlenecks. Implementing vectorized operations in programming languages like Python or R can significantly boost performance by leveraging hardware capabilities to execute multiple operations simultaneously.

For example, Python libraries such as NumPy offer optimized routines for matrix and vector operations. Functions like numpy.dot or numpy.matmul allow traders to efficiently compute inner products across large datasets by reducing computational overhead. These functions offload tasks to compiled C code, leading to faster execution times compared to native Python loops—a crucial advantage in high-frequency trading where milliseconds can affect profit margins.

Additionally, maintaining numerical precision is essential when dealing with floating-point arithmetic common in financial computations. Small errors can propagate through iterative processes, causing significant discrepancies over time. To mitigate these issues, using double precision or implementing error-checking algorithms ensures the reliability of computed results.

Parallel computing further enhances computational capabilities by distributing workloads across multiple processors or cores. Frameworks like Dask or parallel processing modules in R enable traders to scale their analyses without sacrificing speed. By dividing data into chunks processed concurrently, traders can efficiently handle larger datasets—a necessity given the growing volume of market data.

Efficient memory management is also critical as datasets

expand. Proper use of memory prevents unnecessary delays caused by swapping data between disk and RAM. Techniques such as sparse matrix representations minimize memory usage by storing only non-zero elements, which is especially beneficial when working with large covariance matrices typical in portfolio management.

Robust computational infrastructure supports these efforts. Cloud-based solutions offer scalable resources that adapt to varying computational demands, providing flexibility without requiring significant upfront hardware investments. Platforms like AWS or Google Cloud deliver on-demand processing power tailored to specific trading strategies.

In summary, mastering computational considerations within inner product spaces involves a sophisticated blend of mathematical insight and technological expertise. By optimizing algorithms for performance while maintaining precision and leveraging modern computing resources, traders equip themselves with powerful tools capable of confidently and agilely navigating the dynamic landscape of financial markets.

CHAPTER 15: LEAST SQUARES AND REGRESSION

Least Squares Approximations

L east squares approximations are fundamental in financial modeling, offering a powerful approach for making data-driven decisions. By minimizing discrepancies between observed data and predictive models, they become indispensable tools for quantitative analysts and traders. Central to regression analysis, least squares are extensively used for forecasting and risk assessment.

Imagine an analyst tasked with predicting stock prices using historical data. Through least squares, they can fit a line —or even more complex polynomial functions—to the data, ensuring the model closely mirrors historical patterns. This process involves identifying parameters that minimize the sum of squared differences between observed values and model predictions, effectively capturing underlying trends without succumbing to noise.

In practice, implementing least squares requires solving a system of equations derived from the derivative of the sum of squared errors. These normal equations are efficiently solved using matrix algebra methods like LU decomposition or QR factorization, which are particularly useful for handling large-scale systems common in financial datasets with thousands of variables and observations.

For example, in Python, libraries such as NumPy and SciPy simplify this process. A straightforward example might involve using numpy.linalg.lstsq to solve for parameters in a linear regression model:

```python
import numpy as np


\#\# Example dataset: features (X) and target variable (y)

X = np.array([[1, 2], [2, 3], [3, 4], [4, 5]])

y = np.array([2.5, 3.6, 4.5, 5.1])


\#\# Adding a column of ones for intercept term

X_b = np.c_[np.ones((4, 1)), X]


\#\# Calculating least squares solution

theta_best = np.linalg.lstsq(X_b, y, rcond=None)[0]
```

Here, theta_best represents the optimal parameters that minimize the error between predicted and actual values. This approach is not only computationally efficient but also adaptable to various regression analyses beyond linear relationships.

Least squares techniques extend beyond simple regressions to more complex models like polynomial or multivariate regressions. Transforming input data with polynomial features or incorporating multiple predictors can enhance the model's ability to capture intricate market dynamics.

However, caution is necessary to avoid overfitting—where the model becomes too tailored to historical data and loses generalizability. Techniques such as cross-validation help prevent this by partitioning data into training and test sets to ensure robust performance on unseen data.

Additionally, addressing multicollinearity—when independent variables are highly correlated—is vital, as it can distort parameter estimates and reduce model reliability. Regularization methods like Ridge or Lasso regression introduce penalty terms that constrain coefficients, promoting stability and enhancing interpretability.

In summary, least squares approximations enable financial professionals to extract actionable insights from extensive datasets. By utilizing advanced mathematical techniques and computational tools, analysts create predictive models that accurately reflect historical trends while adapting to future market conditions with precision and confidence.

Linear Regression in Finance

Linear regression is a fundamental tool for financial analysts, providing a straightforward method to model relationships between variables. Essentially, it aims to derive a linear equation that predicts a dependent variable based on one or more independent variables. This approach is especially valuable in finance, where it is commonly used to forecast stock prices, assess risk factors, and evaluate economic indicators.

Take this example, when predicting a stock's future performance based on its historical prices and market conditions, linear regression can quantify these relationships. It does this by producing an equation of the form ($y = \beta_0 + \beta_1 x_1 + \beta_2 x_2 + + \beta_n x_n +$), where (y)

is the dependent variable (stock price), ($x\_1, x\_2, , x\_n$) are independent variables (such as interest rates or GDP growth), and ( ) is the error term. The coefficients (\beta_0, \beta_1, , \beta_n) are calculated to minimize the sum of squared residuals, ensuring the best fit line through the data points.

Financial analysts often use tools like Excel or programming languages such as Python to perform these calculations efficiently. Excel offers functions like LINEST and the Data Analysis Toolpak's regression feature for this purpose. However, Python provides a more flexible and robust environment for handling complex datasets:

```python
import numpy as np

import pandas as pd

from sklearn.linear_model import LinearRegression


\#\# Sample dataset

data =

'GDP Growth': [2.5, 3.0, 3.5, 4.0],

'Interest Rate': [1.5, 1.7, 1.8, 2.0],

'Stock Price': [150, 160, 170, 180]



df = pd.DataFrame(data)

X = df[['GDP Growth', 'Interest Rate']]

y = df['Stock Price']


\#\# Linear regression model
```

```
model = LinearRegression()
model.fit(X, y)


\#\# Coefficients and intercept
print("Coefficients:", model.coef_)
print("Intercept:", model.intercept_)
```
` ` `

In this example, model.coef_ reveals the slope coefficients for each predictor variable, while model.intercept_ provides the y-intercept of the fitted line. These results offer insights into how changes in GDP growth or interest rates might affect stock prices.

Beyond prediction, linear regression helps in understanding causality and making informed decisions under uncertainty. Analysts use it to identify key drivers of asset prices and evaluate their sensitivity to economic changes. By analyzing coefficient magnitudes and directions, one can determine whether rising interest rates might positively or negatively impact market performance.

However, real-world financial data often present challenges such as non-linearity and volatility that simple linear models may not adequately capture. Enhancing basic regression with techniques like polynomial regression or adding interaction terms can better reflect complex relationships.

To ensure model reliability, analysts must consider the assumptions underlying linear regression—such as homoscedasticity (constant variance of errors), independence of errors, and normality of residuals. Violating these assumptions can lead to biased estimates and misleading conclusions.

To address these issues and enhance model robustness,

analysts use diagnostic tools like residual plots and statistical tests (e.g., Durbin-Watson for autocorrelation), along with validation strategies such as train-test splits and k-fold cross-validation.

In finance, linear regression remains an essential tool due to its simplicity and interpretability. It enables analysts to distill complex datasets into actionable insights that guide strategic decision-making across various financial domains—from investment banking to corporate finance—providing a competitive edge in a dynamic market environment.

Relationship to Economics

Understanding the interplay between linear regression and economics is essential for financial analysts aiming to decipher complex economic phenomena. Essentially, economics involves grasping and forecasting how various factors impact markets, consumer behavior, and business cycles. Linear regression serves as a powerful tool in modeling these relationships quantitatively, providing clarity amid the complexity of economic data.

Take, for instance, the task of assessing how consumer spending affects GDP growth. An analyst might use linear regression to quantify this relationship, treating consumer spending as an independent variable and GDP growth as the dependent variable. The resulting equation not only aids in making predictions but also helps identify the strength and nature of the connection between these variables. Such insights can guide policymakers in formulating fiscal policies that stimulate economic growth.

Economic indicators like inflation rates, employment levels, and interest rates are often interconnected, influencing each other in ways that are not immediately obvious. Through linear regression analysis, economists and analysts can dissect these interactions to forecast trends and inform decisions. For example, by examining historical data on inflation and unemployment rates, analysts can create models to predict future inflation under different employment scenarios—a concept commonly known as the Phillips curve in economic theory.

Beyond mere prediction, linear regression also facilitates hypothesis testing in economics. Analysts can test economic theories by checking if observed data patterns align with theoretical expectations. Take this example, if a model suggests that interest rate hikes should reduce investment activity, regression analysis can empirically confirm this hypothesis by evaluating historical data across diverse economic contexts.

Incorporating economic theory into regression models enhances their explanatory power. For example, integrating elasticity—how demand for a product responds to price changes—into demand forecasting models allows analysts to more accurately predict consumer behavior under varying market conditions. Understanding these dynamics enables companies to adjust their pricing strategies proactively.

However, it's important to recognize the limitations of linear models when applied to economics. Economic systems are inherently complex and often exhibit nonlinearities that simple linear regression might overlook. Issues like multicollinearity—where independent variables are highly correlated—can obscure individual variable effects and complicate interpretation. Analysts must remain vigilant in diagnosing such issues using statistical tests like variance inflation factors (VIF) and adopting techniques such as ridge regression when necessary.

And, external shocks or structural changes in an economy can render previously reliable models obsolete. Continuous evaluation of models against new data ensures their relevance in evolving economic landscapes. Adapting models to include additional variables or transitioning to more advanced modeling approaches like time series or econometric models may be necessary for accurately capturing new dynamics.

Where X meets Y linear regression with economics highlights how quantitative tools enhance our understanding of multifaceted economic systems. By distilling vast amounts of data into actionable insights, regression analysis empowers analysts and policymakers alike to make informed decisions that shape economic policy and strategy.

In this domain where economics meets finance through quantitative analysis, it becomes evident that despite its simplicity, linear regression remains invaluable. It bridges theory with practice by offering a systematic approach to exploring economic relationships—ultimately deepening our comprehension of how myriad factors interact within global financial markets.

Applying Technology and Software

Technology and software have revolutionized the application of linear regression in the financial sector, significantly enhancing the analytical capabilities of economists and financial analysts. This transformation has streamlined processes and improved the accuracy and depth of insights gleaned from economic data.

Modern analysts face the challenge of managing vast datasets, including real-time market information, historical economic indicators, and consumer behavior patterns. Manually handling these datasets is impractical. This is where software solutions like Python, with libraries such as pandas and statsmodels, or R, with its extensive array of statistical packages, come into play. These tools offer robust frameworks for efficiently importing, cleaning, and analyzing data.

Take Python's pandas library, for instance—it excels at handling structured data by providing functionalities to merge datasets, handle missing values, and perform complex data manipulations seamlessly. When combined with statsmodels or scikit-learn, users can effortlessly conduct linear regression analysis. A typical workflow might involve using pandas to import a CSV file of economic data and then leveraging statsmodels to fit a regression model that predicts future trends based on historical variables. The integration of powerful visualization libraries like Matplotlib further allows analysts to present their findings compellingly, making complex results more accessible to stakeholders.

R is equally powerful in this arena. With functions like lm() for linear modeling and ggplot2 for visualization, R has become indispensable in financial analytics. An analyst can quickly set up a regression model using the lm() function to explore relationships between variables such as interest rates and stock prices, while ggplot2 facilitates the creation of informative plots that highlight patterns and anomalies within data.

Advancements in machine learning software have further expanded the horizons for regression analysis in finance. Tools like TensorFlow and PyTorch enable analysts to develop sophisticated models that capture nonlinear relationships often missed by traditional linear regression. These platforms support the creation of neural networks capable of identifying intricate patterns within large datasets—a capability increasingly utilized in predictive analytics for market trends and risk assessment.

The rise of cloud computing has democratized access to these technological resources. Platforms such as AWS or Google Cloud provide scalable infrastructure for running computationally intensive analyses without requiring significant hardware investments. Analysts can deploy regression models at scale, using cloud-based databases like Amazon RDS or BigQuery to efficiently store and query large volumes of financial data.

In institutional settings, comprehensive solutions like SAS

or SPSS are preferred over piecemeal approaches. These integrated platforms offer end-to-end workflows—from data preprocessing through model deployment—ensuring seamless integration into existing business operations.

While technology undoubtedly enhances analytical capabilities, a strong foundational understanding of economics and statistics is essential for correctly interpreting outputs. Analysts must be skilled at validating models through diagnostic tests such as residual analysis or cross-validation techniques to ensure reliability before application.

To wrap things up, the synergy between technology and linear regression has transformed financial analyses today. By harnessing advanced software tools, analysts can unravel complex economic dynamics with unprecedented precision and speed—transforming raw data into strategic insights that drive informed decision-making across sectors. As technology continues to advance rapidly, so too will its capacity to refine our understanding of economics through enhanced regression techniques—a testament to human ingenuity in leveraging technological progress.

Interpretation of Financial Results

Interpreting financial results from regression analysis is a critical component of financial analytics, transforming numerical data into actionable insights. A deep understanding of economic principles and statistical nuances is essential in this process.

Central to interpreting regression results is discerning the significance of coefficients. Each coefficient indicates the change in the dependent variable for a one-unit change in an independent variable, assuming all other variables remain constant. This relationship is crucial in finance; for example, when assessing how interest rate changes affect stock prices, the coefficient provides strategic foresight into market behavior by quantifying this impact.

Beyond numerical values, analysts must consider the statistical significance of these coefficients using p-values or confidence intervals. A low p-value suggests that an observed effect is unlikely due to chance, enhancing the model's predictive power. Practically, a significant p-value for a GDP growth-related coefficient might indicate a reliable predictor of market trends, aiding investment strategies.

Residual analysis adds another layer of insight. By examining residuals—the differences between observed and predicted values—analysts can assess model fit and identify anomalies. Patterns in residuals may signal data issues or model inadequacies, prompting refinements. Take this example, if residuals display a pattern rather than randomness, it may suggest omitted variables or nonlinear relationships needing attention.

Interpreting results also requires awareness of multicollinearity, where independent variables are highly correlated. This can obscure each predictor's individual effect on the dependent variable, leading to misleading interpretations. Techniques such as variance inflation factor (VIF) analysis help identify multicollinearity issues, allowing analysts to adjust models for more accurate interpretation.

A thorough interpretation considers external factors influencing data trends over time. Economic events like policy changes or geopolitical developments can unpredictably impact financial data. Integrating qualitative insights with quantitative analysis ensures interpretations remain grounded in real-world contexts.

Visualization plays a vital role in effectively interpreting regression results. Tools like scatter plots or regression lines superimposed on data provide intuitive visual cues about relationships between variables and potential outliers that could skew results. These visual aids make complex findings more accessible to stakeholders without technical expertise.

Additionally, sensitivity analysis enhances interpretation by testing how variations in key assumptions affect outcomes. It equips decision-makers with knowledge about potential risks and uncertainties surrounding predictions—essential for developing robust financial strategies that withstand volatile market conditions.

In the end, interpreting financial results from regression models involves balancing quantitative rigor with qualitative judgment. It requires technical proficiency and critical thinking to translate abstract figures into meaningful insights that inform strategic decisions within dynamic financial landscapes.

As analysts continue refining their interpretive skills alongside technological advancements, they solidify their role as pivotal navigators within finance—guiding organizations through complexities with precision and clarity while shaping informed paths forward amidst ever-evolving economic scenarios.

Optimization Techniques

A key concept in financial optimization is linear programming, which optimizes a linear objective function subject to linear constraints. This approach is particularly useful in portfolio management, where the aim is to maximize returns while controlling risk through asset allocation limits. For example, a fund manager can use linear programming to determine the optimal mix of investments across various securities, achieving desired return levels while maintaining acceptable risk thresholds.

Linear programming problems are often solved using algorithms like the simplex method or interior-point methods, which iteratively explore feasible solutions to find an optimal result. Python's SciPy library offers robust capabilities for solving such problems by defining objective functions and constraints, allowing analysts to simulate complex financial environments and derive actionable strategies.

Beyond linear programming, nonlinear optimization is essential for dealing with non-linear relationships among variables common in finance. This includes optimizing utility functions or pricing derivatives where payoff structures aren't strictly linear. Nonlinear optimization uses gradient-based algorithms like conjugate gradient or Newton's method to find optimal solutions.

Take this example, options pricing models often require nonlinear optimization due to their nonlinear payoffs, necessitating advanced approaches for accurate valuation under varying market conditions. Implementing these techniques typically involves numerical libraries such as NumPy or specialized software like MATLAB, enabling precise modeling of intricate financial landscapes.

Another critical aspect of financial optimization is integer programming, which addresses decisions involving discrete variables—a frequent need in scheduling or resource allocation within trading operations or project management. Mixed-integer programming (MIP) models help devise strategies that balance cost-effectiveness with logistical feasibility.

Real-world applications often demand a combination of optimization techniques working together. Consider portfolio optimization scenarios involving risk measures like Value at Risk (VaR) or Conditional Value at Risk (CVaR), which require hybrid approaches combining stochastic elements with deterministic frameworks for comprehensive risk-return assessments.

Multi-objective optimization further expands the scope by tackling situations with multiple competing objectives— such as maximizing returns while minimizing volatility and transaction costs simultaneously. Techniques like Pareto efficiency allow analysts to identify optimal trade-offs among conflicting goals without compromising critical priorities.

The integration of machine learning with traditional optimization techniques marks an exciting advancement in finance, where predictive analytics enhance decision-making by improving forecasting accuracy and model adaptability in dynamic market environments.

In the end, mastering optimization techniques provides quantitative analysts with powerful tools for effectively navigating complex financial systems. This involves balancing precision-driven strategies against real-world uncertainties while fostering innovation and resilience across diverse economic landscapes. Continuous refinement of these skills not only elevates analytical acumen but also empowers informed decision-making that shapes successful financial futures amidst evolving challenges and opportunities.

Case Studies in Trading Strategies

In the high-stakes world of trading, strategies are more than theoretical exercises; they are the lifeblood of decision-making. Each strategy is a blend of mathematical rigor, market intuition, and real-time adaptability. To showcase the practical application of linear algebra and matrix theory in trading, we explore case studies that highlight the transformative power of these tools.

Imagine a hedge fund aiming to optimize its trading portfolio for maximum returns while minimizing risk. The fund adopts a quantitative approach, leveraging historical price data and predictive modeling. Here, matrix theory becomes crucial, enabling efficient handling and analysis of large datasets to identify correlations and potential market trends.

One case involves using a mean-variance optimization model. This strategy relies on calculating expected returns and covariances of various assets. By representing these as matrices, analysts can swiftly compute optimal asset weights to achieve the desired risk-return balance. Tools like Python's

NumPy library facilitate these calculations, allowing seamless integration with live data for real-time adjustments.

In algorithmic trading, eigenvalue decomposition plays a pivotal role in predicting market movements. A trading firm might analyze principal components of asset prices to detect underlying factors driving market behavior. By decomposing covariance matrices into eigenvalues and eigenvectors, the firm isolates key variables impacting price dynamics, gaining a predictive edge. This insight helps develop automated trading strategies that capitalize on anticipated shifts.

Another example highlights singular value decomposition (SVD) in developing pairs trading strategies. Traders look for two correlated securities whose price ratio is expected to revert to a mean over time. Using SVD to filter noise from price series data enables analysts to better identify deviation patterns indicative of profitable entry and exit points.

Global financial markets also demand robust risk management strategies. Take this example, a multinational investment bank uses linear programming to manage currency exposure across its international portfolio. By modeling exchange rate fluctuations and transaction costs, the bank dynamically adjusts currency positions, minimizing risk while ensuring liquidity.

In each case study, we see how theoretical constructs translate into actionable insights driving trading decisions. Practical implementation requires not only mathematical proficiency but also an acute understanding of market mechanics and regulatory environments. Tools like R for statistical analysis or MATLAB for complex modeling become invaluable in executing sophisticated strategies.

These real-world applications emphasize the necessity for continuous learning and adaptation in developing trading strategies. As markets evolve with technological advancements and geopolitical shifts, methodologies employed by quantitative analysts and traders must evolve as well. Embracing innovation while maintaining a firm grasp on foundational principles ensures these strategies remain relevant and effective.

In the end, these case studies reveal the integral role of linear algebra and matrix theory in refining trading strategies. They demonstrate how abstract mathematical concepts become powerful instruments when applied precisely to finance's fast-paced realm, shaping informed decisions that withstand the unpredictable nature of global markets.

Data-Driven Decision Making

In today's fast-paced financial world, data-driven decision making has become essential rather than optional. The ability to quickly and accurately interpret large datasets is what sets successful trading firms apart from the rest. Linear algebra and matrix theory form the core mathematical foundation needed for this analysis, turning raw data into actionable insights.

Imagine a trading desk where analysts continuously analyze streams of market data. These professionals use matrix operations to extract crucial information from background noise. A key component of this process is constructing and manipulating large matrices that represent various financial indicators—such as prices, volumes, and economic metrics—all interconnected.

Take, for instance, how a quantitative analyst employs principal component analysis (PCA) to simplify complex datasets. By identifying the key variables influencing market behavior, PCA reduces dimensionality, focusing on core components that drive asset prices. This streamlined dataset enables traders to concentrate on significant factors without getting bogged down by extraneous details.

Matrix theory is also vital in risk management. Financial institutions use covariance matrices to evaluate portfolio risk by examining how different assets interact under various scenarios. This rigorous analysis allows risk managers to simulate potential market movements and adjust positions proactively, mitigating potential losses.

Machine learning further enhances data-driven decision making. Algorithms trained on historical data can identify patterns and predict future market trends with remarkable accuracy. For example, linear regression models solve linear equations using matrix operations to calculate coefficients that best fit observed data points, providing a quantifiable measure for forecasting prices or returns.

Python's pandas library is often used by analysts to manage financial time series data efficiently. Dataframes facilitate seamless storage and manipulation of multi-dimensional arrays, enabling rapid computations crucial for real-time trading decisions. When combined with NumPy's powerful array processing capabilities, these tools provide an efficient toolkit for sophisticated analyses.

By integrating big data analytics, firms can analyze unstructured datasets such as social media sentiment or news feeds using natural language processing (NLP) techniques rooted in linear algebra concepts like vectorization and similarity measurements between textual elements represented as vectors.

In environments where precision is paramount, every trade decision must be supported by rigorous quantitative methodologies. Stakeholders increasingly demand transparency and assurance that strategies are grounded in solid analyses rather than speculative guesses.

As technology advances rapidly, staying ahead requires adopting innovative approaches while maintaining fundamental principles that ensure reliability across global trading operations. Embracing cutting-edge technologies within a framework rooted in linear algebra allows firms to thrive amid competitive pressures in today's financial markets.

By systematically applying these mathematical frameworks alongside evolving technological solutions like cloud computing or blockchain technology—which enhance data accessibility and security—firms equip themselves with unparalleled capabilities for informed decision-making processes crucial for long-term success in finance's dynamic ecosystem.

CHAPTER 16:
NUMERICAL
METHODS FOR
MATRICES

Direct Solution Techniques

I n the complex world of finance, efficiently and accurately
solving systems of linear equations is essential. Direct
solution techniques offer a straightforward approach to
these problems, delivering reliable outcomes that are crucial
for timely decision-making in high-stakes environments.

Take the Gaussian elimination method, a cornerstone in linear
algebra for solving matrix equations. This method simplifies
a complex system into an upper triangular matrix through a
series of row operations. Its elegance lies in its simplicity; once
reduced, back-substitution easily reveals the solution set. For
financial analysts managing large datasets, this method cuts
through computational noise to deliver precise answers with
clarity and directness.

Take this example, if you're optimizing a portfolio based
on multiple constraints and asset correlations, Gaussian

elimination can systematically simplify the equations representing these constraints into solvable forms. This helps you to efficiently determine the asset allocations that maximize returns while adhering to risk parameters.

Another valuable technique is LU decomposition, which factors a matrix into lower and upper triangular matrices. This approach is particularly useful when dealing with repeated solutions of linear systems where only the right-hand side changes. By precomputing the LU decomposition of the coefficient matrix, subsequent solutions require less computational effort—ideal for scenarios needing rapid recalculations, such as intraday trading adjustments.

Imagine operating within a volatile market where asset prices constantly fluctuate. LU decomposition allows you to quickly adapt by recalculating optimal positions as market conditions shift without having to refactor the entire matrix from scratch each time.

And, direct solution methods are integral in constructing covariance matrices used extensively in risk management. Covariance matrices quantify how different financial instruments move relative to each other—a key component for developing hedging strategies or stress-testing portfolios against hypothetical scenarios. Precise calculations of these matrices ensure robust assessments of potential risk exposures.

Beyond solving static equations, direct methods lay the groundwork for more advanced analytical models. They serve as building blocks for algorithms that power machine learning models or statistical simulations crucial to modern financial analysis.

The efficiency and reliability offered by direct solution techniques make them indispensable tools in finance's quantitative toolkit. Whether optimizing portfolios or evaluating risk scenarios, these methods provide the clarity and confidence needed to successfully navigate complex financial landscapes.

As technology continues to evolve rapidly, mastering these foundational techniques remains vital. Ensuring decisions are informed by solid analytical grounding rather than mere conjecture or intuition-driven guesses is essential in this dynamic arena where precision is paramount. Leveraging direct solution techniques solidifies your competitive edge amidst relentless market shifts.

Iterative Methods

In the financial domain, challenges often arise that require agile and adaptive approaches, especially when dealing with large-scale datasets or systems where direct methods become computationally prohibitive. This is where iterative methods come into play, offering a practical solution by progressively refining results.

Take, for instance, the Jacobi and Gauss-Seidel methods —both are iterative techniques for solving linear systems by approximating solutions through repeated updates. They begin with an initial guess and iteratively move towards convergence. Unlike direct methods, these do not necessitate loading the entire system into memory, making them ideal for managing large matrices frequently encountered in finance.

Picture being tasked with pricing complex derivatives in a market where factors change dynamically. Iterative methods enable you to adjust calculations incrementally as new data arrives, maintaining real-time accuracy without extensive recalculations. Their iterative nature allows solutions to be refined continuously, which is crucial in high-frequency trading environments where every millisecond counts.

In cases involving sparse matrices—common when dealing with financial networks or correlations—iterative techniques excel. The Conjugate Gradient method, for example, efficiently handles large symmetric positive-definite matrices by iteratively reducing the problem size while maintaining computational efficiency. This capability is ideal for evaluating large-scale investment portfolios or assessing interconnected risk exposures across markets.

Also, iterative methods are vital in risk management strategies, particularly when stress-testing portfolios against potential market shocks. By simulating multiple scenarios and refining results iteratively, analysts can gain insights into how portfolios might react under different stress conditions, enabling more robust risk mitigation strategies.

In practice, these methods are often implemented using programming languages like Python or R, leveraging libraries that simplify matrix operations and optimizations. Take this example, using Python's SciPy library, one can easily implement iterative solvers for linear systems:

```python
import numpy as np

from scipy.sparse.linalg import cg


\#\# Define a large sparse matrix 'A' and a vector 'b'

A = np.array([[4, 1], [1, 3]])

b = np.array([1, 2])


\#\# Use Conjugate Gradient method to solve Ax = b

x, info = cg(A, b)


print("Solution:", x)
```

This code snippet illustrates how effortlessly iterative

methods can be deployed to tackle computationally demanding tasks in finance. By providing solutions that evolve with each iteration, they empower analysts to adapt swiftly to new information—an essential skill in dynamic markets.

Iterative techniques also drive innovation within algorithmic trading. Algorithms can incorporate real-time data inputs and adjust trading strategies iteratively as market conditions evolve. This adaptability keeps strategies aligned with current trends and reduces the risk of becoming outdated.

In the end, the flexibility and scalability of iterative methods make them invaluable in a quantitative analyst's toolkit. They enable finance professionals to navigate the complexities of modern markets with agility and precision—traits essential for success in an ever-evolving financial landscape.

As the world of finance grows increasingly intricate and data-driven, mastering iterative approaches is no longer optional but necessary for those aiming to stay ahead in the competitive arena of quantitative analysis.

Numerical Stability in Finance

Numerical stability is crucial in financial computations, influencing the reliability of results from various mathematical operations. It involves understanding how errors propagate through an algorithm. In financial modeling, even minor miscalculations can significantly affect outputs, impacting investment strategies and risk assessments.

Take portfolio optimization as an example, where asset allocations are determined by solving linear equations. Using numerically unstable algorithms can amplify rounding errors or poorly conditioned matrix inputs, leading to inaccurate predictions and suboptimal investment decisions. To mitigate these issues, it's vital to choose computational methods that minimize error propagation and maintain robustness across different datasets.

One effective approach to ensuring stability is using condition numbers. A matrix's condition number indicates the sensitivity of its solution; higher numbers suggest greater susceptibility to numerical errors. Regularly calculating condition numbers in finance helps assess potential risks associated with numerical instability.

Another technique is opting for iterative methods over direct methods when solving linear systems. Iterative techniques, like the Conjugate Gradient Method, offer improvements in both efficiency and stability, particularly with large and sparse matrices typical in financial datasets. These methods refine solutions step by step, controlling and reducing errors rather than allowing them to accumulate.

Additionally, preconditioning can further stabilize iterative solutions by transforming matrices to enhance convergence speed without introducing significant errors. This allows finance professionals to handle larger datasets efficiently while maintaining reliable accuracy—an essential balance in high-stakes environments where precise calculations are crucial.

For practical application, consider matrix factorization used in risk model calibration or derivative pricing. Techniques like Singular Value Decomposition (SVD) or QR Factorization require careful attention to rounding behaviors and the handling of small singular values to prevent dramatic result skewing.

In programming environments like Excel or Python, built-in functions often include checks for numerical stability. However, understanding these processes conceptually helps users anticipate potential issues before they affect financial outcomes.

At its core, numerical stability is foundational for trustworthy financial computations. By integrating stable algorithms and being mindful of their properties—such as condition numbers and error propagation characteristics—financial analysts can enhance the accuracy and reliability of their models. Through diligent application of these principles, complex data environments become navigable, transforming intricate algebraic theories into tangible economic insights.

Dealing with Precision Issues

Precision in financial calculations is crucial for maintaining the integrity and reliability of models. Even minor inaccuracies can escalate through computations, particularly in iterative processes, leading to significant deviations in outputs. Addressing these precision issues requires a solid understanding of numerical methods and the implementation of strategies to minimize errors.

Floating-point arithmetic, commonly used in computational finance, involves rounding errors due to its finite representation of real numbers. Although these errors are often subtle, they can accumulate, especially with repeated operations. For example, slight discrepancies in compound interest calculations or complex derivatives can lead to substantial differences over time.

One effective strategy for mitigating these issues is the use of higher precision data types. Many programming languages and software tools offer double-precision or even arbitrary-precision arithmetic options. While this approach may increase computational load, it enhances accuracy by reducing rounding errors.

Careful algorithm design also plays a vital role in managing precision. Choosing algorithms that are inherently stable reduces susceptibility to error amplification. Take this example, algorithms that avoid subtracting nearly equal numbers can significantly reduce errors—a common problem when calculating differences between large numbers with small results, as seen in variance calculations or sensitivity analysis.

Rearranging calculations to enhance precision is another effective approach. Breaking down calculations into smaller parts that retain greater precision before combining them helps maintain overall accuracy.

In practical applications like financial risk modeling or pricing complex derivatives, precision is paramount. These tasks often involve large datasets and numerous computations, where errors can magnify unnoticed if not carefully controlled. Utilizing numerical libraries specifically designed for financial applications often provides built-in functions for high-precision calculations and error-checking mechanisms.

Thoroughly testing algorithms with various datasets helps identify potential precision pitfalls before deployment in critical decision-making environments. This guarantees models perform reliably across different conditions, boosting confidence in their outputs.

In environments like Python or R, libraries such as NumPy or R's 'Rmpfr' can effectively manage precision. These libraries offer high-level interfaces for precise calculations and include mechanisms to handle common floating-point arithmetic pitfalls.

In the end, dealing with precision issues requires a multifaceted approach—combining careful algorithm selection with strategic computation management ensures robust financial modeling. As analysts become adept at identifying and addressing these challenges, they reinforce the trustworthiness of their models, delivering valuable insights grounded in accuracy rather than approximation.

Algorithms in Practice

In the realm of financial modeling, algorithms play a pivotal role far beyond simple computation; they are integral to decision-making processes, transforming raw data into actionable insights. Mastery of these algorithms is essential to fully harness their potential.

Take algorithmic trading as an example, where speed and precision are crucial. Here, algorithms execute trades based on real-time data analysis, demanding both high accuracy and swift execution. Typically, they employ time-series data, technical indicators, and predictive models to fine-tune trading strategies. Moving averages may be used to identify trends, while stochastic models help assess volatility. The challenge is selecting adaptable algorithms that can navigate the dynamic nature of financial markets without sacrificing performance.

In risk management, algorithms identify potential threats and assess their impact on portfolios. Monte Carlo simulations, for instance, model various outcomes to provide comprehensive risk assessments. By using random sampling and statistical modeling, these simulations predict the effects of uncertainty in market variables. Ensuring accuracy under changing conditions requires careful calibration and validation against historical data.

Portfolio optimization offers another avenue where algorithms are indispensable. The goal is to maximize returns while minimizing risk, often achieved through quadratic programming or linear optimization methods. These techniques adjust asset weights in a portfolio based on expected returns, variances, and covariances. A solid grasp of how these mathematical concepts translate into algorithmic solutions is crucial for optimizing financial outcomes.

Machine learning algorithms have risen in prominence due to their ability to reveal patterns not easily detected by traditional analysis. Techniques like regression trees and neural networks are increasingly utilized for tasks such as credit scoring and fraud detection. These models depend on vast amounts of training data and an iterative approach to refine predictions, underscoring the importance of model selection and parameter tuning.

Implementing these algorithms effectively requires a robust understanding of both their theoretical foundations and computational intricacies. Programming languages like Python or R provide powerful libraries such as SciPy or TensorFlow, which simplify the deployment of complex algorithms. These tools enable practitioners to concentrate on refining models rather than constructing them from scratch.

In the end, deploying algorithms involves more than technical implementation; it requires aligning computational capabilities with business objectives strategically. As financial environments grow more complex and interconnected, leveraging sophisticated algorithms becomes essential—transforming computational power into a strategic advantage.

As we delve deeper into the practicalities of using these algorithms, the importance of continuous monitoring and refinement cannot be overlooked. Financial markets evolve, necessitating that our algorithmic approaches evolve with them. Thus, maintaining an agile framework where feedback loops inform ongoing development is crucial for staying competitive in the financial landscape.

Error Analysis and Measurements

In the intricate world of financial modeling, understanding errors and their implications is as vital as the algorithms themselves. Mistakes in calculations can lead to significant misjudgments, impacting both strategic decisions and financial outcomes. Thus, rigorous error analysis forms the backbone of robust algorithm development.

A common type of error encountered is truncation error, which occurs when an approximation replaces an exact mathematical operation. In finance, this might happen when simplifying a complex model for easier computation. For example, using a finite number of terms in a Taylor series to estimate future cash flows can compromise precision if too few terms are included. Balancing computational efficiency with accuracy becomes crucial, necessitating a careful consideration of trade-offs.

Another significant category is round-off error, resulting from the finite precision with which computers store numbers. This can be particularly challenging in financial computations where large datasets amplify these errors. Take this example, when summing large series of financial transactions, small round-off errors can accumulate, leading to noticeable discrepancies. Ensuring that numerical operations are performed in an order that minimizes such accumulation is key to maintaining result integrity.

In evaluating models and algorithms, it is essential to consider data measurement errors as well. Financial datasets are prone to inaccuracies from incorrect entries or delays in data collection processes. These inaccuracies can skew algorithmic outputs significantly. Applying statistical methods like outlier detection or noise filtering helps mitigate these issues by identifying and correcting anomalous data points before they impact model predictions.

Sensitivity analysis serves as a valuable tool for assessing how variations in input parameters affect outputs. By systematically altering inputs within plausible ranges, one can evaluate how sensitive an algorithm's results are to changes and uncertainties inherent in the market environment. This process provides insights into the robustness and reliability of algorithms under various scenarios—a critical aspect when dealing with volatile markets.

Validation techniques further ensure that models perform accurately across different conditions and datasets. Cross-validation strategies involve dividing data into training and testing subsets to thoroughly assess predictive accuracy. Techniques like k-fold cross-validation generalize findings by iterating this process over multiple data partitions, offering a more comprehensive evaluation than single-instance tests.

In the end, ongoing monitoring and calibration are indispensable parts of error management in financial algorithms. As markets are dynamic, they require adaptable models capable of efficiently responding to new information. Implementing feedback loops where model performance informs successive iterations can refine accuracy over time— a necessity for staying competitive amid ever-evolving market conditions.

Understanding and managing errors allows practitioners not only to enhance model fidelity but also to build trust with stakeholders reliant on these outputs for decision-making purposes. Such diligence ensures that complex financial analyses translate into actionable insights grounded in reliable computations rather than misleading projections —a cornerstone for success within the quantitative finance landscape.

Performance Enhancements

In the fast-paced world of finance, optimizing algorithm performance is not just a preference—it's essential. With vast amounts of data being processed in real-time, even minor inefficiencies can lead to significant delays and missed opportunities. Therefore, enhancing performance is crucial for maintaining a competitive edge.

One critical area for improvement is algorithmic efficiency. Streamlining code to reduce computational complexity is fundamental. For example, instead of using nested loops for matrix operations—which can be computationally expensive —leveraging vectorized operations available in libraries like NumPy for Python can significantly speed up calculations. These libraries are optimized for performance and can handle large-scale data with ease.

Parallel processing also offers substantial performance gains, particularly for tasks that are inherently independent. By distributing computations across multiple processors, parallel algorithms can achieve faster execution times. In practice, this means running Monte Carlo simulations or backtesting trading strategies concurrently rather than sequentially. Tools like Python's multiprocessing module or job scheduling systems in high-performance computing environments facilitate such parallel executions.

Another vital aspect of performance enhancement is memory management. Poor memory utilization can bottleneck processes, especially when handling large datasets typical in financial analysis. Techniques like memory profiling help identify inefficient memory usage, allowing for optimizations such as data type conversion and efficient data storage formats (e.g., using HDF5 files instead of CSVs). By minimizing memory footprint, algorithms can operate more swiftly and reliably.

Algorithmic stability must not be overlooked when considering enhancements. An algorithm that runs quickly but produces erratic results under certain conditions is detrimental. Ensuring numerical stability through careful implementation and validation is essential. This involves selecting appropriate numerical methods and ensuring they are well-conditioned—meaning small changes in input lead to proportional changes in output.

The integration of machine learning models adds new dimensions to performance enhancements. These models can automatically adapt to new data patterns, improving predictive accuracy and reducing the need for manual recalibration. However, their deployment demands thoughtful consideration regarding training time and inference speed—key factors affecting their applicability in real-time trading scenarios.

Adaptive algorithms represent another frontier in performance optimization. These algorithms dynamically adjust parameters based on market conditions or input data characteristics, providing tailored responses rather than static outputs. Techniques like reinforcement learning enable algorithms to learn from past actions and outcomes, enhancing decision-making processes over time.

Finally, continuous monitoring and iterative refinement form the backbone of sustained performance improvement. Regularly assessing algorithm outputs against benchmarks or industry standards ensures alignment with performance goals. Incorporating user feedback into refinement cycles helps uncover practical limitations or unforeseen issues that may not be apparent during initial development stages.

In summary, performance enhancements in financial algorithms are about more than achieving faster computations; they're about building systems that are robust, scalable, and capable of evolving alongside market demands. By focusing on efficiency at every level—from code optimization to strategic adaptation—financial analysts and traders can harness the full power of technology to inform better decisions and drive successful outcomes in an ever-changing landscape.

Financial Data Computation Tools

Financial data computation tools form the backbone of modern quantitative finance, providing essential infrastructure for processing vast datasets and implementing sophisticated models efficiently. Analysts and traders rely on these tools for rapid computations that inform real-time decisions, helping them maintain a competitive edge in the market.

Python has emerged as a cornerstone in financial analytics, largely due to its extensive library ecosystem. Libraries like Pandas facilitate data manipulation and analysis, streamlining complex tasks such as data cleaning and transformation. For example, Pandas offers methods like fillna() or interpolate()

to handle missing data, ensuring datasets are robust before further analysis.

Beyond basic data manipulation, Python's NumPy and SciPy libraries offer powerful numerical computation capabilities. NumPy supports large, multi-dimensional arrays and matrices, along with a comprehensive collection of mathematical functions. SciPy builds on NumPy by adding modules for optimization, integration, interpolation, eigenvalue problems, and more—essential tools for implementing advanced financial models.

For clear visualization of financial data insights, Matplotlib is a go-to option in Python's toolkit. It enables the creation of static, interactive, and animated plots that effectively communicate trends or anomalies in financial datasets. By using Matplotlib alongside Seaborn—a library based on Matplotlib for high-level statistical graphics—users can create detailed visual representations that enhance understanding and decision-making.

R is another language popular among financial analysts due to its strength in statistical computing. R's comprehensive packages like dplyr for data manipulation and ggplot2 for visualization mirror Python's capabilities while offering unique strengths in statistical modeling. Financial practitioners often use R's quantmod package to simplify access to quantitative financial modeling frameworks.

In high-frequency trading environments where speed is critical, C++ remains relevant due to its execution efficiency. Although C++ may not be as user-friendly as interpreted languages like Python or R, its performance benefits are invaluable in scenarios where latency directly affects profitability.

For database management within finance applications, SQL is indispensable because of its robust querying capabilities across relational databases. SQL efficiently handles structured data, supporting backend operations crucial for maintaining comprehensive financial records or executing batch operations on large datasets.

APIs (Application Programming Interfaces) from platforms like Bloomberg or Yahoo Finance provide direct access to up-to-date market data feeds necessary for timely analysis without manual intervention. Integrating these APIs into analytical workflows allows seamless updates that enhance model accuracy by reflecting current market conditions.

And, cloud computing platforms such as AWS (Amazon Web Services) or Google Cloud offer scalable storage solutions alongside parallel processing power. These capabilities are conducive to handling computationally intensive tasks without the hardware constraints typical of on-premises systems.

In the end, choosing the right computation tools is pivotal; the selection depends on specific project requirements, including complexity and real-time processing needs. By effectively harnessing these tools—each tailored to distinct aspects of financial analysis—professionals can extract actionable insights from data more swiftly while optimizing overall workflow efficiency. This approach enables them to achieve desired financial outcomes amidst dynamic market landscapes.

CHAPTER 17:
APPLICATIONS IN
FINANCIAL MARKETS

Market Models and Analysis

Market models are crucial to financial analysis, providing frameworks that help interpret data and guide decision-making. These models aim to simplify the complexities of financial markets by breaking them down into quantifiable elements for analysis and prediction. Their effectiveness relies on balancing statistical rigor with intuitive understanding.

For example, the Capital Asset Pricing Model (CAPM) is a foundational tool used to estimate an asset's expected return based on its market risk. It posits that a security's expected return is a function of the risk-free rate, its beta (which measures sensitivity to market movements), and the expected market return. This helps traders assess whether an asset is overvalued or undervalued.

More advanced scenarios use multi-factor models like the Fama-French Three-Factor Model. This model builds on CAPM by incorporating additional factors such as company size and value metrics, allowing for a more nuanced interpretation of returns by considering elements beyond market risk.

Derivatives pricing also relies heavily on market models. The Black-Scholes model, for instance, is widely used for valuing options, employing differential equations that account for variables like volatility and time decay. While popular, practitioners must be aware of its limitations, especially in markets that deviate from assumptions like lognormal distribution or during extreme conditions.

Quantitative finance often uses stochastic processes to model price movements. The Geometric Brownian Motion (GBM) model is foundational in this area, assuming continuous price changes with constant volatility. This simplification captures broad trends while acknowledging inherent randomness, helping traders simulate future price paths and assess potential outcomes.

In portfolio management, quantitative modeling techniques such as mean-variance optimization are invaluable. Developed by Harry Markowitz, this approach constructs an optimal portfolio by balancing expected returns against risk, measured as variance or standard deviation of portfolio returns. Efficient frontier analysis helps investors identify portfolios offering maximum return for a given level of risk.

Applying these models requires extensive computational support. Python's ecosystem is particularly well-suited for this; libraries like NumPy enable efficient array operations essential for handling large datasets in portfolio optimization. Meanwhile, pandas streamline data manipulation, allowing quick transformation and aggregation of financial datasets—a crucial step in model preparation.

Visualizing financial data enhances analytical efforts by revealing patterns not immediately obvious in raw numbers. Using Python libraries like Matplotlib or Seaborn, analysts can create plots that highlight correlations or anomalies within datasets, aiding strategic decision-making.

In the end, the success of any market model depends on its adaptability and alignment with real-world conditions. Continuous refinement through backtesting— testing strategies against historical data—and stress testing under extreme scenarios ensures robustness and reliability. This iterative process requires careful consideration of each model's assumptions; errors can lead to inaccurate predictions with significant financial implications.

Effective market analysis combines theoretical frameworks with practical insights from experience and empirical evidence. As new data emerges and market conditions evolve, so must our modeling techniques—ensuring they remain relevant tools for navigating the ever-shifting landscape of global finance.

Implementing Strategies with Matrices

In the ever-evolving world of financial markets, using matrices to implement trading strategies offers a robust framework for managing complexity and optimizing decision-making. Central to this approach is the power of matrix algebra, which allows traders and analysts to efficiently process and analyze large datasets, ultimately leading to the development of sophisticated, data-driven strategies.

Matrices play a crucial role in organizing and structuring financial data, enabling seamless manipulation and transformation. Take this example, when a trader analyzes a portfolio with multiple assets, each having its own set of historical returns, organizing these returns into a matrix simplifies calculations. Operations such as summing columns for total returns or multiplying by weight vectors for overall portfolio performance become more streamlined and clear.

A prominent application of matrices is in portfolio optimization, particularly through mean-variance analysis. The covariance matrix is vital here as it captures variances and covariances between asset returns. This information helps traders construct portfolios that maximize expected return for a given level of risk. Efficient algorithms like quadratic programming rely on matrix computations to swiftly solve these optimization problems.

Beyond traditional portfolio management, matrices are essential in building factor models that break down asset returns into systematic components—like market movements or economic indicators—and idiosyncratic elements unique to each security. By formulating these models in matrix notation, analysts can gain insights into underlying risk factors driving performance and adjust portfolios accordingly.

In algorithmic trading, speed and precision are crucial. Strategies often depend on real-time data analysis powered by optimized matrix operations on advanced hardware architectures. High-frequency traders, for example, use singular value decomposition (SVD) on vast arrays of order book data to identify fleeting pricing opportunities that conventional methods might miss.

Statistical arbitrage is another area where matrices excel. This strategy exploits temporary price discrepancies between correlated securities. By representing historical price data in matrix form, traders apply techniques like principal component analysis (PCA) to detect patterns and predict reversion tendencies—capitalizing on mean-reverting behavior for profit.

Implementing these strategies requires not only mathematical expertise but also proficiency with technological tools capable of handling complex computations effortlessly. Python's SciPy library exemplifies such capabilities with its extensive support for linear algebra operations essential in this field. Additionally, Jupyter Notebooks provide an interactive platform for experimenting with models and visualizing results instantly—a valuable resource for refining strategies iteratively.

However, any quantitative approach demands caution regarding model assumptions; relying too heavily on historical correlations without considering regime shifts or structural changes can lead to costly mistakes. Rigorous stress testing under various market conditions is crucial for ensuring resilience across diverse scenarios—a necessary practice for crafting strategies that thrive amid uncertainty.

The ongoing evolution of financial markets calls for adaptive thinking; implementing strategies with matrices combines innovative methodology with practical application. This empowers practitioners to navigate complexities confidently while maintaining an edge over competitors who may not be as attuned to the nuances of quantitative finance.

The synergy between theory and practice highlights the transformative power of linear algebra in finance—pushing boundaries and setting new standards in strategic execution through its versatile applications across global markets today.

Pricing Financial Derivatives

Pricing financial derivatives is a complex task within quantitative finance, demanding both precision and speed. Central to this challenge is matrix theory, which simplifies and enhances the accuracy of derivative pricing.

The process often begins with modeling the underlying asset's price movements using stochastic processes like geometric Brownian motion. Matrices are crucial here, especially when simulating models over multiple time steps. They facilitate the computation of expected values and variances, key components in determining derivative prices. In this role, matrices serve as both guides and calculators, leading analysts through numerous possibilities with mathematical rigor.

The Black-Scholes model, a cornerstone in derivative pricing, greatly benefits from matrix algebra. When evaluating options with varying strike prices and maturities, matrices streamline calculations by efficiently managing the multidimensionality involved. This capability is essential for assessing entire portfolios rather than individual contracts, enabling traders to hedge positions and manage risk more effectively.

Matrix operations are also extensively used in finite difference methods for solving partial differential equations (PDEs). These methods transform the continuous price evolution of an asset into a system solvable by linear algebra techniques, with matrices forming the backbone of algorithms that approximate solutions to PDEs governing option pricing.

In modern quantitative finance, advanced techniques such as Monte Carlo simulations and binomial trees further illustrate the utility of matrices. These tools require large-scale computations to simulate numerous price paths or tree nodes efficiently. For example, parallel computing architectures leverage matrix operations to accelerate Monte Carlo simulations by distributing computations across multiple processors.

Incorporating machine learning into derivative pricing adds sophistication. Training models on historical data necessitates extensive manipulation of feature sets—tasks ideally suited for matrix algebra's ability to manage high-dimensional data. Neural networks often represent layers as matrices, ensuring efficient computation for timely model training and deployment.

Python libraries like NumPy and Pandas are indispensable for practitioners handling these complex tasks. They provide robust support for array-based computations, allowing swift execution of matrix operations integral to derivative pricing models. Visualization tools such as Matplotlib complement this by offering clear graphical representations of results, aiding interpretation and communication with stakeholders.

Accuracy in derivative pricing depends on validation against real market conditions. Backtesting strategies with historical data ensure models are robust against market fluctuations. Stress testing explores how extreme conditions affect derivative values—a crucial step in identifying vulnerabilities before they impact financial positions.

Amidst these technical challenges lies the need for creative thinking; novel approaches can lead to innovative solutions that redefine market standards. This interplay between analytical proficiency and strategic innovation highlights the transformative potential of linear algebra in finance—turning complexity into opportunity by integrating theory with practice.

As markets evolve, so must our methods for navigating them. The agility provided by matrix-based approaches places practitioners at the forefront of financial innovation, crafting solutions that not only meet current demands but also anticipate future trends with foresight and precision.

Matrix theory remains an essential tool for mastering financial derivatives—fueling advancements and inspiring new ways to conquer an ever-changing landscape with confidence and skill.

Hedge Fund Applications

Hedge funds, renowned for their aggressive strategies and intricate portfolios, heavily rely on matrix theory to boost returns while effectively managing risk. Central to this approach is the use of matrices to optimize portfolio allocation, balancing assets to achieve the highest expected return for a specified level of risk.

A pivotal tool in this process is the covariance matrix, which captures relationships between asset returns. By analyzing these relationships, hedge funds can create diversified portfolios that minimize risk. The covariance matrix underpins the calculation of critical metrics like portfolio variance and beta, essential for making informed investment decisions.

In addition to traditional optimization, hedge funds utilize advanced techniques such as principal component analysis (PCA) to condense high-dimensional data into its most crucial components. This method reduces noise and uncovers underlying factors that influence asset performance. PCA relies on eigenvalue decomposition, a fundamental concept in matrix algebra, with eigenvectors highlighting directions of maximum variance—a valuable insight for strategic asset allocation.

Risk management remains a top priority, necessitating robust stress-testing frameworks. Matrix algebra enables scenario analysis by swiftly recalculating potential losses under various market conditions. This predictive ability allows hedge funds to anticipate pitfalls and adjust strategies accordingly, safeguarding against unforeseen downturns.

Also, matrices enhance the execution of algorithmic trading strategies where speed and precision are vital. Trading algorithms often depend on real-time data feeds structured in matrix form, facilitating rapid calculations that inform buy or sell decisions within milliseconds. This high-frequency trading relies on robust computational frameworks supported by modern programming languages like Python and R.

For example, Python libraries such as NumPy allow for efficient handling of large datasets through vectorized operations, essential for quickly processing extensive financial data. R complements this with statistical tools tailored for financial analysis, empowering hedge fund analysts to conduct comprehensive evaluations confidently.

Matrix theory also significantly influences options pricing within hedge funds. Calculating Greeks—sensitivities that measure how options prices react to market changes —is frequently done using matrix-based models. These calculations inform dynamic hedging strategies that adjust positions based on real-time market fluctuations.

The incorporation of machine learning models into trading strategies further illustrates the versatility of matrices. Algorithms trained on historical data can detect patterns predictive of future price movements. In these models, matrices manage input features and weight vectors within neural networks, enabling the development and deployment of sophisticated models that learn from market behavior.

Matrix theory's adaptability equips hedge funds to navigate an ever-evolving financial landscape with agility and precision. By combining mathematical rigor with cutting-edge technology solutions, they maintain a competitive edge —transforming raw data into actionable insights that drive performance.

As markets grow increasingly complex, matrix algebra's role becomes ever more critical. Hedge fund managers equipped with these mathematical tools are better positioned to seize opportunities and mitigate risks effectively—leading the way in financial innovation while maintaining robust safeguards against volatility.

Through strategic applications of linear algebra principles, hedge funds not only enhance operational efficiency but also push the boundaries of quantitative finance—ushering in a new era where creativity meets computation on an unprecedented scale.

Algorithmic Trading and Matrices

Algorithmic trading, a cornerstone of modern finance, relies heavily on matrix theory to enhance the efficiency and speed of trading processes. The architecture of these systems is deeply interwoven with matrices, allowing for the rapid processing and analysis of vast datasets essential for executing trades at lightning speed.

Central to algorithmic trading is the need for real-time

data analysis, where each data point represents a potential opportunity or risk. Matrices structure this data to enable swift computations, empowering traders to execute strategies that react instantly to market changes—often within fractions of a second. Their ability to handle multiple inputs and outputs simultaneously makes matrices indispensable in high-frequency trading (HFT).

Consider a strategy focused on identifying arbitrage opportunities across different markets. Here, matrices model price discrepancies, with rows and columns representing various securities and time intervals. This setup quickly identifies exploitable mispricings, provided trades are executed rapidly enough to outpace competitors.

The integration of machine learning into algorithmic trading further highlights the utility of matrices. These models require large datasets, typically organized in matrix form, for training and prediction purposes. By analyzing historical patterns, machine learning models offer insights that drive decision-making processes. Within these frameworks, matrices manage input variables and model parameters, ensuring efficient computation during model training and inference.

Matrix decompositions like Singular Value Decomposition (SVD) help reduce dimensionality while retaining significant information. This technique compresses datasets without losing critical features—a crucial aspect when dealing with real-time processing constraints in trading systems.

Take this example, suppose we have a large dataset containing historical prices and volumes for numerous assets. SVD can decompose this dataset into principal components that capture the most significant patterns while discarding noise. This reduced representation enables faster computations and more robust predictions when deployed within an algorithmic strategy.

Python's NumPy library is commonly used due to its optimized operations on arrays and matrices. Vectorized operations allow traders to perform complex calculations with minimal latency—crucial for maintaining an edge in competitive markets. Similarly, R provides statistical functions that complement Python's capabilities, especially useful for developing models incorporating stochastic elements reflective of market uncertainties.

Risk management within algorithmic trading also benefits from matrix-based approaches. Scenario simulations use matrices to assess potential market conditions' impacts on portfolio performance. This predictive modeling ensures traders are well-prepared for various contingencies, allowing them to adjust strategies dynamically.

Incorporating algorithmic adjustments based on evolving market conditions is vital for success. Matrix algebra facilitates this adaptability by enabling quick recalculations and strategy modifications as new data emerges—a key requirement for staying competitive in volatile markets.

The seamless integration of matrices into algorithmic trading systems exemplifies their centrality in financial innovation. As technology advances and markets become more interconnected, efficiently processing large quantities of information will grow increasingly important. Traders equipped with matrix theory knowledge will find themselves at the forefront of this evolving landscape—leveraging mathematics as a fundamental component driving their strategic success.

To wrap things up, algorithmic trading's reliance on matrix algebra not only enhances operational efficiency but also unlocks new potential within quantitative finance. By harnessing these mathematical principles alongside technological advancements, traders continue to redefine possibilities—transforming raw data into strategic insights with unmatched precision and agility compared to traditional trading paradigms.

Optimization in Portfolio Theory

Optimization in portfolio theory is a key component of finance that utilizes linear algebra to maximize returns while effectively managing risk. Essentially, portfolio optimization aims to find the ideal combination of assets that achieves a balance between expected returns and risk, commonly assessed through variance or standard deviation.

The main challenge lies in solving the mean-variance optimization problem, which involves choosing asset weights to either minimize the portfolio's variance for a given expected return or maximize the expected return for a specified level of risk. This is mathematically framed as a quadratic programming problem, where matrices are integral.

Take this example, an investor looking to optimize a portfolio using historical return data relies on the covariance matrix. This matrix, which details the variance and covariances of asset returns, is crucial as it describes how asset prices move in relation to each other—information vital for diversification strategies aimed at minimizing risk without reducing returns.

In constructing an optimal portfolio, the investor seeks to minimize the quadratic form ($w^T w$), where (w) denotes the vector of asset weights and ( ) is the covariance matrix. The typical constraints include ($w^T e = 1$) (with (e) as a vector of ones, ensuring the sum of weights equals one) alongside other possible constraints based on investment policies or regulations.

Efficient matrix operations are pivotal in solving this optimization problem. Algorithms leverage matrix decompositions like Cholesky decomposition to expedite calculations by converting the covariance matrix into a simpler form. This efficiency is vital for institutional investors managing large portfolios.

Python libraries such as CVXPY provide powerful tools for these optimization tasks. CVXPY allows for setting up and solving mean-variance optimization with straightforward syntax. For example:

```python
import cvxpy as cp

import numpy as np


\#\# Define problem parameters

n_assets = 4

expected_returns = np.array([0.04, 0.06, 0.08, 0.10])

cov_matrix = np.array([[0.1, 0.02, 0.03, 0.04],

[0.02, 0.2, 0.05, 0.06],

[0.03, 0.05, 0.3, 0.07],

[0.04, 0.06, 0.07, 0.4]])


\#\# Define variables

w = cp.Variable(n_assets)


\#\# Define objective function

objective = cp.Minimize(cp.quad_form(w, cov_matrix))


\#\# Define constraints

constraints = [cp.sum(w) == 1,

w >= 0]
```

```
\#\# Formulate problem and solve

problem = cp.Problem(objective, constraints)

problem.solve()


optimal_weights = w.value
` ` `
```

The cp.quad_form(w, cov_matrix) efficiently calculates the necessary quadratic form for optimization using advanced matrix techniques.

Portfolio theory also addresses more complex scenarios involving constraints such as transaction costs or varying risk appetites over time—a context where matrices remain invaluable due to their ability to handle multi-dimensional data simultaneously.

Real-world applications extend beyond individual portfolios to encompass broader financial systems like mutual funds or pension plans, where managers must meet specific performance metrics while adhering to rigorous risk controls.

And, there is a shift towards multi-period optimization reflecting realistic investment horizons where decisions impact future opportunities and constraints adapt dynamically based on market conditions or changes in investor objectives.

Matrices also enable scenario analysis—essential for anticipating potential future market states under various assumptions about economic conditions or policy changes—and facilitate stress testing portfolios against extreme events.

Overall, linear algebra's role in portfolio theory highlights its significance in modern finance: enabling complex strategies that account for intricate interrelationships among assets while striving for optimal outcomes.

The advancement of computational tools further enhances these capabilities; traders and analysts can apply advanced mathematical techniques with unmatched ease and precision, pushing boundaries in pursuit of financial innovation and excellence across global markets. This mathematical rigor drives strategic asset allocation in their quest for superior returns and minimized risks.

Data Interpretation for Decision Making

Data interpretation is crucial for informed decision-making in finance, enabling quantitative analysts and traders to extract actionable insights from complex datasets. The ability to decipher and leverage this data effectively can differentiate successful strategies from missed opportunities.

Financial market data is multifaceted, covering price movements, trading volumes, economic indicators, and more. Analyzing such information requires not only mathematical skill but also a strategic understanding of market dynamics. Matrices are essential here, organizing large datasets into manageable structures that reveal patterns and correlations that might otherwise be hidden.

Take, for instance, analyzing historical stock returns to forecast future performance. A dataset might include multiple stocks over various time periods, forming a matrix where each row represents a different time point and each column corresponds to a different stock. This setup allows for efficient computation of statistical measures like mean returns or standard deviations, which are critical for risk assessment.

One key technique in data interpretation is Principal Component Analysis (PCA), which reduces dimensionality while preserving variance. This involves transforming the data matrix into a new coordinate system defined by principal components—eigenvectors linked to the largest eigenvalues of the covariance matrix. These components highlight the directions in which the data varies most, providing insights into the underlying factors driving market behavior.

For example, PCA can streamline portfolio construction by reducing thousands of potential asset choices to a few principal components that capture most of the variance. This approach helps identify key drivers without losing important information—a major advantage when dealing with high-dimensional datasets typical in finance.

Correlation matrices offer another valuable application by illustrating how asset prices move relative to one another. These matrices inform diversification strategies by identifying assets with low or negative correlations, minimizing unsystematic risk through strategic asset allocation.

Python libraries like pandas and NumPy make these processes more efficient. Consider the following example:

```python
```python

import numpy as np

import pandas as pd

from sklearn.decomposition import PCA


\#\# Sample data for stocks

data = pd.DataFrame(

'Stock A': [1.2, 1.5, 1.8],

'Stock B': [2.3, 2.6, 2.9],

'Stock C': [0.9, 1.0, 1.1]

)


\#\# Calculate correlation matrix
```
```

```
corr_matrix = data.corr()

\#\# Perform PCA
pca = PCA(n_components=2)
principal_components = pca.fit_transform(data)

\#\# Display principal components
print(principal_components)
` ` `
```

These tools facilitate calculations and enhance visualization through heatmaps or plots that succinctly convey complex data narratives.

Interpreting data goes beyond mere number-crunching; it requires critical thinking to contextualize findings within broader market trends or economic conditions. Analysts must consider questions such as: How do current geopolitical events influence these trends? What are the potential regulatory impacts on asset performance? Addressing these questions refines analytical outputs into practical insights that guide investment decisions and risk management strategies.

And, machine learning algorithms are increasingly integrated into data interpretation frameworks for predictive analytics— using historical patterns to forecast future events with greater accuracy than traditional models alone could achieve.

In the end, effective data interpretation combines technical skills with strategic foresight—transforming raw numbers into valuable intelligence that helps financial institutions navigate ever-evolving markets confidently and decisively.

This analytical prowess supports successful decision-making processes within trading desks and investment management firms worldwide—enabling them to remain agile amidst uncertainties while capitalizing on emerging opportunities for growth and profitability in competitive financial landscapes where precision is paramount.

Current Practices and Innovations

Quantitative analysts and traders use matrix operations to analyze large data sets, uncovering patterns that might otherwise remain hidden. This method streamlines decision-making processes and improves predictive accuracy. Take this example, by employing eigenvalue decomposition, professionals can identify principal components in extensive financial data sets, revealing underlying trends critical for strategic planning.

The rise of algorithmic trading has further propelled innovations in linear algebra usage. Algorithms built on these mathematical foundations enable high-frequency trading strategies that surpass human capabilities. Matrix multiplications are central to such algorithms, facilitating rapid calculations that adapt to real-time market conditions— a necessity for maintaining a competitive edge in fast-paced environments.

Additionally, risk management practices have been revolutionized by advancements in matrix theory. Techniques like Singular Value Decomposition (SVD) assess the stability of financial portfolios by isolating variables with significant impacts on variance. This lets you robust stress testing and scenario analysis, crucial for mitigating potential losses during volatile market periods.

Integrating machine learning with linear algebraic methods represents another innovation frontier. By using vector spaces and transformations, machine learning models can recognize complex patterns and predict market behaviors with increasing accuracy. This synergy is particularly evident in credit risk modeling, where predictive analytics assess borrower default probabilities based on historical data trends.

Practically, these innovations materialize through software platforms incorporating sophisticated mathematical algorithms into user-friendly interfaces for analysts and traders. Tools like Python's NumPy library or MATLAB provide pre-built functions that simplify complex calculations, democratizing access to advanced financial modeling techniques.

However, as technology advances, finance professionals must engage in continuous learning to fully exploit these tools' capabilities while contributing to their evolution. The collaborative nature of modern finance fosters ongoing dialogue between mathematicians, technologists, and market strategists, creating an environment where innovative ideas thrive.

Embracing current practices and innovations not only enhances efficiency but also paves the way for future breakthroughs in financial analysis and strategy formulation. This way, professionals position themselves at the cutting edge of a field where precision meets creativity—a dynamic intersection promising continued growth and opportunity within the ever-expanding world of finance.

CHAPTER 18: ADVANCED TOPICS IN MATRIX THEORY

Tensors and Multilinear Algebra

The exploration of tensors and multilinear algebra represents a significant advancement in financial mathematics, providing a robust framework for analyzing multi-dimensional data sets. As finance becomes more intertwined with data science, understanding tensors is crucial for managing complex datasets that go beyond the traditional two-dimensional matrix structure.

Tensors, essentially multi-dimensional arrays, offer a sophisticated method for representing data across various dimensions. While matrices are confined to rows and columns, tensors introduce additional axes, capturing more intricate relationships within data. This ability is particularly beneficial in finance, where datasets often encompass multiple variables across different time periods, sectors, and geographies.

Multilinear algebra facilitates operations on these tensors, enabling computations that reflect the high-dimensional nature of financial markets. Take this example, when assessing investment portfolios spanning numerous asset classes and regions over time, tensors efficiently encapsulate the dataset's complexity. This helps quantitative analysts to perform operations like tensor decomposition, breaking down data into core components for deeper analysis.

These techniques are especially valuable in risk management scenarios where correlations among various risk factors must be evaluated simultaneously. By leveraging tensor calculus, financial professionals can identify and model complex dependencies among variables—a crucial task when assessing systemic risks or conducting stress tests under varying market conditions.

Consider an analyst assessing the impact of macroeconomic indicators on a diversified portfolio. Tensors can accommodate data inputs like GDP growth rates across countries over several years while integrating sector-specific performance metrics. This comprehensive perspective allows for more accurate modeling and prediction of portfolio behavior under different economic conditions.

A practical application of this approach is seen in derivative pricing models, where multidimensional factors such as interest rates, currency exchange rates, and underlying asset volatilities influence pricing strategies. Tensor-based algorithms enable financial engineers to simulate complex scenarios and compute derivative values with greater precision than traditional models.

Software tools have evolved to support tensor calculations, with libraries like TensorFlow or PyTorch offering powerful functionalities for implementing tensor operations within financial models. These platforms not only streamline computations but also provide scalable solutions to handle large volumes of data efficiently—essential for firms involved in high-frequency trading or managing extensive portfolios.

As financial markets become more complex and interconnected, mastery over tensors and multilinear algebra will become increasingly important. Analysts with this expertise can fully harness their data resources, delivering deeper insights and crafting strategies that leverage every available dimension of information. This approach embraces innovation and complexity as pathways to uncover new opportunities within global markets.

High-Dimensional Data Analysis

High-dimensional data analysis has become a cornerstone of modern financial strategies due to the explosion of available data and the intricate nature of financial systems. Traditional methods, which often rely on two-dimensional datasets, struggle to capture the complexities of today's financial landscapes. High-dimensional data analysis addresses this challenge by offering tools capable of handling and interpreting extensive datasets with multiple variables.

A significant advantage of high-dimensional data analysis is its ability to reveal patterns that remain hidden in lower-dimensional frameworks. For example, a trader aiming to understand the interactions between economic indicators, stock performances, and geopolitical events would find traditional two-dimensional analysis limiting. In contrast, high-dimensional techniques allow for simultaneous examination of these factors, uncovering intricate relationships that lead to more robust trading strategies.

These complex interconnections are often explored through dimensionality reduction techniques like principal component analysis (PCA) and more advanced methods such as t-distributed stochastic neighbor embedding (t-SNE). PCA simplifies datasets by reducing dimensions while preserving variance, enabling analysts to concentrate on the most critical factors affecting their models. This approach is particularly valuable when dealing with large datasets, where excessive information can obscure key insights.

In practice, dimensionality reduction not only streamlines data but also boosts computational efficiency. Financial institutions frequently manage vast amounts of real-time data, so reducing dimensionality without significant information loss accelerates computations and facilitates quicker decision-making. This efficiency is crucial in environments like algorithmic trading, where milliseconds can mean the difference between profit and loss.

The application of high-dimensional data analysis goes beyond trading into areas such as risk assessment and portfolio optimization. By capturing the multidimensional nature of risk factors—such as credit ratings, interest rates, and market volatility—analysts can build comprehensive risk models that accurately reflect market dynamics. These models are essential for stress testing and scenario analysis, helping prepare for potential market shifts by understanding variable interactions under various conditions.

And, high-dimensional tools enhance machine learning algorithms used in predictive analytics. Techniques capable of managing multiple inputs effectively improve model predictions on asset returns or economic trends by considering a broader array of influencing factors. This capability is transformative for quantitative analysts who rely on precise forecasts to craft strategies that maximize returns while mitigating risks.

As technology advances, so do the tools for handling high-dimensional datasets. Software like R and Python offers libraries specifically designed for processing complex data structures efficiently. These libraries enable the implementation of high-dimensional analytics in financial modeling, ensuring analysts remain at the forefront of innovation and insight.

Mastering high-dimensional data analysis distinguishes

successful financial practitioners from their peers. In an industry driven by data and speed, these techniques empower professionals to extract maximum value from their analyses—leading to smarter investment decisions and paving the way for strategic growth opportunities in competitive markets.

In the end, each aspect of high-dimensional data analysis contributes to a deeper understanding of financial complexities, introducing new methodologies that reshape how markets are navigated and understood worldwide.

Financial Applications and Implications

The financial sector has experienced a significant transformation through the integration of high-dimensional data analysis. This advancement has not only improved existing methodologies but also created new opportunities for exploration and innovation in financial applications. A key area where high-dimensional data proves invaluable is in constructing and analyzing complex financial models, which are essential for accurately understanding and predicting market behavior.

Take, for example, the challenge of modeling credit risk. Traditional models often struggle to incorporate the myriad variables influencing creditworthiness, such as borrower income, employment status, economic conditions, and even global geopolitical events. High-dimensional data techniques enable analysts to seamlessly integrate these diverse datasets, allowing for a more nuanced risk assessment that considers multiple influences simultaneously. By utilizing these advanced models, institutions can better anticipate defaults and adjust their lending strategies accordingly, thereby minimizing potential losses.

In portfolio management, high-dimensional data analysis supports the development of multi-factor investment strategies that account for a wide range of asset characteristics. This approach allows portfolio managers to optimize asset allocation by considering correlations and interactions among factors like market size, liquidity, momentum, and volatility. Modeling these relationships comprehensively enhances diversification strategies, mitigating risks while maximizing returns—essentially aligning portfolios more closely with investor objectives.

Derivatives pricing is another domain where high-dimensional analytics play a crucial role. Derivative instruments are inherently complex due to their dependence on multiple underlying assets and factors. Pricing options, for instance, requires considering not only the price movements of the underlying asset but also variables like interest rates, time decay (theta), volatility (vega), and others. High-dimensional techniques provide a framework for accurately and efficiently incorporating these elements into valuation models.

In algorithmic trading strategies, speed and precision are paramount. High-frequency trading systems rely on high-dimensional data analysis to leverage real-time data streams from multiple sources and execute trades within microseconds. These systems use complex algorithms to detect patterns or anomalies across vast datasets—a task made feasible by computational power enabled by dimensionality reduction methods like PCA or machine learning algorithms refined through extensive datasets.

Beyond trading and risk management, regulatory compliance significantly benefits from high-dimensional analytics. Financial institutions face rigorous regulatory requirements that necessitate comprehensive reporting and transparency across all operations. Advanced analytics can automate parts of this process by sifting through enormous volumes of transaction data to identify discrepancies or compliance breaches effectively—ensuring institutions meet regulatory standards while reducing manual oversight costs.

Also, the implications of high-dimensional data extend to predictive modeling for macroeconomic trends. By analyzing comprehensive datasets that encompass everything from consumer spending patterns to industrial production metrics, financial analysts can forecast economic conditions with greater accuracy—providing invaluable insights into future market dynamics that inform investment decisions at both micro and macro levels.

As financial professionals adopt these sophisticated tools, they become better equipped to navigate the complexities of modern markets confidently. High-dimensional data analysis not only enhances traditional practices but transforms them entirely—ushering in an era where informed decision-making is driven by deep analytical insights rather than mere speculation.

This evolution highlights a broader trend within finance: an industry increasingly defined by its ability to harness data's full potential for strategic advantage. As practitioners continue exploring these capabilities further, they stand at the forefront of an ever-evolving landscape—ready to leverage their understanding into tangible successes that redefine financial excellence globally.

Nonlinear Matrix Usage

The use of nonlinear matrices in finance adds a layer of complexity that mirrors the intricate nature of financial markets. While traditional linear models have been effective for many applications, they often fall short in capturing the unpredictable and multifaceted behaviors observed in real-world financial systems. Nonlinear matrices offer a powerful alternative, enabling analysts to delve deeper into these complexities with greater precision and adaptability.

Take, for instance, the modeling of interest rate movements —a classic scenario where nonlinear matrices are invaluable. Interest rates are influenced by various factors, including central bank policies, inflation expectations, and global economic conditions. These factors interact in nonlinear ways, making it challenging for linear models to provide accurate forecasts. By employing nonlinear matrix approaches, such as polynomial or exponential transformations, analysts can capture these interactions more effectively. This leads to more accurate modeling of interest rate changes and better-informed decisions regarding interest rate swaps and related instruments.

In asset pricing, nonlinear matrices play a crucial role in reflecting the true dynamics of market behaviors. Markets often experience sudden shifts due to investor sentiment or geopolitical events, causing asset prices to deviate from predicted trends. Incorporating nonlinear elements into pricing models—using techniques like logistic regression or neural networks—allows analysts to accommodate these abrupt changes more robustly. This capability aids in accurately valuing assets under volatile market conditions, thereby reducing risk exposure.

Risk management strategies also greatly benefit from nonlinear matrix usage. For example, assessing credit default risks across a diverse portfolio of loans involves numerous variables, such as borrower credit scores, loan-to-value ratios, and economic downturns. A nonlinear approach can integrate these disparate variables through techniques like support vector machines or kernel methods. This integration provides a more holistic view of credit risk profiles and supports the development of strategies that better mitigate potential losses.

In portfolio optimization, nonlinear matrices facilitate the exploration of complex landscapes where traditional linear models might struggle. Real-world constraints like transaction costs, tax considerations, and regulatory requirements introduce nonlinearities that must be accounted for in optimization processes. Techniques such as quadratic programming or dynamic optimization using nonlinear matrices help portfolio managers find solutions that align with both investor goals and market realities.

Algorithmic trading strategies also leverage nonlinear matrices to enhance performance in rapidly changing environments. High-frequency trading algorithms utilize complex models capable of identifying patterns within noisy data—patterns that linear approaches might miss. Nonlinear matrix methods like recursive neural networks or deep learning architectures allow these algorithms to swiftly adapt to new information, ensuring trades are executed at optimal moments.

Beyond traditional applications, nonlinear matrices are pivotal in emerging areas like machine learning and artificial intelligence within finance. Predictive models built on nonlinear frameworks can uncover latent variables driving market movements, offering unprecedented insights into future trends. By harnessing these capabilities, financial institutions can anticipate market shifts and develop innovative products and services tailored to evolving client needs.

The adoption of nonlinear matrices marks a significant shift in financial analysis—characterized by increased accuracy and adaptability across diverse contexts. As analysts become more proficient with these tools, they unlock opportunities for deeper insights and strategic advantages that were previously unattainable with linear methods alone.

In the end, embracing nonlinear matrix techniques represents an evolution towards a more nuanced understanding of financial phenomena—a step forward in an industry where precision and foresight define success. As financial professionals refine their mastery of these methods, they will be better equipped to navigate the complexities of modern finance with greater confidence and competence than ever before.

Advances in Algorithm Design

In recent years, advances in algorithm design have significantly transformed financial analysis, equipping analysts and traders with sophisticated tools to navigate the complexities of modern markets. These advancements are not just about optimizing existing processes; they represent a fundamental shift in how financial data is approached, analyzed, and utilized.

A major development in this field is the integration of machine learning algorithms into financial models. Machine learning excels at recognizing patterns in vast datasets that would be unmanageable through traditional methods. By employing algorithms like decision trees or ensemble methods, analysts can uncover hidden trends and correlations that inform investment strategies. These models continuously learn from new data, adapting to market changes and enhancing predictive accuracy over time.

Deep learning techniques have also been transformative. Deep neural networks, with their ability to model complex nonlinear relationships, have opened new avenues for analyzing unstructured data such as news articles and social media sentiment. This capability is crucial in a world where market movements are often swayed by qualitative factors not captured by numerical data alone. Convolutional neural networks (CNNs) for image data analysis and recurrent neural networks (RNNs) for sequential data like time series forecasts further demonstrate how these technologies are reshaping financial analytics.

And, optimization algorithms have evolved to incorporate stochastic elements, better handling the inherent uncertainty of financial markets. Genetic algorithms and particle swarm optimization, inspired by natural processes, efficiently explore potential solutions. These algorithms excel in complex scenarios with multiple objectives or constraints—common in portfolio optimization or derivative pricing.

Algorithmic trading has seen immense benefits from advancements in high-frequency trading (HFT) technology. Designing low-latency algorithms capable of executing trades within microseconds relies on state-of-the-art techniques involving predictive modeling and real-time data processing. In this context, latency optimization is as crucial as model accuracy, driving the development of specialized hardware and software solutions for competitive advantages.

On another frontier, quantum computing promises revolutionary changes in algorithm design with significant implications for finance. Quantum algorithms offer exponential speed-ups for specific problems like portfolio optimization or option pricing through techniques such as Grover's search or quantum annealing. Although still nascent, quantum computing's potential to revolutionize computational finance is a focus of intense research interest.

Beyond sheer computational power, recent advances emphasize interpretability and transparency—essential when deploying models within regulatory frameworks or communicating insights to stakeholders. Explainable AI (XAI) initiatives aim to make machine learning models more transparent by providing clear rationales behind their predictions. This supports trust among users wary of black-box approaches while ensuring compliance with increasingly stringent regulatory standards.

These technological strides create an environment where financial professionals must continually adapt and expand their skill sets. Understanding advanced algorithmic frameworks is essential not only for generating alpha but also for risk management and strategic planning across various domains—from asset management to corporate finance.

In the end, these innovations redefine existing capabilities entirely. As we harness the power of cutting-edge algorithms across all facets of finance—from trading strategies to investment decisions—we move towards unprecedented levels of efficiency and insight within our industry's ever-evolving landscape.

Machine Learning Techniques

Machine learning techniques have become integral to the financial ecosystem, transforming how data is interpreted and decisions are made. Unlike traditional statistical methods that rely on predefined assumptions, machine learning offers flexibility by learning directly from data patterns. This adaptability is especially valuable in the dynamic financial markets where conditions change rapidly.

Central to machine learning's impact on finance are supervised learning algorithms, such as regression and classification models. These algorithms use historical data with known outcomes to train models that predict future events. Take this example, regression models forecast continuous variables like stock prices or economic indicators. A linear regression model might analyze historical market data to predict future price movements based on identified trends. Classification algorithms categorize data into distinct classes and are used for tasks like credit scoring or fraud detection.

Unsupervised learning techniques also play a crucial role by identifying patterns without labeled outcomes. Clustering algorithms, such as K-means, can segment customers into distinct groups based on behaviors or financial profiles, aiding personalized marketing strategies and risk assessments. Dimensionality reduction techniques like principal component analysis (PCA) simplify complex datasets by reducing variables while preserving essential information, which is crucial for visualizing high-dimensional financial data.

Reinforcement learning adds another layer of sophistication

by framing decision-making as a series of actions taken to maximize cumulative reward. In trading contexts, reinforcement learning agents can develop strategies that adaptively respond to market conditions, learning from interactions with the environment to optimize trading performance over time.

Neural networks extend machine learning's capabilities into deep learning domains, where complex structures mimic human brain functions to identify sophisticated patterns in large datasets. Deep neural networks (DNNs) have been applied effectively in algorithmic trading and sentiment analysis, capturing intricate relationships within unstructured data such as news feeds.

In combination with deep learning frameworks, natural language processing (NLP) enables financial institutions to extract insights from textual sources like earnings call transcripts or social media posts. Sentiment analysis using NLP tools helps gauge market sentiment by assessing investor mood and its potential impact on asset prices.

Ensemble methods are another powerful strategy within machine learning toolkits used in finance. By combining predictions from multiple models, techniques like bagging (e.g., random forests) or boosting (e.g., AdaBoost) improve accuracy and robustness across diverse applications, including risk assessment models and algorithmic trading systems.

Transfer learning has emerged as a promising approach where knowledge gained while solving one problem is applied to related problems—beneficial when dealing with limited labeled datasets common in niche financial sectors.

The increasing availability of big data and advances in computational power continue to push machine learning frontiers forward in finance. This progress enables more precise predictions under uncertainty and efficient resource allocation across portfolios while seamlessly adapting to evolving market landscapes through intelligent automation. These cutting-edge technologies are reshaping industry paradigms, moving beyond traditional boundaries and transforming future horizons in ways previously unimaginable.

Innovations in Financial Technology

Financial technology, or fintech, has become a powerful catalyst for innovation within the financial industry, ushering in not just updates but a fundamental transformation in how financial services are conceived, delivered, and consumed. A key player in this revolution is blockchain technology, which underlies cryptocurrencies and offers the potential for secure, transparent transactions without the need for traditional intermediaries. Its decentralized ledger system creates an immutable record of transactions, establishing trust in environments where verification is crucial.

Alongside blockchain, artificial intelligence (AI) is rapidly advancing within fintech applications. AI algorithms enhance customer service through chatbots that provide real-time support and personalized advice. These systems continuously learn from user interactions, evolving to offer increasingly relevant assistance and thereby boosting customer satisfaction and operational efficiency.

Big data analytics has also revolutionized risk management and compliance in financial institutions. With vast amounts of data generated daily, banks and trading firms leverage analytics to detect fraud patterns, assess credit risk with greater accuracy, and ensure regulatory compliance with precision. Predictive models analyze historical data to forecast future trends, enabling proactive strategies that mitigate risks before they arise.

Mobile banking represents another significant frontier of fintech innovation, democratizing access to financial services worldwide. As smartphones become ubiquitous, users can manage their finances on-the-go—transferring funds, paying bills, or investing with just a few taps. This ease of access accelerates financial inclusion by reaching previously underserved populations.

Cloud computing further empowers fintech by providing scalable solutions that reduce costs and enhance flexibility. Financial institutions can rapidly deploy applications without the constraints of physical infrastructure, allowing for swift adaptation to market changes and facilitating collaboration across geographical boundaries.

Digital payment platforms exemplify fintech's transformative power in everyday transactions. Companies like PayPal and Square have reshaped commerce by offering seamless online payment solutions that bypass traditional banking systems, making peer-to-peer transfers effortless and secure.

Biometric authentication technologies are bolstering security measures in digital finance environments. Fingerprint scanning, facial recognition, and voice identification safeguard against unauthorized access while streamlining user experiences by eliminating cumbersome password requirements.

Robo-advisors have disrupted wealth management by providing automated portfolio management services tailored to individual investor preferences and risk tolerances. These platforms offer cost-effective alternatives to traditional advisors while delivering data-driven insights that optimize investment strategies.

Crowdfunding platforms like Kickstarter and Indiegogo demonstrate how fintech enables new business models by connecting entrepreneurs directly with potential investors or customers. This direct engagement fosters innovation by removing barriers typically associated with venture capital or bank loans.

Lastly, open banking initiatives herald a new era of

transparency and competition within the financial sector. By granting third-party developers access to bank data (with user consent), open banking encourages the creation of innovative apps that enhance consumers' financial decision-making.

Collectively, these technological advancements illustrate how fintech continues to redefine global financial landscapes —reshaping consumer expectations, fostering inclusivity, enhancing security measures, and driving unprecedented efficiencies across sectors. As these innovations evolve, they will undoubtedly continue to challenge traditional paradigms while unlocking new potentials within the ever-expanding universe of finance.

Challenges and Frontiers in Research

As the financial industry evolves, researchers encounter a variety of challenges and opportunities that expand the limits of possibility. The integration of cutting-edge technologies with traditional financial systems presents unique hurdles, each requiring innovative solutions. A major concern in this arena is cybersecurity. With the expansion of fintech, the risks associated with digital transactions increase, making the protection of sensitive data from sophisticated cyber threats crucial. This demands constant vigilance and the development of robust encryption methods.

Another challenge is the sheer volume and velocity of data. Big data analytics can reveal deep insights, but it requires advanced processing capabilities to handle complex datasets efficiently. The pursuit of speed and accuracy in analyzing high-frequency trading data or extensive sets of consumer behavior information necessitates continual advancements in both hardware and algorithms.

Additionally, as artificial intelligence becomes more integral to financial decision-making, issues of algorithmic transparency and bias emerge. Ensuring AI-driven decisions are fair and unbiased is essential for maintaining trust and compliance within regulatory frameworks. Addressing this requires not only technical solutions but also ethical considerations in algorithm design and implementation.

Quantum computing offers transformative potential for financial modeling and risk analysis. Although still in its early stages, its ability to process information exponentially faster than classical computers could revolutionize complex computations such as portfolio optimization or derivatives pricing. However, realizing this potential involves overcoming significant technical barriers related to stability and error rates in quantum systems.

In parallel, decentralized finance (DeFi) challenges traditional banking by using blockchain technology to create open, permissionless financial services without intermediaries. While DeFi promises inclusivity and innovation, it also raises regulatory challenges and security concerns that require attention from researchers and policymakers.

As these challenges grow more complex, collaboration across disciplines becomes increasingly important. Financial experts must work alongside computer scientists, ethicists, policymakers, and other stakeholders to develop holistic solutions that are technically sound and socially responsible.

Adding another layer of complexity is the ever-changing landscape of regulation. As new technologies emerge, regulators strive to keep pace by adapting existing rules or crafting new ones—making staying informed about legal requirements as crucial as technological expertise.

And, climate change introduces both risks and opportunities in finance, prompting researchers to develop models that incorporate environmental factors into investment strategies. This area presents significant challenges regarding data availability and model complexity but offers potential for meaningful contributions toward sustainable finance practices.

These challenges highlight a fundamental truth: innovation in financial research goes beyond problem-solving; it's about redefining possibilities in finance. As these frontiers are explored, they will shape the future landscape—where interdisciplinary collaboration fuels breakthroughs that enhance both economic vitality and societal well-being.

CHAPTER 19:
CASE STUDIES
AND PRACTICAL
FINANCIAL MODELS

Real-World Financial Systems

The financial landscape is a dynamic ecosystem, serving as the heartbeat of global commerce. This intricate web encompasses everything from stock exchanges to banking networks, illustrating a complex interplay of transactions, regulations, and technologies. Central to these systems is data—vast and continuously expanding—holding immense potential for those equipped with the right analytical tools.

Grasping the intricacies of real-world financial systems begins with understanding their components and interactions. Take stock markets, for example; they are not merely venues for buying and selling shares. Instead, they function as sophisticated networks of trading strategies, investor behaviors, and regulatory frameworks. Each trade is guided by algorithms that process immense volumes of information in real time, where speed and accuracy are crucial.

Simultaneously, banking systems offer a range of services such as lending, investment, and risk management. The digitization of these services has ushered in unprecedented levels of connectivity and efficiency. Modern banks now rely heavily on advanced algorithms to assess creditworthiness, predict market trends, and optimize asset allocations. These algorithms often employ linear algebraic models to swiftly handle complex datasets.

Consider matrix computations in risk assessment as a practical example of this complexity. When evaluating loan portfolios, banks use matrices to model relationships between different assets. Analyzing these matrices helps determine correlations between asset performances and identify potential risks within the portfolio, enabling strategies that minimize exposure while maximizing returns.

The insurance sector provides another illustration. Actuarial models depend on precise statistical methods to predict future events based on historical data. Linear regression models are frequently used to analyze trends and forecast outcomes such as claim amounts or policyholder behaviors. Matrix operations play a crucial role in handling the large data arrays necessary for accurate modeling.

And, financial systems are deeply intertwined with global economic conditions. Factors like geopolitical events, economic policies, and technological advancements can significantly influence market dynamics. Analysts must stay vigilant, continually integrating new data into their models to accurately reflect these changes.

A particularly fascinating aspect of financial systems is their adaptive nature. As conditions evolve, so do market participants' strategies. During periods of market volatility, traders might adjust their algorithms to exploit short-term price fluctuations through high-frequency trading (HFT), which relies on sophisticated mathematical models capable of executing trades within microseconds.

As we delve deeper into these systems, it's essential to appreciate the synergy between theoretical concepts and practical applications. Linear algebra acts as a bridge between abstract mathematical ideas and tangible financial strategies. By mastering these techniques, analysts can decode financial market complexities and devise innovative solutions that drive success in a competitive landscape.

This exploration into real-world financial systems highlights the importance of continuous learning and adaptation in finance—a field characterized by constant change and abundant opportunities for those ready to harness mathematics and technology to shape the future.

Solving Large-Scale Finance Problems

In the rapidly evolving landscape of finance, large-scale challenges often resemble intricate puzzles that require more than just intuition to solve. These issues are multidimensional, involving vast datasets and complex mathematical models. Successfully addressing them necessitates a combination of computational skill and theoretical insight, particularly through the framework of linear algebra.

Imagine you're tasked with optimizing an extensive investment portfolio spread across global markets. The goal is to maximize returns while minimizing risk—a classic yet daunting problem due to its sheer scale. Here, linear algebra becomes essential. Matrices provide a compact means to represent relationships among thousands of assets, each with its own historical performance metrics and projected future values.

Covariance matrices, for example, capture the variance and covariance of asset returns, offering critical insights into how different assets move in relation to one another. By manipulating these matrices, analysts can identify asset combinations that yield favorable risk-return profiles. The eigenvectors of these matrices reveal principal directions—combinations of assets with significant variance—guiding strategies that balance volatility and growth potential.

Algorithmically, tackling such large-scale optimization problems often involves techniques like matrix factorization or decomposition. LU decomposition, for instance, simplifies complex matrix equations, allowing efficient computation even when dealing with enormous data volumes. This technique breaks down problems into manageable components, streamlining decision-making.

Beyond portfolio management, large-scale challenges are prevalent in areas like risk management and regulatory compliance. Financial institutions must navigate an increasingly stringent regulatory environment while managing risk exposure across multiple dimensions. Linear programming models optimize risk allocations by processing vast datasets representing diverse risk factors and regulatory constraints.

Data visualization tools further enhance these efforts by converting raw numbers into coherent visual narratives that aid decision-making. Consider heat maps derived from matrix data: they visually depict correlations or other critical metrics across asset classes or sectors, highlighting potential investment opportunities or risks that might otherwise remain hidden.

In high-frequency trading (HFT), speed is crucial; trades must be executed in milliseconds based on real-time data from global exchanges. Advanced algorithms powered by matrix operations process this data at lightning speed, identifying patterns or arbitrage opportunities invisible to the human eye.

These endeavors highlight not only computational techniques but also the strategic application of linear algebraic principles.

As finance evolves alongside technological advancements and market shifts, those adept at solving large-scale problems will remain at the forefront, pioneering innovative solutions that redefine possibilities in financial analytics.

Through this intricate interplay between theory and application, we uncover the true power of mathematics in finance—transforming abstract concepts into actionable insights that drive strategic decisions and foster competitive advantage in the global marketplace.

Customized Financial Solutions

Customized financial solutions are essential in a world where one-size-fits-all approaches often fall short. The complex nature of financial challenges requires tailored strategies that address specific client needs, operational hurdles, and market conditions. Linear algebra and matrix theory provide a framework for creating these bespoke solutions with precision and adaptability.

Imagine a financial advisor tasked with developing a personalized investment strategy for a high-net-worth individual. The client's portfolio must mirror their unique risk tolerance, investment goals, and time horizon. Here, matrices are invaluable, modeling diverse asset classes and their historical returns to simulate various allocation strategies.

Through matrix operations such as multiplication and addition, advisors can forecast portfolio performance under different economic scenarios. By adjusting variables like expected returns or volatility, they can visualize outcomes and optimize allocations to meet the client's objectives. This iterative process refines the strategy until it aligns perfectly with the desired criteria.

In corporate finance, businesses often face complex capital budgeting decisions requiring customized approaches. Linear programming techniques help managers determine optimal investment levels across multiple projects while considering constraints like budget limits or resource availability. Matrices efficiently represent these constraints and objectives, facilitating effective problem-solving.

Consider merger and acquisition (M&A) analysis. Companies contemplating acquisitions need detailed insights into potential synergies and risks associated with target firms. By using matrices to compile data on financial metrics—such as revenue growth rates, profit margins, and debt levels—analysts can evaluate different post-acquisition scenarios. This quantitative analysis aids in crafting offers that maximize shareholder value while minimizing integration risks.

Derivatives trading is another area where customization flourishes through mathematics. Traders design complex instruments like options or futures contracts tailored to hedge against specific market risks or capitalize on anticipated asset price movements. Matrices simplify these designs by representing payoff structures and calculating potential gains or losses under various conditions.

In wealth management for institutional clients such as pension funds or insurance companies, customization extends beyond simple asset allocation models to encompass liability-driven investment strategies (LDI). These strategies align assets with future liabilities—a complex task managed through matrix-based models that project cash flows over time, adjusting for inflation or interest rate changes.

The flexibility afforded by linear algebra allows for dynamic adjustments as market conditions evolve or client preferences change. This agility is crucial in today's fast-paced financial environment where static solutions quickly become obsolete.

In the end, crafting customized financial solutions requires more than technical skill; it demands a deep understanding of client needs combined with innovative applications of mathematical principles. Through the careful synthesis of data analysis, strategic thinking, and mathematical rigor facilitated by linear algebraic methods, advisors can deliver solutions that exceed expectations—building lasting relationships founded on trust and success.

This blend of personalization and precision highlights the transformative impact of linear algebra in crafting bespoke financial strategies—enhancing decision-making effectiveness and providing a competitive advantage across the financial industry landscape.

Portfolio Management Techniques

Portfolio management is a vital component of finance where data analysis, strategic insight, and mathematical modeling converge. Linear algebra equips portfolio managers with the tools they need to navigate complex investment landscapes and make informed decisions that align with market dynamics and client objectives.

At the heart of portfolio construction is the creation of an optimal mix of assets to maximize returns while minimizing risk, a process heavily reliant on matrix operations. Managers use matrices to represent correlations between different asset classes, capturing their historical price movements and relationships. This lets you efficient calculation of portfolio variance and expected returns.

A fundamental technique in this process is the Markowitz Efficient Frontier model, which uses matrix algebra to identify portfolios offering the highest expected return for a given level of risk. By organizing asset returns into a covariance matrix, managers apply quadratic programming methods to determine the weights that define these efficient portfolios. The resulting curve visually represents the trade-off between risk and return, guiding allocation decisions.

Adding constraints such as sector exposure limits or ethical considerations introduces complexity but also customization opportunities. Linear algebraic methods can handle these additional constraints seamlessly, modifying the optimization process while keeping overall goals in focus.

Risk management within portfolios also benefits from linear algebra. Stress testing scenarios often require simulating market shocks across asset classes—a task simplified through matrix multiplication. By adjusting variables like interest rates or inflation rates within these models, managers can predict impacts on portfolio value under adverse conditions and devise strategies to mitigate potential losses.

Performance attribution is another area where matrices are invaluable. By breaking down portfolio returns into components attributable to asset allocation, security selection, and other factors, managers can identify strengths and weaknesses in their strategies. This detailed analysis informs future adjustments and enhances overall performance.

For active management strategies that involve frequent rebalancing, linear algebra offers computational efficiency. Calculating optimal rebalancing paths involves solving systems of equations quickly—a task well-suited to matrix operations. This agility ensures that portfolios remain aligned with target allocations despite market fluctuations or cash flows.

And, incorporating alternative investments like hedge funds or private equity into portfolios requires sophisticated modeling techniques facilitated by matrices. These assets often have unique risk-return profiles not easily captured by traditional models; however, linear algebra provides a robust framework for analyzing such diverse investment vehicles.

The emergence of machine learning in finance introduces additional dimensions to portfolio management techniques. Algorithms utilizing neural networks or decision trees rely heavily on matrix computations for data processing— enabling insights into patterns that may elude conventional analysis methods.

At its core, successful portfolio management depends on combining mathematical sophistication with strategic acumen. Linear algebra not only empowers managers with tools for precise calculation but also fosters creativity in designing adaptive strategies responsive to an ever-changing financial landscape. This integration of quantitative rigor with qualitative insight underscores the power of linear algebra in enhancing portfolio management practices, enabling investors to achieve superior outcomes through informed decision-making grounded in mathematical excellence.

Strategic Trading Applications

Strategic trading applications of linear algebra and matrix theory are fundamental to modern financial decision-making, providing tools that enhance the precision and efficiency of complex trading strategies. For a trader assessing a diverse set of financial instruments, the sheer volume of data can be daunting. However, matrices simplify this complexity by organizing and manipulating large datasets, transforming raw data into actionable insights.

One key application is portfolio optimization, where matrix theory plays a crucial role. Using matrix algebra, traders can analyze risk versus return profiles for various asset combinations, efficiently identifying portfolios that maximize expected returns at a given risk level. This involves constructing covariance matrices to assess how asset returns correlate—an essential step in minimizing portfolio variance while maximizing gains.

Take this example, consider constructing a covariance matrix using historical returns data from stocks A, B, and C. Each element of this matrix indicates the covariance between two stocks, offering insights into their relative movements over time. With tools like Excel or programming languages such as Python, traders can easily calculate these matrices. Here's an example in Python:

```python
import numpy as np

\#\# Assume historical returns data
returns = np.array([[0.05, 0.02, 0.01], [0.04, 0.03, 0.02], [0.06, 0.01, 0.03]])

\#\# Compute covariance matrix
covariance_matrix = np.cov(returns.T)
print(covariance_matrix)
```

This snippet illustrates how linear algebra simplifies calculation processes in environments where speed and accuracy are paramount.

Beyond portfolio management, eigenvalues and eigenvectors are pivotal in quantitative trading strategies, particularly in principal component analysis (PCA). PCA reduces the dimensionality of large datasets while preserving essential variability trends, thereby highlighting dominant patterns that may influence trading decisions.

By employing PCA to analyze market sentiment across different sectors, traders can identify underlying factors driving collective price movements—these factors are represented by eigenvectors. Focusing on these components rather than individual asset noise during volatile periods provides strategists with robust market insights—a feat challenging without these mathematical frameworks.

And, arbitrage opportunities emerge through strategic applications of singular value decomposition (SVD). Decomposing price matrices via SVD enables traders to identify mispriced securities and anticipate corrections by leveraging theoretical fair values derived from decomposed structures.

Imagine a pricing matrix composed of prices from various intervals across multiple exchanges; SVD highlights discrepancies between actual traded values and inferred ones after eliminating anomalies identified through singular vectors corresponding to relevant price patterns. This leads to profitable arbitrage setups minus the conventional risks associated with manual identification methods.

The synergy between theoretical applications and algorithmic executions enhances trading significantly. It's not just about crunching numbers but crafting algorithms that respond in real-time to varying market conditions and adapt consistently through iterative learning processes informed by each cycle's outputs.

As technology evolves faster than ever before, we continue to push boundaries and extract maximum value from existing systems using cutting-edge innovations. This ongoing evolution ensures success stories throughout the global financial landscape and decisively shapes the future of markets, now more accessible than ever at our fingertips.

Success Stories in Finance

Success stories in finance often showcase the transformative power of linear algebra and matrix theory, illustrating how these mathematical tools can reshape the financial landscape. A prime example is a hedge fund that successfully turned its fortunes around by optimizing trading strategies through matrix algebra. Initially struggling with volatile returns and inefficiencies, the fund adopted matrix techniques to refine its approach.

The journey began with the implementation of matrix-based risk assessment models, which meticulously evaluated portfolio compositions. By constructing and analyzing covariance matrices, the fund gained a clearer understanding of interdependencies among assets, reducing overall exposure to market fluctuations. This analytical insight was invaluable, enabling precise and agile portfolio rebalancing.

Another compelling case involves a proprietary trading firm that leveraged principal component analysis (PCA) to decode complex market behaviors. Overwhelmed by data from global exchanges, the firm needed a method to identify latent trends influencing asset prices. Through PCA, they distilled thousands of variables into a few principal components, capturing essential market dynamics.

This approach allowed traders to focus on these dominant components, streamlining decision-making processes and enhancing predictive accuracy. The firm's ability to anticipate sector-specific shifts before they appeared in broader indices demonstrated PCA's efficacy in forecasting significant price movements.

Similarly, an investment bank used singular value decomposition (SVD) for arbitrage opportunities in foreign exchange markets. Faced with inconsistent pricing across currency pairs and time zones, they employed SVD to analyze historical price matrices. This decomposition uncovered hidden patterns and discrepancies, enabling traders to capitalize on undervalued currencies while minimizing risks.

These strategies led to substantial profits and established the bank as a leader in innovative currency trading techniques, showcasing how sophisticated mathematical models can uncover lucrative avenues previously hidden by market noise.

Individual traders have also benefited from these methodologies. One retail investor applied matrix factorization techniques to enhance personal stock selection processes. By analyzing historical return matrices through LU decomposition, this investor optimized portfolio allocations based on identified structural patterns within market data.

The investor's application of matrix theory led to consistent outperformance against benchmark indices, highlighting how independent traders can leverage mathematical insights for a competitive edge.

These narratives emphasize that success in finance often relies on distilling complexity into actionable intelligence. Linear algebra and matrix theory provide financial professionals with analytical frameworks to decode intricate systems and develop strategies that adapt dynamically to evolving market conditions.

Embracing mathematical rigor not only enhances immediate performance but also fosters long-term resilience by deepening insights into the mechanics driving financial markets. Through continuous innovation and adaptation informed by these principles, practitioners consistently unlock new pathways for growth and profitability in an ever-changing economic environment.

Analyzing Historical Data

Analyzing historical data is fundamental to financial decision-making, providing vital insights into market trends, risk assessments, and investment strategies. In quantitative finance, linear algebra and matrix theory offer robust frameworks to interpret past market behaviors and predict future movements. This involves delving into extensive datasets, where historical prices, returns, and volumes are more than just numbers—they are keys to unlocking market patterns.

A practical starting point involves constructing matrices that encapsulate historical data. Imagine a matrix where rows represent different time periods and columns correspond to various assets or indices. This configuration allows analysts to apply transformations and operations that reveal underlying relationships. Take this example, calculating a covariance matrix can uncover how assets have historically moved in relation to each other, informing risk diversification strategies.

Portfolio optimization benefits from eigenvalue decomposition, a notable application in finance. By examining the eigenvalues and eigenvectors of a covariance matrix, analysts can identify principal components that capture most of the variance in asset returns. This aids in constructing efficient portfolios by focusing on components with the most significant impact on overall risk-return profiles.

Singular value decomposition (SVD) adds another dimension to data analysis by breaking down matrices into orthogonal components. This technique is particularly useful when dealing with incomplete or noisy data—a common challenge in financial markets. By concentrating on dominant singular values, analysts can filter out noise and extract meaningful patterns from seemingly chaotic datasets.

Matrix-based techniques also enhance historical volatility estimation. Calculating rolling standard deviations or using GARCH models involves sophisticated matrix manipulations that consider past volatility behavior while adjusting for new data inputs. These models help traders anticipate future price swings, aiding strategy formulation for both hedging and speculative activities.

Machine learning algorithms increasingly leverage historical data matrices as input features for predictive modeling. Techniques like linear regression or neural networks use these inputs to train models capable of forecasting asset prices or market trends. Here, the synergy between linear algebra and advanced computation transforms raw historical data into actionable insights through algorithmic processing.

Visualization of analyzed data is an often-overlooked aspect that enhances understanding. By projecting historical data onto lower-dimensional spaces using techniques like PCA or multidimensional scaling (MDS), analysts create visual representations that clarify complex relationships. These visualizations support strategic discussions among decision-makers by providing clear illustrations of historical market dynamics.

These methodologies highlight the importance of robust data analysis in navigating the complexities of financial markets. Historical data acts as both a teacher and guide; its lessons lie within matrices waiting to be explored through mathematical rigor. As analysts refine their techniques, they gain an increasingly nuanced understanding of markets—balancing historical wisdom with forward-looking innovation.

By continuously revisiting and refining analytical approaches grounded in linear algebra, finance professionals enhance their ability to interpret market signals accurately and devise strategies aligned with evolving economic landscapes. Such adaptability ensures they remain at the forefront of financial innovation, effectively bridging past performance with future potential.

Learning from Industry Experts

Gaining insights from industry experts in quantitative finance offers a unique opportunity to understand the practical application of linear algebra and matrix theory. These professionals have honed their skills by applying mathematical models to navigate complex financial landscapes, translating theoretical concepts into actionable strategies.

One critical lesson from these experts is the importance of adaptability. Financial markets are inherently unpredictable, with variables that change rapidly. Experts stress the necessity of flexible models that can adjust to new data and evolving market conditions. This often involves recalibrating matrices and updating algorithms to reflect current realities. By adopting a dynamic approach, analysts can respond effectively to market shifts and seize emerging opportunities.

Additionally, experts underscore the value of interdisciplinary knowledge. While a strong foundation in mathematics is essential, understanding economics, computer science, and finance provides a comprehensive view of market dynamics. This multidisciplinary approach allows analysts to integrate various perspectives when constructing financial models. Take this example, combining economic indicators with statistical analysis can yield deeper insights into asset pricing or risk assessment.

And, seasoned professionals highlight the importance of robust data management practices. In finance, data quality directly influences model accuracy and reliability. Quantitative analysts prioritize maintaining clean, organized datasets to ensure precise inputs for their calculations. Experts recommend implementing rigorous data validation protocols and leveraging advanced software tools to automate this process, minimizing errors that could lead to costly misinterpretations.

Continuous learning and development are also pivotal in this field. Financial markets are ever-evolving due to technological advancements and regulatory changes. Experienced professionals advocate for ongoing education through workshops, conferences, and online courses to stay updated on these developments. Engaging with cutting-edge research helps analysts refine methodologies and introduce innovative solutions.

Collaboration is another key aspect emphasized by industry leaders. Effective communication between quantitative teams and other departments—such as risk management or strategic planning—ensures that mathematical insights align with organizational goals. This collaborative environment fosters the exchange of ideas, leading to informed decision-making that leverages collective expertise.

Practical case studies often demonstrate these principles in action. For example, during volatile market periods, seasoned traders may adjust portfolio allocations by interpreting covariance matrices differently based on emerging trends or geopolitical events—illustrating adaptability in practice. Such examples show how theory-based tools are strategically utilized to manage risk or enhance returns amid uncertainty.

Mentorship also plays a crucial role in professional growth within finance. Learning directly from experienced analysts provides newcomers with guidance beyond what textbooks can offer—insights into real-world problem-solving techniques or strategic decision-making frameworks developed through years of frontline experience in finance.

Embracing these lessons enriches one's ability not only as an individual analyst but also as part of a team striving for financial excellence. By integrating the wisdom shared by experts into daily practices, professionals enhance their proficiency in applying linear algebraic methods effectively within complex financial environments—ensuring they remain competitive amid the ever-evolving challenges of global markets.

At its core, learning from industry experts bridges the gap between theoretical knowledge and practical expertise, empowering financial analysts to excel in deploying sophisticated mathematical frameworks for impactful results within a dynamic marketplace landscape.

Future Prospects in Financial Mathematics

In the dynamic realm of finance, the future of financial mathematics holds both excitement and challenges. As technology advances rapidly, mathematical models are becoming increasingly essential in finance. The incorporation of artificial intelligence and machine learning is transforming how we assess risk, optimize portfolios, and predict market trends.

A significant trend shaping the future is the application of big data analytics. The immense volume of data generated every second offers valuable insights that can lead to more accurate predictions when properly utilized. Linear algebra is crucial here, providing the foundation for efficiently processing and analyzing large datasets. Techniques like singular value decomposition (SVD) help reduce dimensionality and extract meaningful patterns from complex data structures, enhancing our ability to forecast market movements with precision.

Another promising development is the use of quantum computing in financial mathematics. Quantum algorithms have the potential to solve problems currently beyond the reach of classical computers. For example, quantum systems could revolutionize portfolio optimization by evaluating a vast array of potential solutions simultaneously, identifying optimal investment strategies much faster than traditional methods. This breakthrough would improve efficiency and open new avenues for innovation in risk management and derivative pricing.

And, blockchain technology is adding new dimensions to financial mathematics. Decentralized finance (DeFi) platforms are challenging conventional banking systems by offering innovative solutions like smart contracts and automated market makers. These innovations require robust mathematical frameworks to ensure security and stability. Cryptography and game theory are becoming increasingly relevant, providing the foundations for these decentralized systems and requiring analysts to develop new skills to navigate this emerging landscape effectively.

The rise of environmental, social, and governance (ESG) investing also presents opportunities for financial mathematics to contribute positively toward sustainable finance. Mathematical models can assess the impact of investments on environmental and social factors, helping investors make informed decisions that align with their ethical values while achieving financial returns.

With these advancements come challenges that require continuous learning and adaptation. The complexity of new technologies demands that analysts constantly update their knowledge and refine their skills. Collaborative efforts between academia and industry will be essential in developing innovative solutions that meet the practical needs of financial markets while pushing the boundaries of possibility.

The journey into the future of financial mathematics is not just about adopting new tools or technologies; it's about embracing a mindset that values adaptability, interdisciplinary collaboration, and ethical considerations. As we stand on the brink of this new era, professionals equipped with these qualities will be well-positioned to lead the transformation of finance in a digital world.

In the end, success will belong to those who not only understand mathematics but also possess the vision to apply it creatively within an ever-changing environment—ensuring they remain at the forefront of innovation while driving positive change within global markets.

CHAPTER 20:
CONCLUSION AND
FUTURE DIRECTIONS

Recapitulation of Key Concepts

The journey through linear algebra and matrix theory in finance is a multifaceted exploration, rich with concepts that form the bedrock of quantitative analysis. We started by examining the fundamental principles of linear algebra—scalars, vectors, and matrices—which serve as essential building blocks in this mathematical domain. Grasping these elements was not just an academic exercise; it unlocked their potential to succinctly and powerfully encapsulate complex financial data.

Our exploration continued with systems of linear equations, where we unraveled their adept application in financial contexts. We looked into methodologies like the Gauss method, a pivotal tool for solving linear equations, which brings clarity to portfolio analysis. This led us to discuss consistent and inconsistent systems, drawing parallels to financial scenarios where data alignment may vary.

As the narrative unfolded, we ventured into matrix algebra

and its various types, each offering unique properties beneficial to financial modeling. We discovered the elegance of identity matrices and the versatility of block matrices, enabling sophisticated partitioning techniques essential for dissecting financial models.

Matrix operations naturally introduced us to determinants and their profound implications in finance. By exploring calculation methods and understanding Cramer's Rule, we saw how determinants influence investment decisions by providing insights into system stability—a crucial aspect of risk assessment.

Our study then turned to eigenvalues and eigenvectors, exploring their transformative potential in identifying underlying patterns within datasets—patterns that reveal critical insights into risk factors and market behavior. The chapter on diagonalization expanded this knowledge, demonstrating how simplifying matrices aids in more efficient calculations and clearer interpretations of complex systems.

Singular value decomposition (SVD) emerged as a critical tool for approximating financial matrices, adept at handling big data challenges through dimensionality reduction. This technique plays a crucial role in refining predictive models, thereby enhancing decision-making in areas such as credit risk management.

We then explored matrix factorizations like LU decomposition, unlocking further efficiency in computations related to derivative pricing and regression analysis. These factorizations underscored how different matrix breakdowns optimize various financial processes.

The examination of norms highlighted methods for measuring data accuracy and errors—essential for maintaining integrity in financial models. This understanding paved the way for deeper insights into orthogonality's role in minimizing risks, illustrated through practical examples like the Gram-Schmidt process.

Linear transformations opened new perspectives on forecasting market trends, while vector spaces provided a framework for understanding portfolio dimensions. Inner product spaces offered tools for analyzing correlations—a vital aspect for crafting balanced portfolios.

Least squares regression brought clarity to economic relationships by illustrating how precise fits can be achieved between variables—a task made easier by leveraging modern technology's computational power.

Finally, our deep dive into numerical methods underscored the importance of algorithmic approaches for efficiently solving financial problems. With an understanding of direct solutions and iterative methods, we enhanced our ability to tackle real-world challenges with precision and confidence.

Through this journey, we have woven a tapestry of mathematical concepts tightly interlinked with financial applications. These tools not only equip us with the technical skills necessary for success but also inspire a broader perspective on mathematics' potential to drive innovation within the ever-evolving landscape of global finance.

The Future of Linear Algebra in Finance

The future of linear algebra in finance is set for a major transformation, largely due to the growing complexity and scale of financial markets. With rapid technological advancements and an explosion of data, linear algebra is becoming increasingly crucial. Quantitative analysts and traders are now harnessing these mathematical tools to gain new insights and develop innovative strategies.

Linear algebra's role in finance is evolving beyond its traditional uses, intersecting with cutting-edge technologies like machine learning and artificial intelligence. These fields heavily rely on matrix operations, which are reshaping data analysis and decision-making processes in finance. For example, machine learning algorithms often utilize matrix factorizations to optimize models, underscoring the essential role of linear algebra in creating robust and scalable predictive analytics.

One significant area of impact is the management of large datasets. Financial institutions collect massive amounts of data from multiple sources, making efficient processing and analysis critical. Techniques such as singular value decomposition (SVD) are vital for dimensionality reduction, allowing analysts to extract actionable insights from vast datasets without sacrificing important information. This not only enhances the precision of financial models but also improves computational efficiency, enabling real-time handling of larger data volumes.

Quantum computing is poised to further revolutionize the use of linear algebra in finance. Quantum algorithms could solve complex matrix problems at unprecedented speeds, dramatically affecting portfolio optimization, risk assessment, and algorithmic trading strategies. As quantum computing technology evolves, its integration with conventional computational methods could redefine possibilities in financial modeling and analysis.

As global markets become more interconnected, there's an increasing demand for advanced risk management tools. Linear algebra provides a framework for creating models that accurately capture correlations across diverse asset classes and better predict systemic risks. Take this example, eigenvalue analysis is crucial in identifying principal risk components within portfolios, facilitating more effective hedging strategies.

Regulatory changes are also influencing how financial institutions utilize mathematical tools. With heightened scrutiny on transparency and risk management practices, there's a shift towards adopting more rigorous analytical methods. Linear algebra supports compliance by enabling precise models that ensure thorough risk assessment and mitigation.

The fusion of finance with other scientific domains presents promising opportunities for innovation. Cross-disciplinary research initiatives are exploring how principles from fields like physics or biology can enhance financial modeling techniques, potentially leading to novel approaches that incorporate non-linear dynamics or complex systems theory into traditional financial frameworks.

Educational programs are adapting to meet these evolving needs by emphasizing the practical applications of linear algebra in finance. This guarantees that future quantitative professionals are equipped with both theoretical knowledge and the practical skills necessary to implement these concepts effectively within financial environments.

Looking ahead, the trajectory of linear algebra in finance suggests an era marked by integration, innovation, and expansion. By fully leveraging these mathematical tools— amplified by technological advances—finance professionals will be better positioned to navigate a rapidly changing landscape and seize opportunities for growth and success.

Emerging Trends in Financial Mathematics

Emerging trends in financial mathematics are reshaping quantitative finance, propelled by technological advancements and the growing need for sophisticated analytical tools. A key development is the integration of machine learning and artificial intelligence with traditional mathematical models. This fusion allows analysts to process vast amounts of data with unprecedented accuracy and speed.

Notably, deep learning algorithms, a subset of machine learning, excel at detecting complex patterns in large datasets.

These patterns are invaluable for predictive modeling in finance. For example, neural networks have proven effective in forecasting market trends by analyzing historical price movements alongside economic indicators. These techniques reveal hidden relationships within data, offering deeper insights into market dynamics than conventional methods.

Additionally, the use of automated trading systems powered by advanced mathematics is on the rise. High-frequency trading (HFT) algorithms perform complex calculations to execute trades at lightning speed, exploiting minute price discrepancies across markets. These systems rely heavily on linear algebra to optimize performance and ensure rapid decision-making, highlighting the importance of a solid mathematical foundation in developing such technologies.

Blockchain technology is also impacting financial mathematics significantly. Decentralized finance (DeFi) platforms are introducing new models for asset management and investment strategies that challenge traditional systems. Smart contracts—self-executing agreements with terms written in code—are being developed using cryptographic methods that require robust mathematical foundations. As these platforms grow, so will the need for innovative approaches to secure transactions and manage digital assets.

In parallel, there is a shift towards sustainable and responsible investing practices. Environmental, social, and governance (ESG) criteria are becoming integral to investment strategies, necessitating new mathematical models that incorporate non-financial factors alongside traditional metrics. Quantitative analysts are creating tools to better measure ESG impact and integrate these considerations into portfolio optimization processes.

And, real-time data analysis is gaining emphasis as financial markets become more volatile and interconnected. The ability to analyze streaming data rapidly enables traders and analysts to respond swiftly to market changes. Techniques such as Kalman filtering—based on recursive estimation— are becoming popular for processing real-time information efficiently while maintaining accuracy.

The democratization of financial technology is another trend shaping the field. With access to powerful computing resources and open-source software tools, individual traders and small firms can implement complex quantitative strategies previously reserved for large institutions. This accessibility fosters innovation as diverse participants bring fresh perspectives and solutions to traditional financial challenges.

Educational curricula are evolving to incorporate these trends by integrating emerging technologies into their frameworks. Programs now emphasize interdisciplinary skills that blend financial theory with computer science and data analytics competencies, preparing students for the diverse demands of modern finance roles.

As these trends gain momentum, they are not only transforming how financial mathematics is applied but also expanding its scope beyond traditional boundaries. By embracing innovation while maintaining rigorous analytical standards, professionals in this field will continue driving progress within an ever-evolving financial ecosystem.

Integrating Theory with Practice

Integrating theory with practice in financial mathematics is crucial for bridging the gap between abstract concepts and their real-world applications. This synergy enables professionals to transform complex mathematical frameworks into actionable strategies that enhance decision-making and performance in the financial sector.

A key component of this integration is a solid grasp of linear algebra and matrix theory, which underpin many quantitative models. Financial analysts use these mathematical tools to structure data, optimize portfolios, and assess risk. Take matrix multiplication: while it might appear theoretical, in finance, it's an effective technique for computing portfolio returns by multiplying vectors of asset weights with matrices of expected returns.

Practitioners must thoroughly understand these mathematical principles to integrate them effectively. Consider eigenvalues and eigenvectors, which provide insights into system stability and dynamics. They are employed to assess risk factors within a financial portfolio. Analyzing the eigenvectors of a covariance matrix helps identify principal components that contribute most significantly to portfolio variance, guiding diversification strategies.

Technology plays a pivotal role in this integration process. Programming languages like Python or R facilitate the automation of complex calculations and simulations. Take this example, a quantitative analyst might use Python to perform Monte Carlo simulations—a method employing random sampling to estimate statistical properties of potential outcomes—offering a practical approach to model uncertainty in asset prices over time.

Here's a practical example using Python:

```python
import numpy as np


\#\# Simulate asset returns

returns = np.random.normal(0.05, 0.1, (1000, 10))  \# 1000 scenarios for 10 assets


\#\# Calculate expected portfolio return using matrix multiplication
```

```
weights = np.array([0.1]*10) \# Equal weights for simplicity

expected_portfolio_return      =      np.dot(weights, np.mean(returns, axis=0))


print(f"Expected      Portfolio      Return: expected_portfolio_return:.2f")
` ` `
```

This example demonstrates how theoretical concepts are practically applied—using random normal distributions to simulate asset returns and matrix multiplication for expected return calculation.

And, the ongoing dialogue between theory and practice fosters innovation within the field. New mathematical discoveries or evolving theories prompt practitioners to refine established models based on real-world data and experiences. This iterative process not only improves model accuracy but also broadens the applicability of mathematical tools across different market conditions.

Collaboration among professionals from various disciplines —mathematics, finance, computer science—further enriches this integration. By pooling diverse expertise, innovative solutions can tackle complex financial challenges more effectively than traditional methods alone.

Real-world case studies offer valuable insights into this context. Examining past financial crises or successful trading strategies highlights how theoretical principles were applied (or misapplied) in practice. Take this example, during market turmoil such as the 2008 financial crisis or recent volatility due to geopolitical events or pandemics, quantitative models grounded in solid mathematical theories have been instrumental in guiding risk management decisions under uncertainty.

In the end, integrating theory with practice goes beyond applying formulas; it's about fostering a mindset that embraces continuous learning and adaptation. As markets evolve rapidly due to technological advances and global interconnectedness, financial professionals must stay agile—ready to adapt their strategies based on empirical evidence and emerging theoretical insights.

By maintaining this delicate balance between rigorous analysis and pragmatic application, the field continues to evolve—paving the way for future quantitative skills that unlock untold financial success stories.

The Role of Technology in Finance

Technology in finance acts as a powerful catalyst, evolving traditional practices into sophisticated systems that redefine market dynamics. Its role is multifaceted, spanning automation, data analysis, and complex financial modeling. As markets grow more intricate and data-rich, technology provides the tools to navigate these complexities with precision and agility.

Take high-frequency trading (HFT) as an example, where algorithms execute trades within fractions of a second. This speed relies on cutting-edge computational power and robust network infrastructure. HFT utilizes real-time data streams and advanced algorithms to pinpoint and exploit fleeting market inefficiencies—tasks that are unfeasible without state-of-the-art technology.

Beyond trading, automation in finance extends to risk management and compliance. With increasingly stringent regulatory requirements, systems that automate reporting and ensure legal compliance have become essential. Machine learning models now detect anomalies in transaction patterns, flagging potential fraud or compliance breaches more effectively than manual methods.

In portfolio management, technology optimizes investment strategies through machine learning algorithms that analyze vast datasets to uncover subtle patterns and correlations among assets. Predictive models using historical price data can forecast trends, allowing fund managers to proactively adjust their portfolios.

A tangible example of technology's impact is the use of Python in financial modeling. Python libraries like NumPy, pandas, and scikit-learn offer powerful tools for statistical analysis and machine learning applications. Analysts can employ these libraries for tasks such as regression analysis to identify factors influencing asset returns.

Here's a simple Python example illustrating linear regression:

```python
import pandas as pd

from sklearn.linear_model import LinearRegression


\#\# Sample financial data: features are economic indicators; target is asset returns

data = pd.DataFrame(

'GDP_growth': [2.3, 2.5, 2.1, 2.7],

'Inflation_rate': [1.9, 2.1, 2.0, 1.8],

'Asset_return': [5.4, 5.6, 5.3, 5.7]

)


\#\# Define features and target

X = data[['GDP_growth', 'Inflation_rate']]

y = data['Asset_return']
```

```
\#\# Create and train model
model = LinearRegression()
model.fit(X, y)

\#\# Predict asset return based on new economic indicators
predicted_return = model.predict([[2.6, 1.9]])
print(f"Predicted Asset Return: predicted_return[0]:.2f")
` ` `
```

This example demonstrates how regression models predict asset performance based on economic conditions—a critical aspect of strategic financial planning.

Technology also enables the integration of alternative data sources—such as social media sentiment analysis or satellite imagery—into financial models. These non-traditional datasets provide fresh insights into market trends that conventional data might overlook.

In addition to analytics and modeling, blockchain technology is transforming finance by enhancing transparency and security in transactions. Distributed ledger systems offer immutable records that streamline processes like clearing and settlement while reducing counterparty risk.

The fusion of finance and technology has spurred the rise of fintech startups challenging established institutions with innovative solutions tailored for modern consumers—ranging from robo-advisors offering personalized investment advice to peer-to-peer lending platforms democratizing capital access.

However, these advancements also bring challenges—particularly cybersecurity risks associated with digital transformation in finance. Protecting sensitive information from cyber threats requires robust security protocols and constant vigilance against evolving threats.

In the end, technology's role in finance transcends mere toolsets; it empowers professionals with capabilities previously unimaginable—enabling smarter decisions driven by accurate data insights while fostering an environment where innovation thrives alongside tradition.

This synergy between technological advancement and financial expertise ensures the industry remains at the forefront of global economic progress—propelling us into a future where finance operates seamlessly across digital landscapes without losing sight of its foundational principles rooted in trustworthiness and strategic foresight.

Predictions for Market Evolutions

Financial markets are in a constant state of evolution, driven by technological innovations, regulatory changes, and global economic developments. As we navigate these shifts, several transformative trends are emerging that promise to redefine the financial systems of tomorrow.

One key development is the expanding role of artificial intelligence (AI) and machine learning in predictive analytics. AI systems are increasingly capable of analyzing vast datasets to uncover insights that were previously inaccessible. In finance, this translates into more accurate forecasting models that can predict market movements with unprecedented precision. By examining patterns in historical data alongside real-time inputs, AI provides traders with insights that enable more informed decision-making and greater confidence.

Complementing AI advancements is the rise of decentralized finance (DeFi), which is poised to disrupt traditional financial systems through blockchain technology. DeFi platforms enable peer-to-peer transactions without intermediaries, giving users more control and reducing costs associated with conventional banking services. This shift democratizes access to financial products but also introduces new regulatory and security challenges that will influence market dynamics in the coming years.

Another significant trend is the integration of environmental, social, and governance (ESG) factors into investment strategies. As investors increasingly prioritize sustainable practices, assets are being reevaluated based on ESG criteria. This trend is likely to influence capital flows, as funds gravitate toward companies committed to ethical practices and sustainability—aligning financial success with societal impact.

Technological infrastructure continues to advance as well. The proliferation of cloud computing and improved network capabilities enables faster data processing and greater storage solutions, facilitating real-time analytics essential for high-frequency trading and complex financial modeling. These advancements offer potential optimization of trading algorithms and enhanced portfolio management techniques.

Risk management also stands to benefit from enhanced computational power, allowing for more sophisticated stress testing and scenario analysis. Financial institutions can simulate various market conditions to assess potential impacts on their portfolios, adopting proactive rather than reactive measures.

Consider an investment firm using cloud-based systems to run Monte Carlo simulations across multiple asset classes simultaneously. These simulations provide probabilistic forecasts that inform risk assessment strategies, illustrating how infrastructure advancements support decision-making processes.

As technological capabilities expand, so does the reliance on alternative data sources. Non-traditional datasets, such as social media sentiment analysis or geolocation information from mobile devices, are being leveraged to gain competitive edges in trading strategies. These data sources enrich traditional models with nuanced perspectives reflecting consumer behavior trends or geopolitical events impacting markets globally.

However, these opportunities come with challenges—foremost among them are cybersecurity threats that loom over digital finance landscapes. Ensuring robust defenses against cyberattacks is crucial as sensitive information becomes increasingly vulnerable within interconnected systems.

The convergence of these factors suggests a future where markets operate with heightened efficiency yet require vigilance over ethical considerations and security protocols. Professionals equipped with adaptable skillsets will be well-positioned within this evolving ecosystem—a landscape marked by resilience amidst uncertainty and grounded in strategic foresight built upon reliable data insights.

At its core, predicting market evolutions involves recognizing patterns through quantitative metrics while understanding the qualitative shifts shaping tomorrow's financial landscape —ensuring readiness for changes ahead while seizing new opportunities presented by this dynamic era in finance history.

Preparing for Future Challenges

The financial landscape is evolving at a rapid pace, introducing new complexities and uncertainties daily. For professionals in the field, preparing for these future challenges involves building a dynamic toolkit that is both versatile and robust. Central to this preparation is the ability to adapt—a proactive approach that emphasizes continuous learning and strategic foresight.

Ongoing education is crucial in adapting to future challenges. With technologies like AI and machine learning becoming integral to financial analysis, staying updated on these advancements is essential. Financial analysts and traders should participate in regular training sessions and workshops focused on new computational techniques and tools. This continuous learning keeps them at the forefront, allowing for seamless integration of emerging technologies into their workflows.

Equally important is a deep understanding of regulatory landscapes. As decentralized finance gains traction, regulatory bodies worldwide are developing new rules to address the unique challenges posed by these innovations. Financial professionals must stay informed about these changes to ensure compliance while also leveraging new opportunities.

Another critical area is developing resilience against cybersecurity threats. As data breaches become more sophisticated, financial institutions need robust security measures to protect sensitive information and maintain client trust. Investing in cybersecurity infrastructure and conducting regular audits can help mitigate risks associated with digital vulnerabilities.

Building strong analytical capabilities is also vital. The integration of alternative data sources—such as social media sentiment and satellite imagery—requires analysts who can extract valuable insights from vast datasets. This necessitates honing skills in data science and analytics, enabling professionals to convert raw data into actionable intelligence.

And, fostering collaboration across disciplines will be key. The future of finance will likely be shaped by interdisciplinary teams that combine expertise in economics, computer science, mathematics, and behavioral science. Such collaboration promotes innovative problem-solving approaches by drawing on diverse perspectives, essential for tackling multifaceted financial issues.

In addition to technical skills, cultivating soft skills such as adaptability and communication is indispensable. Navigating uncertain markets requires agile thinking and the ability to clearly communicate complex ideas to diverse stakeholders —whether they are clients, regulatory authorities, or team members.

Consider an investment firm facing unexpected market volatility due to geopolitical tensions. Analysts with strong communication skills can effectively convey potential risks and strategic responses to clients, maintaining confidence through transparency. Meanwhile, those skilled in cross-disciplinary collaboration might leverage behavioral insights alongside quantitative models to more accurately forecast market reactions.

Ethical considerations must also remain at the forefront of all financial endeavors. As ESG factors become increasingly important in investment strategies, aligning business practices with societal values enhances both reputational integrity and long-term profitability. This alignment requires a conscientious approach where decisions are evaluated not only for their economic impact but also for their broader ethical implications.

In summary, preparing for future challenges involves more than just reacting to immediate threats; it's about crafting a resilient strategy built on lifelong learning, technological integration, robust security measures, interdisciplinary collaboration, effective communication skills, and unwavering ethical standards. By focusing on these areas, financial professionals can navigate the complexities of tomorrow's markets with confidence and poise—ready not only to face uncertainties but to transform them into opportunities for growth and innovation within the ever-evolving global financial landscape.

Continuous Learning and Development

In the fast-paced world of finance, continuous learning isn't just a strategy—it's essential. As technologies and financial instruments evolve rapidly, professionals must update their skills and knowledge to stay relevant. Lifelong learning serves as the foundation for adaptability, enabling analysts and traders to skillfully navigate both current challenges and future uncertainties.

Cultivating a mindset focused on perpetual education is crucial. Take blockchain technology, for example— it has revolutionized traditional finance. Those who quickly mastered its mechanics were better positioned to seize opportunities in cryptocurrencies and smart contracts. Similarly, embracing emerging trends like quantum computing could transform complex calculations in portfolio management, giving an edge to those eager to explore its depths.

Networking is key to continuous development. Engaging with peers across various sectors encourages the exchange of ideas, fostering innovation and growth. Attending conferences or webinars offers fresh perspectives and insights into cutting-edge practices. These interactions often inspire creativity, leading to novel approaches that enhance financial strategies or risk models.

Mentorship is another critical aspect of professional growth. Experienced mentors provide invaluable guidance by sharing lessons from past market cycles or technological shifts. This wisdom helps mentees avoid common pitfalls while encouraging them to explore unconventional solutions to modern challenges.

Investing in formal education is equally beneficial. Enrolling in courses on machine learning, data analytics, or financial engineering can significantly enhance one's ability to interpret complex datasets or model sophisticated trading algorithms. Universities and online platforms offer flexible learning options tailored for working professionals, making it feasible to integrate study into busy schedules.

However, informal learning shouldn't be underestimated. Reading industry journals, subscribing to newsletters from thought leaders, and engaging with content on digital platforms like podcasts or videos provide quick yet impactful insights that keep professionals informed about global market trends and regulatory changes.

Developing technical skills must go hand-in-hand with refining soft skills such as leadership and emotional intelligence. As financial roles increasingly involve team coordination and client interaction, the ability to inspire others or negotiate effectively becomes just as critical as numerical proficiency.

Consider an analyst who identifies a promising investment opportunity but needs buy-in from senior management skeptical of its unconventional nature. Here, persuasive communication grounded in solid data analysis can sway decision-makers by clearly articulating potential benefits.

Reflection is often an overlooked aspect of continuous improvement. Evaluating past decisions—both successes and failures—yields insights into personal growth areas or strategic adjustments needed moving forward. Reflection fosters self-awareness, ultimately leading to smarter decision-making under pressure.

Technological advancements now enable more personalized learning experiences through AI-driven platforms that tailor content based on individual progress or identified gaps during assessments.

Committing wholeheartedly to lifelong education requires intentionality—a deliberate pursuit of excellence characterized by curiosity-driven exploration combined with disciplined study habits extending beyond immediate goals.

As finance continues its relentless transformation through waves of innovation fueled by technology's forward march, those rooted in dynamic adaptability will find themselves well-prepared for whatever challenges lie ahead on this exhilarating journey toward sustained success amidst uncertainty's ever-present shadow.

PROJECTS

Comprehensive Project: Introduction to Linear Algebra in Finance

Project Overview

This project aims to provide students with a thorough understanding of the fundamental concepts of linear algebra and their application in finance. By the end of this project, students should be able to articulate the importance of linear algebra in financial contexts, understand key terminology, and recognize practical uses in trading and financial analysis.

Project Title: "Exploring Linear Algebra in Finance: A Practical Introduction"

Project Objectives

1. Understand the basic concepts of linear algebra and their relevance to finance.
2. Explore the historical context and importance of linear algebra in financial applications.
3. Recognize the role of quantitative analysts and practical uses in trading.
4. Develop an overview of the book's structure and how each chapter builds on the previous one.

Step-by-Step Instructions

&Step 1: Overview of Linear Algebra (Section 1)

- Task: Research and summarize the fundamental concepts of linear algebra.
- Instructions:
- Define what linear algebra is.
- List and explain basic concepts such as vectors, scalars, matrices, and systems of linear equations.

370

- Use at least three academic resources to support your definitions.
- Deliverables: A 2-page summary report on the fundamentals of linear algebra.

&Step 2: Importance in Financial Applications (Section 2)

- Task: Investigate how linear algebra is applied in finance.
- Instructions:
- Identify various financial applications where linear algebra is utilized (e.g., portfolio optimization, risk management, pricing derivatives).
- Provide detailed explanations of at least two specific examples of linear algebra used in finance.
- Include diagrams or equations to illustrate how linear algebra concepts are applied.
- Deliverables: A 2-page detailed report on the importance of linear algebra in finance with examples.

&Step 3: Key Concepts and Terminology (Section 3)

- Task: Create a glossary of key linear algebra terms and their financial relevance.
- Instructions:
- List and define at least 15 key terms related to linear algebra (e.g., eigenvalues, eigenvectors, matrix inversion).
- For each term, provide a brief explanation of its relevance or application in finance.
- Use visual aids where applicable.
- Deliverables: A comprehensive glossary with definitions and financial applications.

&Step 4: Historical Context (Section 4)

- Task: Research the historical development of linear algebra and its adoption in finance.
- Instructions:

- Identify key historical milestones in the development of linear algebra.
- Explore how these milestones impacted the field of finance.
- Present at least three significant historical events or figures.
- Deliverables: A timeline or infographic highlighting the historical context of linear algebra in finance.

&Step 5: The Role of Quantitative Analysts (Section 5)

- Task: Investigate the role of quantitative analysts in finance and how they use linear algebra.
- Instructions:
- Define what a quantitative analyst (quant) does.
- Identify the skills and knowledge required for a quant, focusing on linear algebra.
- Interview or research a case study of a professional quantitative analyst.
- Deliverables: A 2-page report on the role of quants, including a case study or interview insights.

&Step 6: Practical Uses in Trading (Section 6)

- Task: Identify and explain practical uses of linear algebra in trading.
- Instructions:
- Research at least two practical trading strategies that utilize linear algebra.
- Explain how linear algebra concepts are applied in these strategies.
- Provide examples or case studies to illustrate these applications.
- Deliverables: A 2-page report on practical uses of linear algebra in trading, including examples.

&Step 7: Structure of the Book (Section 7)

- Task: Develop an annotated outline of the book's chapters.

- Instructions:
- Review the table of contents and provide a brief description of each chapter.
- Highlight how each chapter builds on the previous one to develop a comprehensive understanding of linear algebra in finance.
- Identify key learning outcomes for each chapter.
- Deliverables: An annotated outline of the book with descriptions and key learning outcomes.

Evaluation Criteria

- Understanding of Concepts: Demonstrates a strong grasp of linear algebra principles and their financial applications.
- Research Quality: Uses credible sources and provides accurate, well-supported information.
- Clarity and Presentation: Information is clearly presented, well-organized, and free of errors.
- Creativity: Uses visual aids and innovative approaches to explain complex concepts.
- Application: Provides real-world examples and case studies to illustrate theoretical concepts.

Good luck, and enjoy your journey through the fascinating intersection of linear algebra and finance!

Comprehensive Project: Basic Concepts and Notation in Linear Algebra for Finance

Project Overview

This project aims to provide students with a deep understanding of the basic concepts and notation of linear algebra, as applied in the financial context. By the end of this project, students will be able to identify and apply fundamental linear algebra concepts and notations in solving financial problems.

Project Title: "Mastering Basic Concepts and Notation

in Linear Algebra for Financial Applications"

Project Objectives

1. Understand and apply basic concepts of linear algebra such as Scalars, Vectors, and Matrices.
2. Familiarize with the mathematical language and notation used in linear algebra.
3. Explore matrix operations and their financial applications.
4. Recognize the encapsulation of financial data using vectors and matrices.
5. Understand key properties of matrices and their practical applications in finance.

Step-by-Step Instructions

&Step 1: Scalars, Vectors, and Matrices (Section 1)

- Task: Define and illustrate the basic building blocks of linear algebra.
- Instructions:
- Define Scalars, Vectors, and Matrices.
- Provide examples of each and their representation in financial contexts (e.g., a scalar representing interest rate, a vector representing a portfolio, a matrix representing stock returns).
- Create visual aids (diagrams or charts) to illustrate these concepts.
- Deliverables: A 2-page document with definitions, examples, and visual aids for Scalars, Vectors, and Matrices.

&Step 2: The Language of Mathematics (Section 2)

- Task: Understand the mathematical language and notation used in linear algebra.
- Instructions:
- List common notations used in linear algebra (e.g., matrix notation, vector notation).
- Explain each notation with an example.

- Provide a brief guide on how to read and interpret these notations in financial problems.
- Deliverables: A 1-page guide on the language and notation in linear algebra.

&Step 3: Notation and Symbols in Linear Algebra (Section 3)

- Task: Create a glossary of important symbols and notations in linear algebra.
- Instructions:
- List at least 20 common symbols and notations used in linear algebra (e.g., (A) for a matrix, (v) for a vector).
- Define each symbol and provide an example of its use in a financial context.
- Use visual aids where necessary to illustrate complex notations.
- Deliverables: A comprehensive glossary with definitions and examples of symbols and notations.

&Step 4: Matrix Operations (Section 4)

- Task: Explore various matrix operations and their applications in finance.
- Instructions:
- Define basic matrix operations (addition, subtraction, multiplication, inversion, and transposition).
- Provide examples of each operation with step-by-step calculations.
- Explain the financial significance of these operations (e.g., matrix multiplication in portfolio analysis, inversion in solving linear systems).
- Deliverables: A 3-page report on matrix operations with examples and financial significance.

&Step 5: Vector Spaces (Section 5)

- Task: Understand the concept of vector spaces and their importance in finance.

- Instructions:
- Define what a vector space is.
- Explain the properties of vector spaces (closure, associativity, etc.).
- Provide examples of vector spaces in financial contexts (e.g., portfolio space).
- Deliverables: A 2-page document explaining vector spaces with financial examples.

&Step 6: Encapsulation of Financial Data (Section 6)

- Task: Investigate how financial data can be encapsulated using vectors and matrices.
- Instructions:
- Identify different types of financial data that can be represented as vectors or matrices (e.g., stock prices, returns, covariances).
- Provide examples of encapsulating financial data in vectors and matrices.
- Create visual aids to show how data is organized in these structures.
- Deliverables: A 2-page report with examples and visual aids on encapsulating financial data.

&Step 7: Key Properties of Matrices (Section 7)

- Task: Examine key properties of matrices and their relevance in financial applications.
- Instructions:
- Define properties such as determinant, rank, trace, and inverse.
- Explain the importance of each property in financial contexts (e.g., determinant in stability analysis, rank in data dimensions).
- Provide examples and calculations to illustrate these properties.
- Deliverables: A 2-page document on key properties of matrices with examples and financial applications.

&Step 8: Row and Column Interpretations (Section 8)

- Task: Explore the significance of row and column interpretations in matrices.
- Instructions:
- Explain the difference between row and column interpretations.
- Provide examples of each interpretation in financial contexts (e.g., rows representing different assets, columns representing different time periods).
- Create visual aids to illustrate these interpretations.
- Deliverables: A 1-page document with examples and visual aids on row and column interpretations.

&Step 9: Practical Applications in Finance (Section 9)

- Task: Identify and explain practical applications of basic linear algebra concepts in finance.
- Instructions:
- Research at least three practical applications (e.g., risk management, portfolio optimization, market analysis).
- Explain how linear algebra concepts are used in each application.
- Provide case studies or real-world examples to illustrate these applications.
- Deliverables: A 3-page report on practical applications of linear algebra in finance with case studies.

Step 10: Challenges in Understanding Notation (Section 10)

- Task: Identify common challenges students face in understanding linear algebra notation.
- Instructions:
- List and describe at least five common challenges.
- Provide strategies or tips to overcome these challenges.
- Include examples and visual aids to support your

strategies.

- Deliverables: A 2-page guide on overcoming challenges in understanding linear algebra notation.

Final Deliverable

Compile all sections into a comprehensive project report titled "Mastering Basic Concepts and Notation in Linear Algebra for Financial Applications." Ensure the report is well-organized with a table of contents, proper citations, and references. The final report should be professionally formatted and submitted in both print and digital formats.

Evaluation Criteria

- Understanding of Concepts: Demonstrates a strong grasp of basic linear algebra concepts and their financial applications.
- Research Quality: Uses credible sources and provides accurate, well-supported information.
- Clarity and Presentation: Information is clearly presented, well-organized, and free of errors.
- Creativity: Uses visual aids and innovative approaches to explain complex concepts.
- Application: Provides real-world examples and case studies to illustrate theoretical concepts.

Good luck, and enjoy your journey through the fascinating world of linear algebra and its applications in finance!

Comprehensive Project: Systems of Linear Equations in Financial Contexts

Project Overview

This project is designed to help students gain a deep understanding of solving systems of linear equations, with a specific focus on their applications in finance. By the end of this project, students will be able to represent financial systems using linear equations, solve these systems using various methods, and interpret the results in a financial context.

Project Title: "Solving Systems of Linear Equations for Financial Applications"

Project Objectives

1. Represent financial systems using linear equations.
2. Solve systems of linear equations using different methods (e.g., Gaussian elimination, matrix methods).
3. Interpret the solutions of these systems in the context of financial applications.
4. Explore the practical implications of consistent and inconsistent systems in finance.
5. Understand the complexity and algorithmic methods for solving large systems of equations.

Step-by-Step Instructions

&Step 1: Representation of Financial Systems (Section 1)

- Task: Define and illustrate how financial systems can be represented using linear equations.
- Instructions:
- Identify a financial problem that can be modeled using a system of linear equations (e.g., portfolio optimization, asset allocation).
- Formulate the problem as a system of linear equations.
- Provide a clear explanation and visual representation of how the financial problem translates into linear equations.
- Deliverables: A 2-page document detailing the financial problem, the system of linear equations, and visual aids.

&Step 2: Gauss Method (Section 2)

- Task: Solve systems of linear equations using Gaussian elimination.
- Instructions:

- Briefly explain the Gaussian elimination method.
- Solve the system of linear equations formulated in Step 1 using Gaussian elimination, showing each step of the process.
- Interpret the financial implications of the solution.
- Deliverables: A 2-page report with the step-by-step Gaussian elimination process and interpretation of results.

&Step 3: Matrices in Linear Systems (Section 3)

- Task: Use matrix methods to solve systems of linear equations.
- Instructions:
- Represent the system of linear equations from Step 1 in matrix form.
- Solve the system using matrix methods (e.g., matrix inversion, LU decomposition).
- Compare the results with those obtained using Gaussian elimination and discuss any differences.
- Deliverables: A 2-page report with the matrix representation, solution using matrix methods, and comparison with Gaussian elimination.

&Step 4: Applications in Portfolio Analysis (Section 4)

- Task: Apply the concepts learned to analyze a portfolio of assets.
- Instructions:
- Select a portfolio of at least three assets.
- Formulate a system of linear equations representing constraints and objectives for portfolio optimization (e.g., minimizing risk, achieving a target return).
- Solve the system and interpret the results in terms of asset allocation.
- Deliverables: A 3-page report with the portfolio analysis, system of equations, solution, and interpretation.

&Step 5: Consistent and Inconsistent Systems (Section 5)

- Task: Explore the concepts of consistent and inconsistent systems in the context of finance.
- Instructions:
- Define consistent and inconsistent systems of linear equations.
- Provide examples of each in financial contexts (e.g., solvable and unsolvable investment strategies).
- Discuss the implications of each type of system for financial decision-making.
- Deliverables: A 1-page document with definitions, examples, and discussion of implications.

&Step 6: Testing Solutions (Section 6)

- Task: Verify the solutions obtained for the systems of linear equations.
- Instructions:
- Explain the methods for testing the solutions of systems of linear equations (e.g., substitution, residual calculation).
- Test the solutions obtained in Steps 2 and 3.
- Discuss the significance of verifying solutions in financial contexts.
- Deliverables: A 1-page report on testing methods, verification of solutions, and discussion.

&Step 7: Financial Interpretation of Solutions (Section 7)

- Task: Interpret the solutions of systems of linear equations in financial terms.
- Instructions:
- Take the solutions obtained in Steps 2 and 3.
- Explain what the solutions mean in the context of the original financial problem (e.g., optimal asset weights, feasibility of investment strategies).
- Use visual aids to enhance the interpretation (e.g., charts, graphs).

- Deliverables: A 2-page document with financial interpretations and visual aids.

&Step 8: Complexity and Algorithmic Methods (Section 8)

- Task: Explore the complexity and algorithmic methods for solving large systems of linear equations.
- Instructions:
- Discuss the computational complexity of solving large systems of linear equations.
- Explore advanced algorithmic methods (e.g., iterative methods, parallel computing).
- Provide examples of large-scale financial problems that require these methods.
- Deliverables: A 2-page report on complexity, algorithmic methods, and examples of large-scale financial problems.

Final Deliverable

Compile all sections into a comprehensive project report titled "Solving Systems of Linear Equations for Financial Applications." Ensure the report is well-organized with a table of contents, proper citations, and references. The final report should be professionally formatted and submitted in both print and digital formats.

Evaluation Criteria

- Understanding of Concepts: Demonstrates a strong grasp of solving systems of linear equations and their financial applications.
- Research Quality: Uses credible sources and provides accurate, well-supported information.
- Clarity and Presentation: Information is clearly presented, well-organized, and free of errors.
- Creativity: Uses visual aids and innovative approaches to explain complex concepts.
- Application: Provides real-world examples and case

studies to illustrate theoretical concepts.

Good luck, and enjoy your journey through the fascinating world of solving systems of linear equations and their applications in finance!

Comprehensive Project: Matrix Algebra and Types in Financial Contexts

Project Overview

This project is designed to guide students through the application of matrix algebra in finance. By the end of this project, students will have a solid understanding of various matrix operations, types, and their practical implications in financial modeling and analysis.

Project Title: "Exploring Matrix Algebra and Types for Financial Analysis"

Project Objectives

1. Understand and perform important matrix operations.
2. Identify and utilize different types of matrices in financial contexts.
3. Apply matrix algebra to solve real-world financial problems.
4. Analyze the implications of matrix operations on financial models.
5. Explore the practical applications of matrices in financial modeling and decision-making.

Step-by-Step Instructions

&Step 1: Important Matrix Operations (Section 1)

- Task: Learn and perform basic matrix operations.
- Instructions:
- Review the basic matrix operations: addition, subtraction, multiplication, and scalar multiplication.
- Provide examples of each operation using financial

data (e.g., returns of different assets).

- Explain the significance of each operation in financial analysis.
- Deliverables: A 2-page document with examples, explanations, and significance of basic matrix operations.

&Step 2: Identity and Diagonal Matrices (Section 2)

- Task: Understand and apply identity and diagonal matrices.
- Instructions:
- Define identity and diagonal matrices and explain their properties.
- Provide examples of how these matrices are used in finance (e.g., identity matrix in portfolio scaling, diagonal matrix in risk assessment).
- Perform calculations using identity and diagonal matrices with financial data.
- Deliverables: A 2-page report with definitions, examples, and calculations using identity and diagonal matrices.

&Step 3: Inverse Matrices and Their Use (Section 3)

- Task: Learn about inverse matrices and their applications.
- Instructions:
- Explain the concept of an inverse matrix and the conditions for its existence.
- Demonstrate how to calculate the inverse of a matrix.
- Provide a financial application where the inverse matrix is used (e.g., solving linear systems in financial models).
- Solve a financial problem using an inverse matrix.
- Deliverables: A 2-page report with explanations, calculations, and a solved financial problem using an inverse matrix.

&Step 4: Transpose and Symmetric Matrices (Section 4)

- Task: Explore transpose and symmetric matrices and their significance in finance.
- Instructions:
- Define transpose and symmetric matrices and illustrate their properties.
- Provide examples of how these matrices are relevant in financial contexts (e.g., covariance matrices).
- Perform calculations involving transpose and symmetric matrices using financial data.
- Deliverables: A 2-page document with definitions, examples, and calculations involving transpose and symmetric matrices.

&Step 5: Special Matrices in Finance (Section 5)

- Task: Identify and apply special matrices in financial modeling.
- Instructions:
- Describe special matrices such as orthogonal, stochastic, and permutation matrices.
- Explain their properties and significance in finance.
- Provide examples of financial models where these special matrices arc applied (e.g., orthogonal matrices in principal component analysis).
- Deliverables: A 2-page report with descriptions, properties, and examples of special matrices in financial modeling.

&Step 6: Block Matrices and Partitioning (Section 6)

- Task: Understand block matrices and their applications in finance.
- Instructions:
- Define block matrices and explain the concept of partitioning.
- Provide examples of how block matrices are used in financial contexts (e.g., breaking down large financial

datasets).

- Perform calculations using block matrices with financial data.
- Deliverables: A 2-page document with definitions, examples, and calculations using block matrices.

&Step 7: Application in Financial Modelling (Section 7)

- Task: Apply matrix algebra to a comprehensive financial modeling scenario.
- Instructions:
- Choose a complex financial problem that can be modeled using matrix algebra (e.g., Markowitz portfolio optimization).
- Formulate the problem using matrix algebra techniques learned in previous steps.
- Solve the problem and interpret the results in a financial context.
- Deliverables: A 3-page report with the financial problem, matrix algebra formulation, solution, and interpretation of results.

Final Deliverable

Compile all sections into a comprehensive project report titled "Exploring Matrix Algebra and Types for Financial Analysis." Ensure the report is well-organized with a table of contents, proper citations, and references. The final report should be professionally formatted and submitted in both print and digital formats.

Evaluation Criteria

- Understanding of Concepts: Demonstrates a strong grasp of matrix algebra and its applications in finance.
- Research Quality: Uses credible sources and provides accurate, well-supported information.
- Clarity and Presentation: Information is clearly presented, well-organized, and free of errors.

- Creativity: Uses visual aids and innovative approaches to explain complex concepts.
- Application: Provides real-world examples and case studies to illustrate theoretical concepts.

Good luck, and enjoy your journey through the intricate and fascinating world of matrix algebra and types in finance!

Comprehensive Project: Determinants and Their Financial Implications

Project Overview

This project aims to provide a comprehensive understanding of determinants and their applications in finance. By the end of the project, students will have mastered the calculation of determinants, understood their properties, and explored their practical uses in financial decision-making and risk assessment.

Project Title: "Determinants in Financial Analysis: Calculations, Properties, and Applications"

Project Objectives

1. Learn and perform determinant calculations.
2. Understand the mathematical properties of determinants.
3. Apply determinants in financial contexts such as investment decisions and risk assessment.
4. Explore the implications of determinants in matrix inversion and Cramer's Rule.
5. Analyze real-world financial problems using determinants.

Step-by-Step Instructions

&Step 1: Introduction to Determinants (Section 1)

- Task: Gain a fundamental understanding of determinants.
- Instructions:
- Define determinants and explain their importance in

linear algebra.

- Provide a step-by-step guide on how to calculate the determinant of a 2x2 and a 3x3 matrix.
- Illustrate the concept with simple numerical examples.
- Deliverables: A 2-page document including definitions, step-by-step calculations, and example problems.

&Step 2: Calculation Methods (Section 2)

- Task: Explore various methods for calculating determinants.
- Instructions:
- Describe different methods of calculating determinants (e.g., Laplace expansion, row reduction).
- Solve several determinant problems using each method.
- Compare the efficiency and applicability of each method in different scenarios.
- Deliverables: A 3-page report with descriptions, solved examples, and a comparison of calculation methods.

&Step 3: Properties of Determinants (Section 3)

- Task: Understand the key properties of determinants.
- Instructions:
- List and explain the main properties of determinants (e.g., linearity, product rule, effect of row swaps).
- Provide proofs or intuitive explanations for these properties.
- Demonstrate the properties with practical examples, particularly in the context of financial matrices.
- Deliverables: A 3-page document with property explanations, proofs, and practical examples.

&Step 4: Application to Investment Decisions (Section 4)

- Task: Apply determinants to financial decision-making processes.
- Instructions:
- Explain how determinants can be used to analyze investment decisions (e.g., stability of systems, risk assessment).
- Develop a hypothetical investment scenario and demonstrate the application of determinants.
- Interpret the results and discuss their implications for investment strategies.
- Deliverables: A 3-page report including the hypothetical scenario, determinant application, results, and interpretations.

&*Step 5: Cramer's Rule (Section 5)*

- Task: Learn and apply Cramer's Rule in solving linear systems.
- Instructions:
- Explain Cramer's Rule and its prerequisites.
- Provide step-by-step instructions for solving a system of linear equations using Cramer's Rule.
- Apply Cramer's Rule to a financial problem, such as determining the weights of assets in a diversified portfolio.
- Deliverables: A 3-page document with explanations, step-by-step solutions, and a financial application example.

&*Step 6: Determinant and Matrix Inversion (Section 6)*

- Task: Explore the relationship between determinants and matrix inversion.
- Instructions:
- Explain how determinants are used in finding the inverse of a matrix.
- Provide examples of matrix inversion using determinants.

- Discuss the implications of matrix inversion in financial modeling, such as solving linear systems in risk models.
- Deliverables: A 3-page report with explanations, examples, and financial implications of matrix inversion using determinants.

&*Step 7: Interpretations in Risk Assessment (Section 7)*

- Task: Analyze the role of determinants in financial risk assessment.
- Instructions:
- Explain how determinants can be used to assess the stability and risk of financial systems.
- Provide a case study where determinants are used to evaluate financial risk.
- Interpret the results and discuss their significance for financial decision-making.
- Deliverables: A 3-page report with explanations, a case study, and interpretations of risk assessment using determinants.

&*Step 8: Economic Implications (Section 8)*

- Task: Explore the broader economic implications of determinants in finance.
- Instructions:
- Discuss how determinants can be used to understand economic relationships and models.
- Provide examples of economic models that utilize determinants (e.g., input-output models).
- Analyze a real-world economic problem using determinants and interpret the results.
- Deliverables: A 3-page document with discussions, examples, and analysis of an economic problem using determinants.

Final Deliverable

Compile all sections into a comprehensive project report titled

"Determinants in Financial Analysis: Calculations, Properties, and Applications." Ensure the report is well-organized with a table of contents, proper citations, and references. The final report should be professionally formatted and submitted in both print and digital formats.

Evaluation Criteria

- Understanding of Concepts: Demonstrates a strong grasp of determinants and their applications in finance.
- Research Quality: Uses credible sources and provides accurate, well-supported information.
- Clarity and Presentation: Information is clearly presented, well-organized, and free of errors.
- Creativity: Uses visual aids and innovative approaches to explain complex concepts.
- Application: Provides real-world examples and case studies to illustrate theoretical concepts.

Good luck, and enjoy your exploration into the fascinating world of determinants and their financial implications!

Comprehensive Project: Eigenvalues and Eigenvectors

Project Overview

This project is designed to provide an in-depth understanding of eigenvalues and eigenvectors and their applications in finance. By the end of this project, students will have a solid grasp of calculating eigenvalues and eigenvectors, understanding their properties, and applying them to various financial contexts, such as risk analysis, portfolio management, and algorithmic trading.

Project Title: "Eigenvalues and Eigenvectors in Financial Analysis: Calculations, Properties, and Applications"

Project Objectives

1. Learn and perform calculations of eigenvalues and eigenvectors.

2. Understand the mathematical properties of eigenvalues and eigenvectors.

3. Apply eigenvalues and eigenvectors in financial contexts such as risk assessment and portfolio optimization.

4. Explore the implications of eigenvalues and eigenvectors in stability analysis and financial modeling.

5. Analyze real-world financial problems using eigenvalues and eigenvectors.

Step-by-Step Instructions

&Step 1: Characteristics and Properties of
Eigenvalues and Eigenvectors (Section 1)

- Task: Gain a fundamental understanding of eigenvalues and eigenvectors.
- Instructions:
- Define eigenvalues and eigenvectors and explain their significance in linear algebra.
- Provide a step-by-step guide on how to calculate the eigenvalues and eigenvectors of a 2x2 and a 3x3 matrix.
- Illustrate the concepts with simple numerical examples.
- Deliverables: A 2-page document including definitions, step-by-step calculations, and example problems.

&Step 2: Financial Interpretation of Eigenvalues
and Eigenvectors (Section 2)

- Task: Understand the financial implications of eigenvalues and eigenvectors.
- Instructions:
- Explain how eigenvalues and eigenvectors can be used to analyze financial systems, such as identifying dominant factors in a financial model.

- Develop a hypothetical financial scenario and demonstrate the application of eigenvalues and eigenvectors.
- Interpret the results and discuss their implications for financial decision-making.
- Deliverables: A 3-page report including the hypothetical scenario, eigenvalue and eigenvector application, results, and interpretations.

&Step 3: Calculation Techniques (Section 3)

- Task: Explore various methods for calculating eigenvalues and eigenvectors.
- Instructions:
- Describe different methods of calculating eigenvalues and eigenvectors (e.g., characteristic polynomial, power iteration).
- Solve several eigenvalue and eigenvector problems using each method.
- Compare the efficiency and applicability of each method in different scenarios.
- Deliverables: A 3-page report with descriptions, solved examples, and a comparison of calculation methods.

&Step 4: Diagonalization and Its Use (Section 4)

- Task: Learn and apply the concept of diagonalization.
- Instructions:
- Explain the process of diagonalizing a matrix and its prerequisites.
- Provide step-by-step instructions for diagonalizing a matrix.
- Apply diagonalization to a financial problem, such as simplifying a covariance matrix in portfolio optimization.
- Deliverables: A 3-page document with explanations, step-by-step solutions, and a financial application

example.

&*Step 5: Risk and Eigen Analysis (Section 5)*

- Task: Analyze the role of eigenvalues and eigenvectors in financial risk assessment.
- Instructions:
- Explain how eigenvalues and eigenvectors can be used to assess the stability and risk of financial systems.
- Provide a case study where eigenvalues and eigenvectors are used to evaluate financial risk.
- Interpret the results and discuss their significance for financial decision-making.
- Deliverables: A 3-page report with explanations, a case study, and interpretations of risk assessment using eigenvalues and eigenvectors.

&*Step 6: Stability of Systems (Section 6)*

- Task: Explore the implications of eigenvalues and eigenvectors in stability analysis.
- Instructions:
- Explain how eigenvalues can indicate the stability of a financial system or model.
- Provide examples of stability analysis using eigenvalues in financial contexts, such as stress testing a financial portfolio.
- Discuss the implications of these analyses for financial planning and risk management.
- Deliverables: A 3-page report with explanations, examples, and implications of stability analysis using eigenvalues.

&*Step 7: Portfolio Implications (Section 7)*

- Task: Analyze the impact of eigenvalues and eigenvectors on portfolio management.
- Instructions:
- Explain how eigenvalues and eigenvectors can be

used to optimize a financial portfolio.

- Provide a step-by-step guide on using eigenvalue decomposition in portfolio diversification.
- Develop a hypothetical portfolio and demonstrate the optimization process.
- Deliverables: A 3-page report with explanations, step-by-step guidance, and a hypothetical portfolio optimization example.

&Step 8: Sensitivity and Analysis (Section 8)

- Task: Explore the sensitivity of financial models using eigenvalues and eigenvectors.
- Instructions:
- Explain how the sensitivity of a financial model can be analyzed using eigenvalues.
- Provide examples of sensitivity analysis in financial contexts, such as assessing the impact of market changes on a financial model.
- Discuss the implications of sensitivity analysis for financial decision-making and risk management.
- Deliverables: A 3-page document with explanations, examples, and implications of sensitivity analysis using eigenvalues.

Final Deliverable

Compile all sections into a comprehensive project report titled "Eigenvalues and Eigenvectors in Financial Analysis: Calculations, Properties, and Applications." Ensure the report is well-organized with a table of contents, proper citations, and references. The final report should be professionally formatted and submitted in both print and digital formats.

Evaluation Criteria

- Understanding of Concepts: Demonstrates a strong grasp of eigenvalues and eigenvectors and their applications in finance.
- Research Quality: Uses credible sources and provides

accurate, well-supported information.

- Clarity and Presentation: Information is clearly presented, well-organized, and free of errors.
- Creativity: Uses visual aids and innovative approaches to explain complex concepts.
- Application: Provides real-world examples and case studies to illustrate theoretical concepts.

Good luck, and enjoy your exploration into the fascinating world of eigenvalues, eigenvectors, and their financial implications!

Comprehensive Project: Diagonalization and Jordan Form

Project Overview

This project aims to provide students with a deep understanding of diagonalization and Jordan form, critical concepts in linear algebra, and their applications in finance. By the end of this project, students will be proficient in performing matrix diagonalization, understanding the significance of Jordan form, and applying these techniques to solve real-world financial problems.

Project Title: "Diagonalization and Jordan Form in Financial Analysis: Techniques, Properties, and Applications"

Project Objectives

1. Learn and perform matrix diagonalization.
2. Understand the Jordan canonical form and its properties.
3. Apply diagonalization and Jordan form to financial models.
4. Analyze the implications of these techniques in simplifying complex financial systems.
5. Explore practical examples and case studies in finance.

Step-by-Step Instructions

&Step 1: Introduction to Diagonalization (Section 1)

- Task: Understand the basics of matrix diagonalization.
- Instructions:
- Define matrix diagonalization and explain its significance in linear algebra.
- Provide a step-by-step guide on how to diagonalize a 2x2 and a 3x3 matrix.
- Illustrate the concept with simple numerical examples.
- Deliverables: A 2-page document including definitions, step-by-step calculations, and example problems.

&*Step 2: Eigen Decomposition (Section 2)*

- Task: Learn the process of eigen decomposition.
- Instructions:
- Explain the relationship between eigenvalues, eigenvectors, and matrix diagonalization.
- Provide a step-by-step guide on performing eigen decomposition.
- Solve example problems to illustrate the process.
- Deliverables: A 3-page document with explanations, step-by-step solutions, and example problems.

&*Step 3: Application to Asset Pricing (Section 3)*

- Task: Apply diagonalization techniques to asset pricing models.
- Instructions:
- Explain how matrix diagonalization can simplify asset pricing models.
- Develop a hypothetical asset pricing scenario and demonstrate the application of diagonalization.
- Interpret the results and discuss their implications for asset pricing.
- Deliverables: A 3-page report including the hypothetical scenario, diagonalization application,

results, and interpretations.

&*Step 4: Block Matrices in Finance (Section 4)*

- Task: Explore the use of block matrices in financial modeling.
- Instructions:
- Define block matrices and explain their significance in finance.
- Provide examples of block matrices in financial contexts, such as risk management and portfolio analysis.
- Solve example problems to illustrate the use of block matrices.
- Deliverables: A 3-page document with definitions, examples, and solved problems.

&*Step 5: The Jordan Canonical Form (Section 5)*

- Task: Understand the concept of the Jordan canonical form.
- Instructions:
- Define the Jordan canonical form and explain its significance in linear algebra.
- Provide a step-by-step guide on how to find the Jordan form of a matrix.
- Illustrate the concept with simple numerical examples.
- Deliverables: A 2-page document including definitions, step-by-step calculations, and example problems.

&*Step 6: Practical Considerations in Finance (Section 6)*

- Task: Explore the practical applications of diagonalization and Jordan form in finance.
- Instructions:
- Discuss the practical considerations and challenges of applying these techniques in financial modeling.
- Provide real-world examples and case studies where

diagonalization and Jordan form are used.

- Analyze the implications of these techniques for financial decision-making and risk management.
- Deliverables: A 3-page report including discussions, examples, case studies, and implications.

&Step 7: Limitations and Computational Complexity (Section 7)

- Task: Understand the limitations and computational complexity of these techniques.
- Instructions:
- Discuss the limitations of matrix diagonalization and Jordan form in financial contexts.
- Explore the computational complexity of these techniques and their impact on financial modeling.
- Provide strategies to overcome these limitations in practice.
- Deliverables: A 3-page report with discussions, complexity analysis, and practical strategies.

&Step 8: Final Project Compilation

- Task: Compile all sections into a comprehensive project report.
- Instructions:
- Ensure the report is well-organized with a table of contents, proper citations, and references.
- Format the report professionally, ensuring clarity and readability.
- Submit the final report in both print and digital formats.
- Deliverables: A complete project report titled "Diagonalization and Jordan Form in Financial Analysis: Techniques, Properties, and Applications."

Final Deliverable

Compile all sections into a comprehensive project report titled "Diagonalization and Jordan Form in Financial Analysis: Techniques, Properties, and Applications." Ensure the report is well-organized with a table of contents, proper citations, and references. The final report should be professionally formatted and submitted in both print and digital formats.

Evaluation Criteria

- Understanding of Concepts: Demonstrates a strong grasp of diagonalization and Jordan form and their applications in finance.
- Research Quality: Uses credible sources and provides accurate, well-supported information.
- Clarity and Presentation: Information is clearly presented, well-organized, and free of errors.
- Creativity: Uses visual aids and innovative approaches to explain complex concepts.
- Application: Provides real-world examples and case studies to illustrate theoretical concepts.

Good luck, and enjoy your exploration into the fascinating world of diagonalization, Jordan form, and their financial implications!

Comprehensive Project: Singular Value Decomposition (SVD) in Financial Analysis

Project Overview

This project aims to provide students with a deep understanding of Singular Value Decomposition (SVD), a powerful matrix factorization technique, and its applications in finance. By the end of this project, students will be proficient in performing SVD, understanding its mathematical underpinnings, and applying these techniques to solve real-world financial problems.

Project Title: "Singular Value Decomposition in Financial Analysis: Techniques, Properties, and Applications"

Project Objectives

1. Learn the mathematical foundations of Singular Value Decomposition.

2. Perform SVD on various matrices.

3. Apply SVD to financial models and data compression.

4. Analyze implications of SVD in risk management and predictive analytics.

5. Explore practical examples and case studies in finance.

Step-by-Step Instructions

&Step 1: Understanding Singular Value Decomposition (Section 1)

- Task: Understand the basics and properties of Singular Value Decomposition.
- Instructions:
- Define Singular Value Decomposition and explain its significance in linear algebra and finance.
- Provide the mathematical formulation of SVD: $(A = U V^\wedge T)$.
- Illustrate the concept with a simple numerical example.
- Deliverables: A 2-page document including definitions, mathematical formulations, and example problems.

&Step 2: Approximating Financial Matrices (Section 2)

- Task: Learn how SVD can be used to approximate financial matrices.
- Instructions:
- Explain the concept of rank-k approximation using SVD.
- Provide a step-by-step guide on how to approximate a financial matrix using SVD.
- Solve example problems to illustrate the process.
- Deliverables: A 3-page document with explanations, step-by-step solutions, and example problems.

&Step 3: SVD and Data Compression (Section 3)

- Task: Apply SVD for data compression in financial

datasets.

- Instructions:
- Explain how SVD can be used for data compression and noise reduction.
- Develop a hypothetical financial dataset and demonstrate the application of SVD for data compression.
- Interpret the results and discuss their implications for financial data analysis.
- Deliverables: A 3-page report including the hypothetical dataset, SVD application, results, and interpretations.

&Step 4: Covariance and Correlation (Section 4)

- Task: Explore the use of SVD in analyzing covariance and correlation matrices.
- Instructions:
- Define covariance and correlation matrices and explain their significance in finance.
- Provide examples of how SVD can be applied to these matrices to extract meaningful financial insights.
- Solve example problems to illustrate the use of SVD in covariance and correlation analysis.
- Deliverables: A 3-page document with definitions, examples, and solved problems.

&Step 5: Applications in Credit Risk Models (Section 5)

- Task: Apply SVD techniques to credit risk modeling.
- Instructions:
- Discuss how SVD can be used in credit risk models to identify key risk factors.
- Develop a hypothetical credit risk scenario and demonstrate the application of SVD.
- Interpret the results and discuss their implications for credit risk management.
- Deliverables: A 3-page report including the

hypothetical scenario, SVD application, results, and interpretations.

&*Step 6: Stability and Predictive Applications (Section 6)*

- Task: Explore the stability and predictive applications of SVD in financial modeling.
- Instructions:
- Discuss the stability properties of SVD and its importance in financial modeling.
- Provide examples of predictive applications of SVD in finance, such as forecasting financial trends.
- Solve example problems to illustrate the predictive power of SVD.
- Deliverables: A 3-page report with discussions, examples, and solved problems.

&*Step 7: Numerical Stability (Section 7)*

- Task: Understand the numerical stability of SVD and its implications for financial computations.
- Instructions:
- Discuss the numerical stability of SVD and its importance in financial computations.
- Explore strategies for ensuring numerical stability in SVD computations.
- Provide examples of numerical stability issues and their solutions.
- Deliverables: A 3-page document with discussions, stability analysis, and practical strategies.

&*Step 8: Practical Examples in Finance (Section 8)*

- Task: Explore practical examples of SVD applications in finance.
- Instructions:
- Provide real-world examples and case studies where SVD is used in financial analysis.
- Analyze the implications of these examples for financial decision-making and risk management.

- Discuss the lessons learned from these real-world applications.
- Deliverables: A 3-page report including examples, case studies, and implications.

&Step 9: Final Project Compilation

- Task: Compile all sections into a comprehensive project report.
- Instructions:
- Ensure the report is well-organized with a table of contents, proper citations, and references.
- Format the report professionally, ensuring clarity and readability.
- Submit the final report in both print and digital formats.
- Deliverables: A complete project report titled "Singular Value Decomposition in Financial Analysis: Techniques, Properties, and Applications."

Final Deliverable

Compile all sections into a comprehensive project report titled "Singular Value Decomposition in Financial Analysis: Techniques, Properties, and Applications." Ensure the report is well-organized with a table of contents, proper citations, and references. The final report should be professionally formatted and submitted in both print and digital formats.

Evaluation Criteria

- Understanding of Concepts: Demonstrates a strong grasp of SVD and its applications in finance.
- Research Quality: Uses credible sources and provides accurate, well-supported information.
- Clarity and Presentation: Information is clearly presented, well-organized, and free of errors.
- Creativity: Uses visual aids and innovative approaches to explain complex concepts.
- Application: Provides real-world examples and case

studies to illustrate theoretical concepts.

Good luck, and enjoy your exploration into the fascinating world of Singular Value Decomposition and its financial implications!

Comprehensive Project: Singular Value Decomposition (SVD) in Financial Analysis

Project Overview

This project aims to provide students with a deep understanding of Singular Value Decomposition (SVD), a powerful matrix factorization technique, and its applications in finance. By the end of this project, students will be proficient in performing SVD, understanding its mathematical underpinnings, and applying these techniques to solve real-world financial problems.

Project Title: "Singular Value Decomposition in Financial Analysis: Techniques, Properties, and Applications"

Project Objectives

1. Learn the mathematical foundations of Singular Value Decomposition.
2. Perform SVD on various matrices.
3. Apply SVD to financial models and data compression.
4. Analyze implications of SVD in risk management and predictive analytics.
5. Explore practical examples and case studies in finance.

Step-by-Step Instructions

&Step 1: Understanding Singular Value Decomposition (Section 1)

- Task: Understand the basics and properties of Singular Value Decomposition.
- Instructions:
- Research and Define:
- Define Singular Value Decomposition and explain its

significance in linear algebra and finance.

- Provide the mathematical formulation of SVD: (A = U V^T).
- Include visual aids or diagrams to illustrate the decomposition.
- Example Problem:
- Provide a simple numerical example to demonstrate SVD.
- Calculate the SVD for a 3x3 matrix and interpret the results.
- Deliverables: A 2-page document including definitions, mathematical formulations, visual aids, and example problems.

&Step 2: Approximating Financial Matrices (Section 2)

- Task: Learn how SVD can be used to approximate financial matrices.
- Instructions:
- Concept Explanation:
- Explain the concept of rank-k approximation using SVD.
- Discuss why approximation is useful in finance.
- Step-by-Step Guide:
- Provide a step-by-step guide on how to approximate a financial matrix using SVD.
- Use a hypothetical financial matrix (e.g., a matrix representing stock prices) for demonstration.
- Example Problems:
- Solve example problems to illustrate the process.
- Deliverables: A 3-page document with explanations, step-by-step solutions, and example problems.

&Step 3: SVD and Data Compression (Section 3)

- Task: Apply SVD for data compression in financial datasets.
- Instructions:

- Concept Explanation:
- Explain how SVD can be used for data compression and noise reduction.
- Discuss the benefits of data compression in financial analysis.
- Hypothetical Dataset:
- Develop a hypothetical financial dataset (e.g., historical stock prices).
- Demonstrate the application of SVD for data compression on this dataset.
- Results Interpretation:
- Interpret the results and discuss their implications for financial data analysis.
- Deliverables: A 3-page report including the hypothetical dataset, SVD application, results, and interpretations.

&Step 4: Covariance and Correlation (Section 4)

- Task: Explore the use of SVD in analyzing covariance and correlation matrices.
- Instructions:
- Definitions and Significance:
- Define covariance and correlation matrices.
- Explain their significance in finance.
- SVD Application:
- Provide examples of how SVD can be applied to these matrices to extract meaningful financial insights.
- Example Problems:
- Solve example problems to illustrate the use of SVD in covariance and correlation analysis.
- Deliverables: A 3-page document with definitions, examples, and solved problems.

&Step 5: Applications in Credit Risk Models (Section 5)

- Task: Apply SVD techniques to credit risk modeling.
- Instructions:

- Application Explanation:
- Discuss how SVD can be used in credit risk models to identify key risk factors.
- Hypothetical Scenario:
- Develop a hypothetical credit risk scenario (e.g., assessing the risk of a portfolio of loans).
- Demonstrate the application of SVD in this scenario.
- Results Interpretation:
- Interpret the results and discuss their implications for credit risk management.
- Deliverables: A 3-page report including the hypothetical scenario, SVD application, results, and interpretations.

&*Step 6: Stability and Predictive Applications (Section 6)*

- Task: Explore the stability and predictive applications of SVD in financial modeling.
- Instructions:
- Stability Properties:
- Discuss the stability properties of SVD and their importance in financial modeling.
- Predictive Applications:
- Provide examples of predictive applications of SVD in finance, such as forecasting financial trends.
- Use real or hypothetical data to illustrate these applications.
- Example Problems:
- Solve example problems to illustrate the predictive power of SVD.
- Deliverables: A 3-page report with discussions, examples, and solved problems.

&*Step 7: Numerical Stability (Section 7)*

- Task: Understand the numerical stability of SVD and its implications for financial computations.
- Instructions:

- Numerical Stability Discussion:
- Discuss the numerical stability of SVD and its importance in financial computations.
- Ensuring Stability:
- Explore strategies for ensuring numerical stability in SVD computations.
- Examples:
- Provide examples of numerical stability issues and their solutions.
- Deliverables: A 3-page document with discussions, stability analysis, and practical strategies.

&Step 8: Practical Examples in Finance (Section 8)
- Task: Explore practical examples of SVD applications in finance.
- Instructions:
- Real-World Examples:
- Provide real-world examples and case studies where SVD is used in financial analysis.
- Implications Analysis:
- Analyze the implications of these examples for financial decision-making and risk management.
- Lessons Learned:
- Discuss the lessons learned from these real-world applications.
- Deliverables: A 3-page report including examples, case studies, and implications.

&Step 9: Final Project Compilation
- Task: Compile all sections into a comprehensive project report.
- Instructions:
- Organization:
- Ensure the report is well-organized with a table of contents, proper citations, and references.
- Formatting:

- Format the report professionally, ensuring clarity and readability.
- Submission:
- Submit the final report in both print and digital formats.
- Deliverables: A complete project report titled "Singular Value Decomposition in Financial Analysis: Techniques, Properties, and Applications."

Final Deliverable

Compile all sections into a comprehensive project report titled "Singular Value Decomposition in Financial Analysis: Techniques, Properties, and Applications." Ensure the report is well-organized with a table of contents, proper citations, and references. The final report should be professionally formatted and submitted in both print and digital formats.

Evaluation Criteria

- Understanding of Concepts: Demonstrates a strong grasp of SVD and its applications in finance.
- Research Quality: Uses credible sources and provides accurate, well-supported information.
- Clarity and Presentation: Information is clearly presented, well-organized, and free of errors.
- Creativity: Uses visual aids and innovative approaches to explain complex concepts.
- Application: Provides real-world examples and case studies to illustrate theoretical concepts.

Good luck, and enjoy your exploration into the fascinating world of Singular Value Decomposition and its financial implications!

Comprehensive Project: Norms and Metrics in Financial Analysis

Project Overview

This project aims to provide students with an in-depth understanding of norms and metrics, essential tools in linear algebra, and their applications in finance. By the end of this project, students will be proficient in using various norms and metrics to analyze financial data, optimize portfolios, and assess the stability of financial models.

Project Title: "Norms and Metrics in Financial Analysis: Tools for Quantitative Finance"

Project Objectives

1. Learn the mathematical foundations of vector and matrix norms.
2. Perform norm calculations on financial datasets.
3. Apply norms and metrics to measure financial data and errors.
4. Analyze the conditioning of financial models using norms.
5. Explore practical examples and case studies in finance.

Step-by-Step Instructions

&Step 1: Understanding Vector Norms (Section 1)

- Task: Understand the basics and properties of vector norms.
- Instructions:
- Research and Define:
- Define vector norms and explain their significance.
- Provide the mathematical formulation for different types of vector norms (e.g., L1 norm, L2 norm, infinity norm).
- Include visual aids or diagrams to illustrate the norms.
- Example Problem:
- Provide a simple numerical example to demonstrate each type of norm.
- Calculate the L1, L2, and infinity norms for a given vector and interpret the results.
- Deliverables: A 2-page document including

definitions, mathematical formulations, visual aids, and example problems.

&*Step 2: Understanding Matrix Norms (Section 2)*

- Task: Learn the basics and properties of matrix norms.
- Instructions:
- Concept Explanation:
- Explain the concept of matrix norms and their importance in finance.
- Provide the mathematical formulation for common matrix norms (e.g., Frobenius norm, operator norm).
- Step-by-Step Guide:
- Provide a step-by-step guide on how to calculate these matrix norms.
- Use a hypothetical financial matrix (e.g., a matrix representing stock returns) for demonstration.
- Example Problems:
- Solve example problems to illustrate the process.
- Deliverables: A 3-page document with explanations, step-by-step solutions, and example problems.

&*Step 3: Measuring Financial Data (Section 3)*

- Task: Apply norms to measure financial data.
- Instructions:
- Concept Explanation:
- Explain how norms can be used to measure financial data and assess data quality.
- Discuss the benefits of using norms in financial analysis.
- Hypothetical Dataset:
- Develop a hypothetical financial dataset (e.g., daily closing prices of a stock).
- Demonstrate the application of norms to measure this dataset.
- Results Interpretation:

- Interpret the results and discuss their implications for financial data analysis.
- Deliverables: A 3-page report including the hypothetical dataset, norm application, results, and interpretations.

&*Step 4: Errors and Approximations (Section 4)*

- Task: Explore the use of norms in measuring errors and approximations.
- Instructions:
- Definitions and Significance:
- Define errors and approximations in the context of financial models.
- Explain the significance of measuring these errors using norms.
- Step-by-Step Guide:
- Provide a step-by-step guide on how to use norms to measure errors in financial models.
- Use a hypothetical financial model (e.g., a linear regression model) for demonstration.
- Example Problems:
- Solve example problems to illustrate the use of norms in error measurement.
- Deliverables: A 3-page document with definitions, examples, and solved problems.

&*Step 5: Conditioning of Financial Models (Section 5)*

- Task: Analyze the conditioning of financial models using norms.
- Instructions:
- Application Explanation:
- Discuss how norms can be used to assess the conditioning of financial models.
- Explain the concept of condition numbers and their importance in finance.
- Hypothetical Scenario:

- Develop a hypothetical scenario (e.g., assessing the conditioning of a portfolio optimization model).
- Demonstrate the application of norms and condition numbers in this scenario.
- Results Interpretation:
- Interpret the results and discuss their implications for financial model stability.
- Deliverables: A 3-page report including the hypothetical scenario, norm application, results, and interpretations.

&Step 6: *Stability of Algorithms (Section 6)*

- Task: Explore the stability of financial algorithms using norms.
- Instructions:
- Stability Properties:
- Discuss the stability properties of financial algorithms and their importance.
- Explain how norms can be used to assess the stability of these algorithms.
- Hypothetical Example:
- Develop a hypothetical example (e.g., the stability of an algorithm for option pricing).
- Demonstrate the application of norms to assess the stability of this algorithm.
- Example Problems:
- Solve example problems to illustrate the stability assessment.
- Deliverables: A 3-page report with discussions, examples, and solved problems.

&Step 7: *Portfolio Optimization Strategies (Section 7)*

- Task: Apply norms to optimize financial portfolios.
- Instructions:
- Concept Explanation:
- Explain how norms can be used in portfolio

optimization.

- Discuss the benefits of using norms to develop robust portfolio strategies.
- Hypothetical Portfolio:
- Develop a hypothetical portfolio of financial assets.
- Demonstrate the application of norms to optimize this portfolio.
- Results Interpretation:
- Interpret the results and discuss their implications for portfolio management.
- Deliverables: A 3-page report including the hypothetical portfolio, norm application, results, and interpretations.

&Step 8: Practical Examples in Finance (Section 8)

- Task: Explore practical examples of norms and metrics applications in finance.
- Instructions:
- Real-World Examples:
- Provide real-world examples and case studies where norms and metrics are used in financial analysis.
- Implications Analysis:
- Analyze the implications of these examples for financial decision-making and risk management.
- Lessons Learned:
- Discuss the lessons learned from these real-world applications.
- Deliverables: A 3-page report including examples, case studies, and implications.

&Step 9: Final Project Compilation

- Task: Compile all sections into a comprehensive project report.
- Instructions:
- Organization:
- Ensure the report is well-organized with a table of

contents, proper citations, and references.
- Formatting:
- Format the report professionally, ensuring clarity and readability.
- Submission:
- Submit the final report in both print and digital formats.
- Deliverables: A complete project report titled "Norms and Metrics in Financial Analysis: Tools for Quantitative Finance."

Final Deliverable

Compile all sections into a comprehensive project report titled "Norms and Metrics in Financial Analysis: Tools for Quantitative Finance." Ensure the report is well-organized with a table of contents, proper citations, and references. The final report should be professionally formatted and submitted in both print and digital formats.

Evaluation Criteria

- Understanding of Concepts: Demonstrates a strong grasp of norms and metrics and their applications in finance.
- Research Quality: Uses credible sources and provides accurate, well-supported information.
- Clarity and Presentation: Information is clearly presented, well-organized, and free of errors.
- Creativity: Uses visual aids and innovative approaches to explain complex concepts.
- Application: Provides real-world examples and case studies to illustrate theoretical concepts.

Good luck, and enjoy your exploration into the fascinating world of norms and metrics and their financial implications!

Comprehensive Project: Orthogonality and Orthogonal Matrices in Financial Analysis

Project Overview

This project is designed to provide students with a thorough understanding of orthogonality and orthogonal matrices, which are fundamental concepts in linear algebra with significant applications in finance. By the end of this project, students will be able to apply orthogonality principles to minimize risks, optimize portfolios, and enhance computational efficiency in financial models.

Project Title: "Orthogonality and Orthogonal Matrices in Financial Analysis: Enhancing Risk Management and Optimization"

Project Objectives

1. Understand the concepts and properties of orthogonality and orthogonal matrices.
2. Apply orthogonality to minimize financial risks.
3. Use orthogonal matrices in practical financial problems.
4. Implement the Gram-Schmidt process to orthogonalize vectors.
5. Explore least squares solutions and their financial applications.
6. Analyze the efficiency of computational methods involving orthogonal matrices.

Step-by-Step Instructions

&Step 1: Concepts of Orthogonality (Section 1)

- Task: Understand the basic concepts and significance of orthogonality.
- Instructions:
- Research and Define:
- Define orthogonality in the context of vectors and matrices.
- Explain the geometrical interpretation of orthogonality.
- Provide examples of orthogonal vectors and

orthogonal matrices.

- Example Problem:
- Given two vectors, show how to check if they are orthogonal.
- Provide a step-by-step solution and interpret the results.
- Deliverables: A 2-page document with definitions, explanations, and example problems.

&Step 2: Transition to Orthogonal Finance (Section 2)

- Task: Explore how orthogonality principles transition into financial applications.
- Instructions:
- Concept Explanation:
- Discuss the relevance of orthogonality in financial contexts.
- Explain how orthogonal principles can be applied to financial data analysis and risk management.
- Hypothetical Scenario:
- Develop a hypothetical scenario where orthogonality is used to analyze financial data.
- Demonstrate the application and discuss the benefits.
- Deliverables: A 2-page report with explanations and hypothetical scenarios.

&Step 3: Application in Minimizing Risks (Section 3)

- Task: Apply orthogonality to minimize financial risks.
- Instructions:
- Risk Minimization Techniques:
- Explain how orthogonal matrices can be used to minimize risks in portfolio management.
- Provide mathematical formulations and risk metrics.
- Example Problems:
- Develop example problems where orthogonal matrices are used to construct a risk-minimized

portfolio.
- Solve the problems and interpret the results.
- Deliverables: A 3-page document with explanations, formulations, and example problems.

&*Step 4: Economic Insights Possibilities (Section 4)*
- Task: Explore economic insights through orthogonal matrices.
- Instructions:
- Insight Exploration:
- Discuss how orthogonal matrices can provide economic insights into market behavior.
- Explain the implications for financial decision-making.
- Case Study Analysis:
- Analyze a case study where orthogonal matrices were used to gain economic insights.
- Discuss the findings and their impact on financial strategies.
- Deliverables: A 3-page report with discussions and case study analysis.

&*Step 5: Gram-Schmidt Process (Section 5)*
- Task: Implement the Gram-Schmidt process to orthogonalize vectors.
- Instructions:
- Process Explanation:
- Explain the Gram-Schmidt process and its importance.
- Provide the step-by-step procedure for orthogonalizing a set of vectors.
- Example Problems:
- Provide example problems where the Gram-Schmidt process is applied to a set of vectors.
- Solve the problems and show the orthogonalized vectors.

- Deliverables: A 2-page document with explanations, procedures, and example problems.

&*Step 6: The Role of Least Squares (Section 6)*

- Task: Explore the role of least squares solutions in financial models.
- Instructions:
- Concept Explanation:
- Explain the least squares method and its significance in finance.
- Discuss how orthogonality plays a role in least squares solutions.
- Example Problems:
- Develop example problems where least squares solutions are used in financial models.
- Solve the problems and interpret the results.
- Deliverables: A 3-page document with explanations and example problems.

&*Step 7: Efficiency in Computations (Section 7)*

- Task: Analyze computational efficiency using orthogonal matrices.
- Instructions:
- Efficiency Analysis:
- Discuss the computational benefits of using orthogonal matrices in financial algorithms.
- Explain how orthogonal matrices improve algorithm stability and efficiency.
- Hypothetical Example:
- Develop a hypothetical example where orthogonal matrices are used to enhance computational efficiency.
- Demonstrate the process and results.
- Deliverables: A 3-page report with discussions and hypothetical examples.

&*Step 8: Practical Applications (Section 8)*

- Task: Explore practical applications of orthogonal matrices in finance.
- Instructions:
- Real-World Examples:
- Provide real-world examples and case studies where orthogonal matrices are used in financial analysis.
- Implications Analysis:
- Analyze the implications of these applications for financial decision-making and risk management.
- Lessons Learned:
- Discuss the lessons learned from these real-world applications.
- Deliverables: A 3-page report including examples, case studies, and implications.

&Step 9: Final Project Compilation

- Task: Compile all sections into a comprehensive project report.
- Instructions:
- Organization:
- Ensure the report is well-organized with a table of contents, proper citations, and references.
- Formatting:
- Format the report professionally, ensuring clarity and readability.
- Submission:
- Submit the final report in both print and digital formats.
- Deliverables: A complete project report titled "Orthogonality and Orthogonal Matrices in Financial Analysis: Enhancing Risk Management and Optimization."

Final Deliverable

Compile all sections into a comprehensive project report titled "Orthogonality and Orthogonal Matrices in Financial

Analysis: Enhancing Risk Management and Optimization." Ensure the report is well-organized with a table of contents, proper citations, and references. The final report should be professionally formatted and submitted in both print and digital formats.

Evaluation Criteria

- Understanding of Concepts: Demonstrates a strong grasp of orthogonality and orthogonal matrices and their applications in finance.
- Research Quality: Uses credible sources and provides accurate, well-supported information.
- Clarity and Presentation: Information is clearly presented, well-organized, and free of errors.
- Creativity: Uses visual aids and innovative approaches to explain complex concepts.
- Application: Provides real-world examples and case studies to illustrate theoretical concepts.

Good luck, and enjoy your exploration into the fascinating world of orthogonality and orthogonal matrices and their financial implications!

Comprehensive Project: Orthogonality and Orthogonal Matrices in Financial Analysis

Project Overview

This project is designed to provide students with a thorough understanding of orthogonality and orthogonal matrices, which are fundamental concepts in linear algebra with significant applications in finance. By the end of this project, students will be able to apply orthogonality principles to minimize risks, optimize portfolios, and enhance computational efficiency in financial models.

Project Title: "Orthogonality and Orthogonal Matrices in Financial Analysis: Enhancing Risk Management and Optimization"

Project Objectives

1. Understand the concepts and properties of orthogonality and orthogonal matrices.
2. Apply orthogonality to minimize financial risks.
3. Use orthogonal matrices in practical financial problems.
4. Implement the Gram-Schmidt process to orthogonalize vectors.
5. Explore least squares solutions and their financial applications.
6. Analyze the efficiency of computational methods involving orthogonal matrices.

Step-by-Step Instructions

&Step 1: Concepts of Orthogonality (Section 1)

- Task: Understand the basic concepts and significance of orthogonality.
- Instructions:
- Research and Define:
- Define orthogonality in the context of vectors and matrices.
- Explain the geometrical interpretation of orthogonality.
- Provide examples of orthogonal vectors and orthogonal matrices.
- Example Problem:
- Given two vectors, show how to check if they are orthogonal.
- Provide a step-by-step solution and interpret the results.
- Deliverables: A 2-page document with definitions, explanations, and example problems.

&Step 2: Transition to Orthogonal Finance (Section 2)

- Task: Explore how orthogonality principles transition into financial applications.
- Instructions:

- Concept Explanation:
- Discuss the relevance of orthogonality in financial contexts.
- Explain how orthogonal principles can be applied to financial data analysis and risk management.
- Hypothetical Scenario:
- Develop a hypothetical scenario where orthogonality is used to analyze financial data.
- Demonstrate the application and discuss the benefits.
- Deliverables: A 2-page report with explanations and hypothetical scenarios.

&*Step 3: Application in Minimizing Risks (Section 3)*

- Task: Apply orthogonality to minimize financial risks.
- Instructions:
- Risk Minimization Techniques:
- Explain how orthogonal matrices can be used to minimize risks in portfolio management.
- Provide mathematical formulations and risk metrics.
- Example Problems:
- Develop example problems where orthogonal matrices are used to construct a risk-minimized portfolio.
- Solve the problems and interpret the results.
- Deliverables: A 3-page document with explanations, formulations, and example problems.

&*Step 4: Economic Insights Possibilities (Section 4)*

- Task: Explore economic insights through orthogonal matrices.
- Instructions:
- Insight Exploration:
- Discuss how orthogonal matrices can provide economic insights into market behavior.
- Explain the implications for financial decision-

making.
- Case Study Analysis:
- Analyze a case study where orthogonal matrices were used to gain economic insights.
- Discuss the findings and their impact on financial strategies.
- Deliverables: A 3-page report with discussions and case study analysis.

&Step 5: Gram-Schmidt Process (Section 5)

- Task: Implement the Gram-Schmidt process to orthogonalize vectors.
- Instructions:
- Process Explanation:
- Explain the Gram-Schmidt process and its importance.
- Provide the step-by-step procedure for orthogonalizing a set of vectors.
- Example Problems:
- Provide example problems where the Gram-Schmidt process is applied to a set of vectors.
- Solve the problems and show the orthogonalized vectors.
- Deliverables: A 2-page document with explanations, procedures, and example problems.

&Step 6: The Role of Least Squares (Section 6)

- Task: Explore the role of least squares solutions in financial models.
- Instructions:
- Concept Explanation:
- Explain the least squares method and its significance in finance.
- Discuss how orthogonality plays a role in least squares solutions.
- Example Problems:

- Develop example problems where least squares solutions are used in financial models.
- Solve the problems and interpret the results.
- Deliverables: A 3-page document with explanations and example problems.

&Step 7: *Efficiency in Computations (Section 7)*

- Task: Analyze computational efficiency using orthogonal matrices.
- Instructions:
- Efficiency Analysis:
- Discuss the computational benefits of using orthogonal matrices in financial algorithms.
- Explain how orthogonal matrices improve algorithm stability and efficiency.
- Hypothetical Example:
- Develop a hypothetical example where orthogonal matrices are used to enhance computational efficiency.
- Demonstrate the process and results.
- Deliverables: A 3-page report with discussions and hypothetical examples.

&Step 8: *Practical Applications (Section 8)*

- Task: Explore practical applications of orthogonal matrices in finance.
- Instructions:
- Real-World Examples:
- Provide real-world examples and case studies where orthogonal matrices are used in financial analysis.
- Implications Analysis:
- Analyze the implications of these applications for financial decision-making and risk management.
- Lessons Learned:
- Discuss the lessons learned from these real-world applications.

- Deliverables: A 3-page report including examples, case studies, and implications.

&Step 9: Final Project Compilation

- Task: Compile all sections into a comprehensive project report.
- Instructions:
- Organization:
- Ensure the report is well-organized with a table of contents, proper citations, and references.
- Formatting:
- Format the report professionally, ensuring clarity and readability.
- Submission:
- Submit the final report in both print and digital formats.
- Deliverables: A complete project report titled "Orthogonality and Orthogonal Matrices in Financial Analysis: Enhancing Risk Management and Optimization."

Final Deliverable

Compile all sections into a comprehensive project report titled "Orthogonality and Orthogonal Matrices in Financial Analysis: Enhancing Risk Management and Optimization." Ensure the report is well-organized with a table of contents, proper citations, and references. The final report should be professionally formatted and submitted in both print and digital formats.

Evaluation Criteria

- Understanding of Concepts: Demonstrates a strong grasp of orthogonality and orthogonal matrices and their applications in finance.
- Research Quality: Uses credible sources and provides accurate, well-supported information.
- Clarity and Presentation: Information is clearly

presented, well-organized, and free of errors.

- Creativity: Uses visual aids and innovative approaches to explain complex concepts.
- Application: Provides real-world examples and case studies to illustrate theoretical concepts.

Good luck, and enjoy your exploration into the fascinating world of orthogonality and orthogonal matrices and their financial implications!

Comprehensive Project: Orthogonality and Orthogonal Matrices in Financial Analysis

Project Overview

This project is designed to provide students with a thorough understanding of orthogonality and orthogonal matrices, which are fundamental concepts in linear algebra with significant applications in finance. By the end of this project, students will be able to apply orthogonality principles to minimize risks, optimize portfolios, and enhance computational efficiency in financial models.

Project Title: "Orthogonality and Orthogonal Matrices in Financial Analysis: Enhancing Risk Management and Optimization"

Project Objectives

1. Understand the concepts and properties of orthogonality and orthogonal matrices.
2. Apply orthogonality to minimize financial risks.
3. Use orthogonal matrices in practical financial problems.
4. Implement the Gram-Schmidt process to orthogonalize vectors.
5. Explore least squares solutions and their financial applications.
6. Analyze the efficiency of computational methods involving orthogonal matrices.

Step-by-Step Instructions

&*Step 1: Concepts of Orthogonality (Section 1)*

- Task: Understand the basic concepts and significance of orthogonality.
- Instructions:
- Research and Define:
- Define orthogonality in the context of vectors and matrices.
- Explain the geometrical interpretation of orthogonality.
- Provide examples of orthogonal vectors and orthogonal matrices.
- Example Problem:
- Given two vectors, show how to check if they are orthogonal.
- Provide a step-by-step solution and interpret the results.
- Deliverables: A 2-page document with definitions, explanations, and example problems.

&*Step 2: Transition to Orthogonal Finance (Section 2)*

- Task: Explore how orthogonality principles transition into financial applications.
- Instructions:
- Concept Explanation:
- Discuss the relevance of orthogonality in financial contexts.
- Explain how orthogonal principles can be applied to financial data analysis and risk management.
- Hypothetical Scenario:
- Develop a hypothetical scenario where orthogonality is used to analyze financial data.
- Demonstrate the application and discuss the benefits.
- Deliverables: A 2-page report with explanations and hypothetical scenarios.

&*Step 3: Application in Minimizing Risks (Section 3)*

- Task: Apply orthogonality to minimize financial risks.
- Instructions:
- Risk Minimization Techniques:
- Explain how orthogonal matrices can be used to minimize risks in portfolio management.
- Provide mathematical formulations and risk metrics.
- Example Problems:
- Develop example problems where orthogonal matrices are used to construct a risk-minimized portfolio.
- Solve the problems and interpret the results.
- Deliverables: A 3-page document with explanations, formulations, and example problems.

&Step 4: Economic Insights Possibilities (Section 4)

- Task: Explore economic insights through orthogonal matrices.
- Instructions:
- Insight Exploration:
- Discuss how orthogonal matrices can provide economic insights into market behavior.
- Explain the implications for financial decision-making.
- Case Study Analysis:
- Analyze a case study where orthogonal matrices were used to gain economic insights.
- Discuss the findings and their impact on financial strategies.
- Deliverables: A 3-page report with discussions and case study analysis.

&Step 5: Gram-Schmidt Process (Section 5)

- Task: Implement the Gram-Schmidt process to orthogonalize vectors.
- Instructions:

- Process Explanation:
- Explain the Gram-Schmidt process and its importance.
- Provide the step-by-step procedure for orthogonalizing a set of vectors.
- Example Problems:
- Provide example problems where the Gram-Schmidt process is applied to a set of vectors.
- Solve the problems and show the orthogonalized vectors.
- Deliverables: A 2-page document with explanations, procedures, and example problems.

&Step 6: The Role of Least Squares (Section 6)

- Task: Explore the role of least squares solutions in financial models.
- Instructions:
- Concept Explanation:
- Explain the least squares method and its significance in finance.
- Discuss how orthogonality plays a role in least squares solutions.
- Example Problems:
- Develop example problems where least squares solutions are used in financial models.
- Solve the problems and interpret the results.
- Deliverables: A 3-page document with explanations and example problems.

&Step 7: Efficiency in Computations (Section 7)

- Task: Analyze computational efficiency using orthogonal matrices.
- Instructions:
- Efficiency Analysis:
- Discuss the computational benefits of using orthogonal matrices in financial algorithms.

- Explain how orthogonal matrices improve algorithm stability and efficiency.
- Hypothetical Example:
- Develop a hypothetical example where orthogonal matrices are used to enhance computational efficiency.
- Demonstrate the process and results.
- Deliverables: A 3-page report with discussions and hypothetical examples.

&Step 8: Practical Applications (Section 8)

- Task: Explore practical applications of orthogonal matrices in finance.
- Instructions:
- Real-World Examples:
- Provide real-world examples and case studies where orthogonal matrices are used in financial analysis.
- Implications Analysis:
- Analyze the implications of these applications for financial decision-making and risk management.
- Lessons Learned:
- Discuss the lessons learned from these real-world applications.
- Deliverables: A 3-page report including examples, case studies, and implications.

&Step 9: Final Project Compilation

- Task: Compile all sections into a comprehensive project report.
- Instructions:
- Organization:
- Ensure the report is well-organized with a table of contents, proper citations, and references.
- Formatting:
- Format the report professionally, ensuring clarity and readability.

- Submission:
- Submit the final report in both print and digital formats.
- Deliverables: A complete project report titled "Orthogonality and Orthogonal Matrices in Financial Analysis: Enhancing Risk Management and Optimization."

Final Deliverable

Compile all sections into a comprehensive project report titled "Orthogonality and Orthogonal Matrices in Financial Analysis: Enhancing Risk Management and Optimization." Ensure the report is well-organized with a table of contents, proper citations, and references. The final report should be professionally formatted and submitted in both print and digital formats.

Evaluation Criteria

- Understanding of Concepts: Demonstrates a strong grasp of orthogonality and orthogonal matrices and their applications in finance.
- Research Quality: Uses credible sources and provides accurate, well-supported information.
- Clarity and Presentation: Information is clearly presented, well-organized, and free of errors.
- Creativity: Uses visual aids and innovative approaches to explain complex concepts.
- Application: Provides real-world examples and case studies to illustrate theoretical concepts.

Good luck, and enjoy your exploration into the fascinating world of orthogonality and orthogonal matrices and their financial implications!

Comprehensive Project: Inner Product Spaces in Financial Analysis

Project Overview

This project aims to deepen your understanding of inner product spaces and their application in finance. By the end, you will be able to employ inner product spaces to analyze correlations, perform orthogonal projections, and apply these concepts to real-world financial data.

Project Title: "Inner Product Spaces in Financial Analysis: From Theory to Application"

Project Objectives

1. Understand the foundational concepts of inner product spaces.
2. Explore the financial contexts where inner product spaces are useful.
3. Analyze angles and orthogonality within financial data.
4. Apply inner product spaces to correlation analysis.
5. Implement orthogonal projections in financial models.
6. Conduct case studies demonstrating real-world applications.
7. Consider computational aspects of inner product spaces in finance.

Step-by-Step Instructions

&Step 1: Introduction to Inner Products (Section 1)

- Task: Gain a foundational understanding of inner products.
- Instructions:
- Research and Define:
- Define inner products and inner product spaces.
- Discuss the properties of inner products (linearity, symmetry, positive-definiteness).
- Example Problem:
- Given vectors ($u = [1, 2]$) and ($v = [3, 4]$), calculate their inner product.

- Deliverables: A 2-page document with definitions, explanations, and example problems.

&Step 2: Financial Contexts (Section 2)

- Task: Investigate the relevance of inner product spaces in finance.
- Instructions:
- Concept Explanation:
- Discuss how inner product spaces are employed in financial contexts.
- Provide specific examples such as portfolio optimization or risk assessment.
- Hypothetical Scenario:
- Develop a scenario where inner product spaces are used in financial decision-making.
- Deliverables: A 2-page report with explanations and hypothetical scenarios.

&Step 3: Angles and Orthogonality (Section 3)

- Task: Analyze angles and orthogonality within financial data.
- Instructions:
- Concept Explanation:
- Explain how angles between vectors in inner product spaces relate to orthogonality.
- Discuss the significance of orthogonal vectors in finance.
- Example Problems:
- Provide example problems where you calculate angles between financial vectors and determine orthogonality.
- Deliverables: A 3-page document with explanations, formulations, and example problems.

&Step 4: Applications in Correlation Analysis (Section 4)

- Task: Apply inner product spaces to correlation analysis.

- Instructions:
- Concept Explanation:
- Explain the relationship between inner products and correlation coefficients.
- Discuss how this relationship is used in finance.
- Example Problems:
- Calculate the correlation coefficient between two financial time series using inner products.
- Deliverables: A 3-page report with explanations and example problems.

&Step 5: Implications for Financial Data (Section 5)

- Task: Explore the implications of inner product spaces for financial data.
- Instructions:
- Insight Exploration:
- Discuss how inner product spaces can provide insights into financial data.
- Explain the implications for financial decision-making and risk management.
- Case Study Analysis:
- Analyze a case study where inner product spaces were used to gain insights into financial data.
- Deliverables: A 3-page report with discussions and case study analysis.

&Step 6: Orthogonal Projections (Section 6)

- Task: Implement orthogonal projections in financial models.
- Instructions:
- Process Explanation:
- Explain the process of orthogonal projection in inner product spaces.
- Provide the step-by-step procedure for projecting a vector onto a subspace.
- Example Problems:

- Provide example problems where orthogonal projection is used in financial models.
- Deliverables: A 2-page document with explanations, procedures, and example problems.

&*Step 7: Case Studies in Finance (Section 7)*

- Task: Conduct case studies demonstrating real-world applications of inner product spaces.
- Instructions:
- Case Study Selection:
- Select case studies from academic journals or real-world financial reports.
- Analysis:
- Analyze the selected case studies, focusing on the application of inner product spaces.
- Discuss the outcomes and implications of the case studies.
- Deliverables: A 3-page report including case study analysis and implications.

&*Step 8: Real-World Applications in Trading (Section 8)*

- Task: Explore real-world applications of inner product spaces in trading.
- Instructions:
- Application Exploration:
- Discuss how inner product spaces are used in trading algorithms and strategies.
- Provide specific examples and explain their significance.
- Implications Analysis:
- Analyze the implications of these applications for trading efficiency and profitability.
- Lessons Learned:
- Discuss the lessons learned from these real-world applications.
- Deliverables: A 3-page report including examples,

analysis, and lessons learned.

&Step 9: Computational Considerations (Section 9)

- Task: Consider computational aspects of inner product spaces in finance.
- Instructions:
- Efficiency Analysis:
- Discuss computational efficiency and stability when using inner product spaces in financial algorithms.
- Explain how inner product spaces improve algorithm performance.
- Hypothetical Example:
- Develop a hypothetical example where inner product spaces enhance computational efficiency.
- Deliverables: A 3-page report with discussions and hypothetical examples.

Step 10: Final Project Compilation

- Task: Compile all sections into a comprehensive project report.
- Instructions:
- Organization:
- Ensure the report is well-organized with a table of contents, proper citations, and references.
- Formatting:
- Format the report professionally, ensuring clarity and readability.
- Submission:
- Submit the final report in both print and digital formats.
- Deliverables: A complete project report titled "Inner Product Spaces in Financial Analysis: From Theory to Application."

Final Deliverable

Compile all sections into a comprehensive project report titled

"Inner Product Spaces in Financial Analysis: From Theory to Application." Ensure the report is well-organized with a table of contents, proper citations, and references. The final report should be professionally formatted and submitted in both print and digital formats.

Evaluation Criteria

- Understanding of Concepts: Demonstrates a thorough understanding of inner product spaces and their applications in finance.
- Research Quality: Uses credible sources and provides accurate, well-supported information.
- Clarity and Presentation: Information is clearly presented, well-organized, and free of errors.
- Creativity: Utilizes visual aids and innovative approaches to explain complex concepts.
- Application: Provides real-world examples and case studies to illustrate theoretical concepts.

Good luck, and enjoy your exploration into the fascinating world of inner product spaces and their financial implications!

Comprehensive Project: Inner Product Spaces in Financial Analysis

Project Overview

This project aims to deepen your understanding of inner product spaces and their application in finance. By the end, you will be able to employ inner product spaces to analyze correlations, perform orthogonal projections, and apply these concepts to real-world financial data.

Project Title: "Inner Product Spaces in Financial Analysis: From Theory to Application"

Project Objectives

1. Understand the foundational concepts of inner product spaces.
2. Explore the financial contexts where inner product

spaces are useful.

3. Analyze angles and orthogonality within financial data.
4. Apply inner product spaces to correlation analysis.
5. Implement orthogonal projections in financial models.
6. Conduct case studies demonstrating real-world applications.
7. Consider computational aspects of inner product spaces in finance.

Step-by-Step Instructions

&Step 1: Introduction to Inner Products (Section 1)

- Task: Gain a foundational understanding of inner products.
- Instructions:
- Research and Define:
- Define inner products and inner product spaces.
- Discuss properties of inner products (linearity, symmetry, positive-definiteness).
- Example Problem:
- Given vectors ($u = [1, 2]$) and ($v = [3, 4]$), calculate their inner product.
- Deliverables: A 2-page document with definitions, explanations, and example problems.

&Step 2: Financial Contexts (Section 2)

- Task: Investigate the relevance of inner product spaces in finance.
- Instructions:
- Concept Explanation:
- Discuss how inner product spaces are employed in financial contexts.
- Provide specific examples such as portfolio optimization or risk assessment.
- Hypothetical Scenario:

- Develop a scenario where inner product spaces are used in financial decision-making.
- Deliverables: A 2-page report with explanations and hypothetical scenarios.

&Step 3: Angles and Orthogonality (Section 3)

- Task: Analyze angles and orthogonality within financial data.
- Instructions:
- Concept Explanation:
- Explain how angles between vectors in inner product spaces relate to orthogonality.
- Discuss the significance of orthogonal vectors in finance.
- Example Problems:
- Provide example problems where you calculate angles between financial vectors and determine orthogonality.
- Deliverables: A 3-page document with explanations, formulations, and example problems.

&Step 4: Applications in Correlation Analysis (Section 4)

- Task: Apply inner product spaces to correlation analysis.
- Instructions:
- Concept Explanation:
- Explain the relationship between inner products and correlation coefficients.
- Discuss how this relationship is used in finance.
- Example Problems:
- Calculate the correlation coefficient between two financial time series using inner products.
- Deliverables: A 3-page report with explanations and example problems.

&Step 5: Implications for Financial Data (Section 5)

- Task: Explore the implications of inner product

spaces for financial data.

- Instructions:
- Insight Exploration:
- Discuss how inner product spaces can provide insights into financial data.
- Explain the implications for financial decision-making and risk management.
- Case Study Analysis:
- Analyze a case study where inner product spaces were used to gain insights into financial data.
- Deliverables: A 3-page report with discussions and case study analysis.

&Step 6: Orthogonal Projections (Section 6)

- Task: Implement orthogonal projections in financial models.
- Instructions:
- Process Explanation:
- Explain the process of orthogonal projection in inner product spaces.
- Provide the step-by-step procedure for projecting a vector onto a subspace.
- Example Problems:
- Provide example problems where orthogonal projection is used in financial models.
- Deliverables: A 2-page document with explanations, procedures, and example problems.

&Step 7: Case Studies in Finance (Section 7)

- Task: Conduct case studies demonstrating real-world applications of inner product spaces.
- Instructions:
- Case Study Selection:
- Select case studies from academic journals or real-world financial reports.
- Analysis:

- Analyze the selected case studies, focusing on the application of inner product spaces.
- Discuss the outcomes and implications of the case studies.
- Deliverables: A 3-page report including case study analysis and implications.

&Step 8: Real-World Applications in Trading (Section 8)

- Task: Explore real-world applications of inner product spaces in trading.
- Instructions:
- Application Exploration:
- Discuss how inner product spaces are used in trading algorithms and strategies.
- Provide specific examples and explain their significance.
- Implications Analysis:
- Analyze the implications of these applications for trading efficiency and profitability.
- Lessons Learned:
- Discuss the lessons learned from these real-world applications.
- Deliverables: A 3-page report including examples, analysis, and lessons learned.

&Step 9: Computational Considerations (Section 9)

- Task: Consider computational aspects of inner product spaces in finance.
- Instructions:
- Efficiency Analysis:
- Discuss computational efficiency and stability when using inner product spaces in financial algorithms.
- Explain how inner product spaces improve algorithm performance.
- Hypothetical Example:
- Develop a hypothetical example where inner product

spaces enhance computational efficiency.

- Deliverables: A 3-page report with discussions and hypothetical examples.

Step 10: Final Project Compilation

- Task: Compile all sections into a comprehensive project report.
- Instructions:
- Organization:
- Ensure the report is well-organized with a table of contents, proper citations, and references.
- Formatting:
- Format the report professionally, ensuring clarity and readability.
- Submission:
- Submit the final report in both print and digital formats.
- Deliverables: A complete project report titled "Inner Product Spaces in Financial Analysis: From Theory to Application."

Final Deliverable

Compile all sections into a comprehensive project report titled "Inner Product Spaces in Financial Analysis: From Theory to Application." Ensure the report is well-organized with a table of contents, proper citations, and references. The final report should be professionally formatted and submitted in both print and digital formats.

Evaluation Criteria

- Understanding of Concepts: Demonstrates a thorough understanding of inner product spaces and their applications in finance.
- Research Quality: Uses credible sources and provides accurate, well-supported information.
- Clarity and Presentation: Information is clearly presented, well-organized, and free of errors.

- Creativity: Utilizes visual aids and innovative approaches to explain complex concepts.
- Application: Provides real-world examples and case studies to illustrate theoretical concepts.

Good luck, and enjoy your exploration into the fascinating world of inner product spaces and their financial implications!

Comprehensive Project: Numerical Methods for Matrices in Finance

Project Overview

This project aims to deepen your understanding of numerical methods for matrices and their application in finance. By the end, you will be able to employ numerical techniques to solve matrix problems, analyze stability and precision, and apply these methods to real-world financial data.

Project Title: "Numerical Methods for Matrices in Financial Analysis: Practical Applications"

Project Objectives

1. Understand the foundational concepts of numerical methods for matrices.
2. Explore the financial contexts where these methods are useful.
3. Analyze direct solution techniques and their applications.
4. Investigate iterative methods for solving matrix problems.
5. Examine numerical stability and precision issues in financial computations.
6. Conduct case studies demonstrating real-world applications.
7. Consider computational aspects and performance enhancements in matrix methods.

Step-by-Step Instructions

&Step 1: Introduction to Numerical Methods (Section 1)

- Task: Gain a foundational understanding of numerical methods for matrices.
- Instructions:
- Research and Define:
- Define numerical methods for matrices.
- Discuss the importance of these methods in financial computations.
- Example Problem:
- Provide a simple matrix problem and solve it using a basic numerical method.
- Deliverables: A 2-page document with definitions, explanations, and example problems.

&Step 2: Financial Contexts (Section 2)

- Task: Investigate the relevance of numerical methods for matrices in finance.
- Instructions:
- Concept Explanation:
- Discuss how numerical methods for matrices are employed in financial contexts.
- Provide specific examples such as risk assessment or derivative pricing.
- Hypothetical Scenario:
- Develop a scenario where numerical methods are used in financial decision-making.
- Deliverables: A 2-page report with explanations and hypothetical scenarios.

&Step 3: Direct Solution Techniques (Section 3)

- Task: Analyze direct solution techniques and their applications.
- Instructions:
- Concept Explanation:
- Explain direct solution techniques such as Gaussian elimination.
- Discuss their applications in solving financial matrix

problems.
- Example Problems:
- Provide example problems where direct solution techniques are applied.
- Deliverables: A 3-page document with explanations, formulations, and example problems.

&*Step 4: Iterative Methods (Section 4)*
- Task: Investigate iterative methods for solving matrix problems.
- Instructions:
- Concept Explanation:
- Explain iterative methods such as the Jacobi and Gauss-Seidel methods.
- Discuss their advantages and limitations in financial computations.
- Example Problems:
- Provide example problems where iterative methods are used.
- Deliverables: A 3-page report with explanations and example problems.

&*Step 5: Numerical Stability in Finance (Section 5)*
- Task: Examine numerical stability and precision issues in financial computations.
- Instructions:
- Insight Exploration:
- Discuss the importance of numerical stability in financial algorithms.
- Explain common precision issues and how they affect financial computations.
- Case Study Analysis:
- Analyze a case study where numerical stability played a critical role.
- Deliverables: A 3-page report with discussions and case study analysis.

&Step 6: Dealing with Precision Issues (Section 6)

- Task: Explore methods for dealing with precision issues in financial data.
- Instructions:
- Process Explanation:
- Explain techniques for improving precision in matrix computations.
- Provide the step-by-step procedure for implementing these techniques.
- Example Problems:
- Provide example problems where precision issues are addressed.
- Deliverables: A 2-page document with explanations, procedures, and example problems.

&Step 7: Algorithms in Practice (Section 7)

- Task: Conduct case studies demonstrating real-world applications of numerical algorithms.
- Instructions:
- Case Study Selection:
- Select case studies from academic journals or real-world financial reports.
- Analysis:
- Analyze the selected case studies, focusing on the application of numerical methods.
- Discuss the outcomes and implications of the case studies.
- Deliverables: A 3-page report including case study analysis and implications.

&Step 8: Error Analysis and Measurements (Section 8)

- Task: Explore error analysis and measurement techniques in financial computations.
- Instructions:
- Application Exploration:
- Discuss methods for analyzing and measuring errors

in financial matrix computations.

- Provide specific examples and explain their significance.
- Implications Analysis:
- Analyze the implications of these error analysis techniques for financial decision-making.
- Lessons Learned:
- Discuss the lessons learned from these real-world applications.
- Deliverables: A 3-page report including examples, analysis, and lessons learned.

&Step 9: Performance Enhancements (Section 9)

- Task: Consider computational aspects and performance enhancements in matrix methods.
- Instructions:
- Efficiency Analysis:
- Discuss computational efficiency and stability when using numerical methods in financial algorithms.
- Explain how performance enhancements improve financial computations.
- Hypothetical Example:
- Develop a hypothetical example where performance enhancements are applied.
- Deliverables: A 3-page report with discussions and hypothetical examples.

Step 10: Final Project Compilation

- Task: Compile all sections into a comprehensive project report.
- Instructions:
- Organization:
- Ensure the report is well-organized with a table of contents, proper citations, and references.
- Formatting:
- Format the report professionally, ensuring clarity

and readability.
- Submission:
- Submit the final report in both print and digital formats.
- Deliverables: A complete project report titled "Numerical Methods for Matrices in Financial Analysis: Practical Applications."

Final Deliverable

Compile all sections into a comprehensive project report titled "Numerical Methods for Matrices in Financial Analysis: Practical Applications." Ensure the report is well-organized with a table of contents, proper citations, and references. The final report should be professionally formatted and submitted in both print and digital formats.

Evaluation Criteria

- Understanding of Concepts: Demonstrates a thorough understanding of numerical methods for matrices and their applications in finance.
- Research Quality: Uses credible sources and provides accurate, well-supported information.
- Clarity and Presentation: Information is clearly presented, well-organized, and free of errors.
- Creativity: Utilizes visual aids and innovative approaches to explain complex concepts.
- Application: Provides real-world examples and case studies to illustrate theoretical concepts.

Good luck, and enjoy your exploration into the fascinating world of numerical methods for matrices and their financial implications!

Comprehensive Project: Numerical Methods for Matrices in Financial Analysis

Project Overview

This project aims to deepen your understanding of numerical

methods for matrices and their application in finance. By the end, you will be able to employ numerical techniques to solve matrix problems, analyze stability and precision, and apply these methods to real-world financial data.

Project Title: "Numerical Methods for Matrices in Financial Analysis: Practical Applications"

Project Objectives

1. Understand the foundational concepts of numerical methods for matrices.
2. Explore the financial contexts where these methods are useful.
3. Analyze direct solution techniques and their applications.
4. Investigate iterative methods for solving matrix problems.
5. Examine numerical stability and precision issues in financial computations.
6. Conduct case studies demonstrating real-world applications.
7. Consider computational aspects and performance enhancements in matrix methods.

Step-by-Step Instructions

&Step 1: Introduction to Numerical Methods (Section 1)

- Task: Gain a foundational understanding of numerical methods for matrices.
- Instructions:
- Research and Define:
- Define numerical methods for matrices.
- Discuss the importance of these methods in financial computations.
- Example Problem:
- Provide a simple matrix problem and solve it using a basic numerical method.
- Deliverables: A 2-page document with definitions,

explanations, and example problems.

&Step 2: Financial Contexts (Section 2)

- Task: Investigate the relevance of numerical methods for matrices in finance.
- Instructions:
- Concept Explanation:
- Discuss how numerical methods for matrices are employed in financial contexts.
- Provide specific examples such as risk assessment or derivative pricing.
- Hypothetical Scenario:
- Develop a scenario where numerical methods are used in financial decision-making.
- Deliverables: A 2-page report with explanations and hypothetical scenarios.

&Step 3: Direct Solution Techniques (Section 3)

- Task: Analyze direct solution techniques and their applications.
- Instructions:
- Concept Explanation:
- Explain direct solution techniques such as Gaussian elimination.
- Discuss their applications in solving financial matrix problems.
- Example Problems:
- Provide example problems where direct solution techniques are applied.
- Deliverables: A 3-page document with explanations, formulations, and example problems.

&Step 4: Iterative Methods (Section 4)

- Task: Investigate iterative methods for solving matrix problems.
- Instructions:
- Concept Explanation:

- Explain iterative methods such as the Jacobi and Gauss-Seidel methods.
- Discuss their advantages and limitations in financial computations.
- Example Problems:
- Provide example problems where iterative methods are used.
- Deliverables: A 3-page report with explanations and example problems.

&*Step 5: Numerical Stability in Finance (Section 5)*

- Task: Examine numerical stability and precision issues in financial computations.
- Instructions:
- Insight Exploration:
- Discuss the importance of numerical stability in financial algorithms.
- Explain common precision issues and how they affect financial computations.
- Case Study Analysis:
- Analyze a case study where numerical stability played a critical role.
- Deliverables: A 3-page report with discussions and case study analysis.

&*Step 6: Dealing with Precision Issues (Section 6)*

- Task: Explore methods for dealing with precision issues in financial data.
- Instructions:
- Process Explanation:
- Explain techniques for improving precision in matrix computations.
- Provide the step-by-step procedure for implementing these techniques.
- Example Problems:
- Provide example problems where precision issues are

addressed.

- Deliverables: A 2-page document with explanations, procedures, and example problems.

&Step 7: Algorithms in Practice (Section 7)

- Task: Conduct case studies demonstrating real-world applications of numerical algorithms.
- Instructions:
- Case Study Selection:
- Select case studies from academic journals or real-world financial reports.
- Analysis:
- Analyze the selected case studies, focusing on the application of numerical methods.
- Discuss the outcomes and implications of the case studies.
- Deliverables: A 3-page report including case study analysis and implications.

&Step 8: Error Analysis and Measurements (Section 8)

- Task: Explore error analysis and measurement techniques in financial computations.
- Instructions:
- Application Exploration:
- Discuss methods for analyzing and measuring errors in financial matrix computations.
- Provide specific examples and explain their significance.
- Implications Analysis:
- Analyze the implications of these error analysis techniques for financial decision-making.
- Lessons Learned:
- Discuss the lessons learned from these real-world applications.
- Deliverables: A 3-page report including examples, analysis, and lessons learned.

&Step 9: Performance Enhancements (Section 9)

- Task: Consider computational aspects and performance enhancements in matrix methods.
- Instructions:
- Efficiency Analysis:
- Discuss computational efficiency and stability when using numerical methods in financial algorithms.
- Explain how performance enhancements improve financial computations.
- Hypothetical Example:
- Develop a hypothetical example where performance enhancements are applied.
- Deliverables: A 3-page report with discussions and hypothetical examples.

Step 10: Final Project Compilation

- Task: Compile all sections into a comprehensive project report.
- Instructions:
- Organization:
- Ensure the report is well-organized with a table of contents, proper citations, and references.
- Formatting:
- Format the report professionally, ensuring clarity and readability.
- Submission:
- Submit the final report in both print and digital formats.
- Deliverables: A complete project report titled "Numerical Methods for Matrices in Financial Analysis: Practical Applications."

Final Deliverable

Compile all sections into a comprehensive project report titled "Numerical Methods for Matrices in Financial Analysis:

Practical Applications." Ensure the report is well-organized with a table of contents, proper citations, and references. The final report should be professionally formatted and submitted in both print and digital formats.

Evaluation Criteria

- Understanding of Concepts: Demonstrates a thorough understanding of numerical methods for matrices and their applications in finance.
- Research Quality: Uses credible sources and provides accurate, well-supported information.
- Clarity and Presentation: Information is clearly presented, well-organized, and free of errors.
- Creativity: Utilizes visual aids and innovative approaches to explain complex concepts.
- Application: Provides real-world examples and case studies to illustrate theoretical concepts.

Good luck, and enjoy your exploration into the fascinating world of numerical methods for matrices and their financial implications!

Comprehensive Project: Advanced Topics in Matrix Theory

Project Title: "Advanced Topics in Matrix Theory:
Financial Applications and Innovations"

Project Overview

This project will explore advanced topics in matrix theory, focusing on their financial applications and innovative use cases. By the end, you will have a deep understanding of complex matrix concepts and their practical implications in finance, along with experience in conducting research and presenting findings.

Project Objectives

1. Understand the advanced concepts of matrix theory.
2. Explore financial applications of these advanced concepts.

3. Investigate innovations in matrix theory and their implications for finance.
4. Conduct case studies demonstrating real-world financial applications.
5. Develop a comprehensive understanding of advanced matrix algorithms and their performance.

Step-by-Step Instructions

&Step 1: Introduction to Advanced Matrix Theory (Section 1)

- Task: Gain a foundational understanding of advanced topics in matrix theory.
- Instructions:
- Research and Define:
- Define key advanced topics in matrix theory, such as tensors, multilinear algebra, and high-dimensional data analysis.
- Discuss the importance of these topics in the context of modern financial analysis.
- Example Problem:
- Provide a simple problem involving an advanced matrix concept and solve it.
- Deliverables: A 2-page document with definitions, explanations, and example problems.

&Step 2: Tensors and Multilinear Algebra (Section 2)

- Task: Investigate the role of tensors and multilinear algebra in financial analysis.
- Instructions:
- Concept Explanation:
- Explain the mathematical foundations of tensors and multilinear algebra.
- Discuss how these concepts are applied in financial contexts.
- Hypothetical Scenario:
- Develop a scenario where tensors are used to model complex financial systems.

- Deliverables: A 3-page report with explanations and hypothetical scenarios.

&*Step 3: High-Dimensional Data Analysis (Section 3)*

- Task: Explore high-dimensional data analysis and its financial implications.
- Instructions:
- Concept Explanation:
- Explain high-dimensional data analysis techniques.
- Discuss their applications in financial modeling and risk assessment.
- Case Study Analysis:
- Analyze a case study involving high-dimensional data analysis in finance.
- Deliverables: A 3-page report with explanations and case study analysis.

&*Step 4: Financial Applications and Implications (Section 4)*

- Task: Investigate the financial applications of advanced matrix theory.
- Instructions:
- Concept Explanation:
- Discuss various financial applications of advanced matrix concepts, such as portfolio optimization and algorithmic trading.
- Example Problems:
- Provide example problems demonstrating these applications.
- Deliverables: A 3-page document with explanations and example problems.

&*Step 5: Nonlinear Matrix Usage (Section 5)*

- Task: Examine the use of nonlinear matrices in financial computations.
- Instructions:
- Concept Explanation:
- Explain how nonlinear matrices are used in financial

modeling.

- Discuss the advantages and challenges of using nonlinear matrices.
- Example Problems:
- Provide example problems involving nonlinear matrices.
- Deliverables: A 2-page report with explanations and example problems.

&Step 6: Advances in Algorithm Design (Section 6)

- Task: Explore recent advances in matrix algorithm design and their impact on financial analysis.
- Instructions:
- Research and Explain:
- Research recent advancements in matrix algorithm design.
- Explain how these advancements enhance financial computations.
- Hypothetical Example:
- Develop a hypothetical example illustrating the impact of a new algorithm on financial modeling.
- Deliverables: A 3-page report with research findings and hypothetical examples.

&Step 7: Machine Learning Techniques (Section 7)

- Task: Investigate the intersection of matrix theory and machine learning in finance.
- Instructions:
- Concept Explanation:
- Explain how matrix theory is applied in machine learning models used for financial analysis.
- Discuss specific financial applications, such as predictive modeling and anomaly detection.
- Case Study Analysis:
- Analyze a case study where machine learning techniques were used in financial modeling.

- Deliverables: A 3-page report with explanations and case study analysis.

&*Step 8: Innovations in Financial Technology (Section 8)*

- Task: Explore innovations in financial technology driven by matrix theory.
- Instructions:
- Research and Explain:
- Research recent innovations in financial technology that leverage advanced matrix theory.
- Explain how these innovations are transforming the financial industry.
- Example Problems:
- Provide example problems that showcase these innovations.
- Deliverables: A 3-page document with research findings and example problems.

&*Step 9: Challenges and Frontiers in Research (Section 9)*

- Task: Discuss the challenges and future directions in matrix theory research.
- Instructions:
- Insight Exploration:
- Identify current challenges in advanced matrix theory research.
- Discuss potential future directions and areas for innovation.
- Implications Analysis:
- Analyze the implications of these challenges and future directions for financial analysis.
- Deliverables: A 3-page report with discussion and analysis.

Step 10: Final Project Compilation

- Task: Compile all sections into a comprehensive project report.
- Instructions:

- Organization:
- Ensure the report is well-organized with a table of contents, proper citations, and references.
- Formatting:
- Format the report professionally, ensuring clarity and readability.
- Submission:
- Submit the final report in both print and digital formats.
- Deliverables: A complete project report titled "Advanced Topics in Matrix Theory: Financial Applications and Innovations."

Final Deliverable

Compile all sections into a comprehensive project report titled "Advanced Topics in Matrix Theory: Financial Applications and Innovations." Ensure the report is well-organized with a table of contents, proper citations, and references. The final report should be professionally formatted and submitted in both print and digital formats.

Evaluation Criteria

- Understanding of Concepts: Demonstrates a thorough understanding of advanced matrix theory and its applications in finance.
- Research Quality: Uses credible sources and provides accurate, well-supported information.
- Clarity and Presentation: Information is clearly presented, well-organized, and free of errors.
- Creativity: Utilizes visual aids and innovative approaches to explain complex concepts.
- Application: Provides real-world examples and case studies to illustrate theoretical concepts.

Good luck, and enjoy your exploration into the fascinating world of advanced matrix theory and its financial implications!

Comprehensive Project: Advanced Topics in Matrix Theory

Project Title: "Advanced Topics in Matrix Theory:
Financial Applications and Innovations"

Project Overview

This project will explore advanced topics in matrix theory, focusing on their financial applications and innovative use cases. By the end, you will have a deep understanding of complex matrix concepts and their practical implications in finance, along with experience in conducting research and presenting findings.

Project Objectives

1. Understand the advanced concepts of matrix theory.
2. Explore financial applications of these advanced concepts.
3. Investigate innovations in matrix theory and their implications for finance.
4. Conduct case studies demonstrating real-world financial applications.
5. Develop a comprehensive understanding of advanced matrix algorithms and their performance.

Step-by-Step Instructions

&Step 1: Introduction to Advanced Matrix Theory (Section 1)

- Task: Gain a foundational understanding of advanced topics in matrix theory.
- Instructions:
- Research and Define:
- Define key advanced topics in matrix theory, such as tensors, multilinear algebra, and high-dimensional data analysis.
- Discuss the importance of these topics in the context of modern financial analysis.
- Example Problem:

- Provide a simple problem involving an advanced matrix concept and solve it.
- Deliverables: A 2-page document with definitions, explanations, and example problems.

&Step 2: Tensors and Multilinear Algebra (Section 2)

- Task: Investigate the role of tensors and multilinear algebra in financial analysis.
- Instructions:
- Concept Explanation:
- Explain the mathematical foundations of tensors and multilinear algebra.
- Discuss how these concepts are applied in financial contexts.
- Hypothetical Scenario:
- Develop a scenario where tensors are used to model complex financial systems.
- Deliverables: A 3-page report with explanations and hypothetical scenarios.

&Step 3: High-Dimensional Data Analysis (Section 3)

- Task: Explore high-dimensional data analysis and its financial implications.
- Instructions:
- Concept Explanation:
- Explain high-dimensional data analysis techniques.
- Discuss their applications in financial modeling and risk assessment.
- Case Study Analysis:
- Analyze a case study involving high-dimensional data analysis in finance.
- Deliverables: A 3-page report with explanations and case study analysis.

&Step 4: Financial Applications and Implications (Section 4)

- Task: Investigate the financial applications of advanced matrix theory.

- Instructions:
- Concept Explanation:
- Discuss various financial applications of advanced matrix concepts, such as portfolio optimization and algorithmic trading.
- Example Problems:
- Provide example problems demonstrating these applications.
- Deliverables: A 3-page document with explanations and example problems.

&*Step 5: Nonlinear Matrix Usage (Section 5)*

- Task: Examine the use of nonlinear matrices in financial computations.
- Instructions:
- Concept Explanation:
- Explain how nonlinear matrices are used in financial modeling.
- Discuss the advantages and challenges of using nonlinear matrices.
- Example Problems:
- Provide example problems involving nonlinear matrices.
- Deliverables: A 2-page report with explanations and example problems.

&*Step 6: Advances in Algorithm Design (Section 6)*

- Task: Explore recent advances in matrix algorithm design and their impact on financial analysis.
- Instructions:
- Research and Explain:
- Research recent advancements in matrix algorithm design.
- Explain how these advancements enhance financial computations.
- Hypothetical Example:

- Develop a hypothetical example illustrating the impact of a new algorithm on financial modeling.
- Deliverables: A 3-page report with research findings and hypothetical examples.

&Step 7: Machine Learning Techniques (Section 7)

- Task: Investigate the intersection of matrix theory and machine learning in finance.
- Instructions:
- Concept Explanation:
- Explain how matrix theory is applied in machine learning models used for financial analysis.
- Discuss specific financial applications, such as predictive modeling and anomaly detection.
- Case Study Analysis:
- Analyze a case study where machine learning techniques were used in financial modeling.
- Deliverables: A 3-page report with explanations and case study analysis.

&Step 8: Innovations in Financial Technology (Section 8)

- Task: Explore innovations in financial technology driven by matrix theory.
- Instructions:
- Research and Explain:
- Research recent innovations in financial technology that leverage advanced matrix theory.
- Explain how these innovations are transforming the financial industry.
- Example Problems:
- Provide example problems that showcase these innovations.
- Deliverables: A 3-page document with research findings and example problems.

&Step 9: Challenges and Frontiers in Research (Section 9)

- Task: Discuss the challenges and future directions in

matrix theory research.

- Instructions:
- Insight Exploration:
- Identify current challenges in advanced matrix theory research.
- Discuss potential future directions and areas for innovation.
- Implications Analysis:
- Analyze the implications of these challenges and future directions for financial analysis.
- Deliverables: A 3-page report with discussion and analysis.

Step 10: Final Project Compilation

- Task: Compile all sections into a comprehensive project report.
- Instructions:
- Organization:
- Ensure the report is well-organized with a table of contents, proper citations, and references.
- Formatting:
- Format the report professionally, ensuring clarity and readability.
- Submission:
- Submit the final report in both print and digital formats.
- Deliverables: A complete project report titled "Advanced Topics in Matrix Theory: Financial Applications and Innovations."

Final Deliverable

Compile all sections into a comprehensive project report titled "Advanced Topics in Matrix Theory: Financial Applications and Innovations." Ensure the report is well-organized with a table of contents, proper citations, and references. The final report should be professionally formatted and submitted in both print and digital formats.

Evaluation Criteria

- Understanding of Concepts: Demonstrates a thorough understanding of advanced matrix theory and its applications in finance.
- Research Quality: Uses credible sources and provides accurate, well-supported information.
- Clarity and Presentation: Information is clearly presented, well-organized, and free of errors.
- Creativity: Utilizes visual aids and innovative approaches to explain complex concepts.
- Application: Provides real-world examples and case studies to illustrate theoretical concepts.

Good luck, and enjoy your exploration into the fascinating world of advanced matrix theory and its financial implications!

Comprehensive Project: Conclusion and Future Directions in Linear Algebra for Finance

Project Title: "Charting the Future of Linear Algebra in Finance"

Project Overview

This project aims to synthesize your understanding of linear algebra applications in finance, focusing on future directions and innovative trends. By the end, you will have conducted thorough research, engaged with emerging trends, and proposed innovative applications of linear algebra in the evolving financial landscape.

Project Objectives

1. Recapitulate key concepts of linear algebra in finance.
2. Investigate emerging trends and future directions.
3. Propose innovative applications and strategies using linear algebra.
4. Develop a comprehensive understanding of the role

of technology in finance.

5. Create a forward-looking plan for continuous learning and development.

Step-by-Step Instructions

&Step 1: Recapitulation of Key Concepts (Section 1)

- Task: Summarize the key concepts of linear algebra covered in previous chapters.
- Instructions:
- Concept Summary:
- Summarize major topics such as matrix operations, eigenvalues, vector spaces, and their financial applications.
- Highlight Key Insights:
- Highlight the most significant insights and takeaways from each chapter.
- Create Visual Aids:
- Develop visual aids like mind maps or flowcharts to represent the relationships among key concepts.
- Deliverables: A 5-page document summarizing key concepts with visual aids.

&Step 2: The Future of Linear Algebra in Finance (Section 2)

- Task: Explore the future of linear algebra in finance.
- Instructions:
- Research Emerging Trends:
- Research current and emerging trends in financial mathematics, focusing on linear algebra.
- Identify Key Areas of Growth:
- Identify areas where linear algebra is expected to play a critical role in the future.
- Prepare a Report:
- Prepare a detailed report on the future directions of linear algebra in finance, including potential challenges and opportunities.
- Deliverables: A 4-page report on future trends and

directions.

&*Step 3: Emerging Trends in Financial Mathematics (Section 3)*

- Task: Investigate new trends in financial mathematics.
- Instructions:
- Trend Analysis:
- Identify and analyze new trends such as machine learning integration, big data analytics, and blockchain.
- Financial Applications:
- Discuss how these trends impact financial analysis and decision-making.
- Create Case Studies:
- Develop case studies illustrating the impact of these trends on financial markets.
- Deliverables: A 4-page document with trend analysis and case studies.

&*Step 4: Integrating Theory with Practice (Section 4)*

- Task: Propose innovative applications of linear algebra in finance.
- Instructions:
- Innovative Applications:
- Brainstorm and propose innovative applications of linear algebra in areas such as risk management, portfolio optimization, and algorithmic trading.
- Develop Models:
- Develop mathematical models for these applications, demonstrating their potential effectiveness.
- Example Problems:
- Provide example problems and solutions to illustrate these applications.
- Deliverables: A 5-page report with innovative applications, models, and example problems.

&*Step 5: The Role of Technology in Finance (Section 5)*

- Task: Explore the impact of technology on financial analysis.
- Instructions:
- Technology Overview:
- Provide an overview of key technologies transforming finance, such as artificial intelligence, quantum computing, and fintech innovations.
- Impact Analysis:
- Analyze the impact of these technologies on financial analysis and modeling.
- Case Study:
- Develop a case study illustrating the integration of technology and linear algebra in finance.
- Deliverables: A 4-page report on the role of technology in finance, including a case study.

&Step 6: Predictions for Market Evolutions (Section 6)

- Task: Make predictions about future market evolutions influenced by linear algebra.
- Instructions:
- Market Analysis:
- Analyze current market trends and predict how they might evolve with advancements in linear algebra.
- Scenario Planning:
- Develop scenarios showing different paths the market could take based on these predictions.
- Implications:
- Discuss the implications of these predictions for financial analysts and traders.
- Deliverables: A 4-page document with market predictions and scenario planning.

&Step 7: Preparing for Future Challenges (Section 7)

- Task: Identify and prepare for future challenges in financial mathematics.
- Instructions:

- Challenge Identification:
- Identify potential challenges that financial analysts might face in the future.
- Strategy Development:
- Develop strategies to address these challenges, focusing on continuous learning and adaptation.
- Toolkit Creation:
- Create a toolkit with resources and best practices for future financial analysts.
- Deliverables: A 3-page report on future challenges and strategies, including a toolkit.

&*Step 8: Continuous Learning and Development (Section 8)*

- Task: Develop a plan for continuous learning and professional development.
- Instructions:
- Learning Plan:
- Create a detailed plan for continuous learning, including courses, certifications, and professional development opportunities.
- Resource Compilation:
- Compile a list of resources such as books, online courses, and industry publications.
- Career Roadmap:
- Develop a career roadmap outlining milestones for professional growth.
- Deliverables: A 3-page continuous learning and development plan.

&*Step 9: Final Project Compilation*

- Task: Compile all sections into a comprehensive project report.
- Instructions:
- Organization:
- Ensure the report is well-organized with a table of contents, proper citations, and references.

- Formatting:
- Format the report professionally, ensuring clarity and readability.
- Submission:
- Submit the final report in both print and digital formats.
- Deliverables: A complete project report titled "Charting the Future of Linear Algebra in Finance."

Final Deliverable

Compile all sections into a comprehensive project report titled "Charting the Future of Linear Algebra in Finance." Ensure the report is well-organized with a table of contents, proper citations, and references. The final report should be professionally formatted and submitted in both print and digital formats.

Evaluation Criteria

- Understanding of Concepts: Demonstrates a thorough understanding of linear algebra concepts and their future applications in finance.
- Research Quality: Uses credible sources and provides accurate, well-supported information.
- Clarity and Presentation: Information is clearly presented, well-organized, and free of errors.
- Creativity: Utilizes visual aids and innovative approaches to explain complex concepts.
- Application: Provides real-world examples and case studies to illustrate theoretical concepts.

Good luck, and enjoy your exploration into the future of linear algebra and its transformative potential in finance!

www.ingramcontent.com/pod-product-compliance
Lightning Source LLC
LaVergne TN
LVHW051219050326
832903LV00028B/2169